THE DAILY STUDY BIBLE

(OLD TESTAMENT)

General Editor: John C. L. Gibson

EZEKIEL

EZEKIEL

PETER C. CRAIGIE

THE SAINT ANDREW PRESS
EDINBURGH

THE WESTMINSTER PRESS
PHILADELPHIA

Published by
The Saint Andrew Press
Edinburgh, Scotland
and
The Westminster Press ®
Philadelphia, Pennsylvania

Printed and bound in Great Britain
by Thomson Litho Ltd., East Kilbride, Scotland

ISBN (Great Britain) 0 7152 0530 7

Reprinted 1986

GENERAL PREFACE

This series of commentaries on the Old Testament, to which Professor Craigie's volume on *Ezekiel* belongs, has been planned as a companion series to the much-acclaimed New Testament series of the late Professor William Barclay. As with that series, each volume is arranged in successive headed portions suitable for daily study. The Biblical text followed is that of the Revised Standard Version or Common Bible. Eleven contributors share the work, each being responsible for from one to three volumes. The series is issued in the hope that it will do for the Old Testament what Professor Barclay's series succeeded so splendidly in doing for the New Testament—make it come alive for the Christian believer in the twentieth century.

Its two-fold aim is the same as his. Firstly, it is intended to introduce the reader to some of the more important results and fascinating insights of modern Old Testament scholarship. Most of the contributors are already established experts in the field with many publications to their credit. Some are younger scholars who have yet to make their names but who in my judgment as General Editor are now ready to be tested. I can assure those who use these commentaries that they are in the hands of competent teachers who know what is of real consequence in their subject and are able to present it in a form that will appeal to the general public.

The primary purpose of the series, however, is *not* an academic one. Professor Barclay summed it up for his New Testament series in the words of Richard of Chichester's prayer—to enable men and women "to know Jesus Christ more clearly, to love Him more dearly, and to follow Him more nearly." In the case of the Old Testament we have to be a little more circumspect than that. The Old Testament was completed long before the time of Our Lord, and it was (as it still is) the sole Bible of the Jews, God's first people, before it became part of the Christian Bible. We must take this fact seriously.

Yet in its strangely compelling way, sometimes dimly and sometimes directly, sometimes charmingly and sometimes embarrassingly, it holds up before us the things of Christ. It should not be forgotten that Jesus Himself was raised on this Book, that He based His whole ministry on what it says, and that He approached His death with its words on His lips. Christian men and women have in this ancient collection of Jewish writings a uniquely illuminating avenue not only into the will and purposes of God the Father, but into the mind and heart of Him who is named God's Son, who was Himself born a Jew but went on through the Cross and Resurrection to become the Saviour of the world. Read reverently and imaginatively the Old Testament can become a living and relevant force in their everyday lives.

It is the prayer of myself and my colleagues that this series may be used by its readers and blessed by God to that end.

New College
Edinburgh

JOHN C. L. GIBSON
General Editor

CONTENTS

INTRODUCTION

Some books are easy to read and easily forgotten; others are difficult to read, but somehow they are not forgotten and their essence remains with the reader for the remainder of life. The Book of Ezekiel belongs to the latter category; its difficulties have been recognised frequently over the centuries, but its rewards have also been reaped. In the first century A.D., a debate took place among the learned Jewish rabbis concerning whether or not the Book of Ezekiel should be included in the canon of Scripture. Rabbi Hanina ben Hezekiah supported the acceptance of the Book of Ezekiel; he is said to have burned three hundred jars of oil in his night lamp, while studying the book in order to defend it before his colleagues. In recent years, many commentators on the book have expressed their sense of difficulty in coming to grips with its message. The late A. B. Davidson, Professor of Old Testament at New College, Edinburgh, published a commentary on Ezekiel in 1892; he wrote in the preface that "the student of the book must take leave of his task with a certain sense of defeat."

From Hanina to Davidson, and on into the twentieth century, students of Ezekiel's book have sensed the difficulty of grasping fully its message. Yet it is also true, though not always stated, that those who have grappled with Ezekiel have come away the richer from their struggle, for Ezekiel has provided an insight into the nature of God that is not easily found in such depth in the other Old Testament books. It is wise to be aware of the difficulties of reading the Book of Ezekiel from the start, but it would be folly to refuse to read it because of its difficulty. We may never grasp its message fully, but in the attempt we shall be enriched enormously.

Not least of the difficulties in understanding the Book of

Ezekiel lies in its use of language, symbol and allegory. Norman Perrin once noted the difficulty that scientific scholars had in understanding the Book of Revelation, "while poets and artists have found it an unending source of inspiration precisely because it uses images of immense evocative power." The same is true to some extent of the Book of Ezekiel. Scholars have become swamped in their literary analyses, literalist interpreters have bemused themselves in their attempts to relate Ezekiel's "prophecies" to the events in the weekend newspapers, and one supposedly serious writer has even found evidence of spaceships and astronauts in the wheels of Ezekiel's vision. But the singers of the traditional American spirituals were closer to the vitality of Ezekiel's message, when they sang of "wheels going round" and "dem dry bones". The symbolism and allegory, the mystery and vitality of the message, are more susceptible to understanding among those sensitive to the level of Ezekiel's communication.

The difficulty of the book pertains not only to understanding it in its own time, but also in applying its truths to the modern world. The continuing vitality of the book is vividly illustrated in modern Israel. In Ezekiel's day, there were some Jews who said in desperation "our hope is lost" (37:11); but the message of Ezekiel was one of hope that the dry bones would be clothed in life again. And Ezekiel's message of hope has survived into the twentieth century; it is embodied in the words of the national anthem of the state of Israel:

> . . . our hope is not yet lost,
> the hope of two thousand years
> to be a free people in our land,
> in the land of Zion and Jerusalem.

The anthem embodies Ezekiel's hope, some two and a half millennia after his death. Within the Christian Church, a similar sense of contemporary vitality must be sought, but it is not a simple task. Ezekiel is rarely quoted in the New Testament, apart from the Book of Revelation, and hence the starting point for finding contemporary relevance is difficult to locate. And yet the relevance of the book both for contemporary theology and life is considerable; like a precious pearl, it must be prized from the encasing shell.

EZEKIEL, THE PRIEST AND THE PROPHET

Nothing is known of Ezekiel beyond the information contained in the book named after him. His father was a priest named Buzi, and so, in the hereditary tradition of the priesthood, Ezekiel would have been educated as a young man for priestly service. Though no biography of Buzi has survived, he was probably a man of some influence and importance in priestly circles, and to some extent Ezekiel inherited this family influence in his own life.

Ezekiel was born about 623 B.C., probably in Jerusalem where his father served in the great temple. But he was born in troubled times. He grew up during the last years of relative independence for his home state of Judah, which was constantly threatened with military subjugation by the superpower of that time, the Babylonian Empire. When Ezekiel was about twenty-six years of age, his native city of Jerusalem was attacked and quickly defeated by the powerful armies of the Babylonian Emperor, Nebuchadrezzar. Although the state of Judah was to survive, after a fashion, for a further decade after the defeat of Jerusalem in 597 B.C., the end was already in view. In 597 B.C., many of Jerusalem's key citizens and families, Ezekiel included, were taken off as exiles to live in Babylon, a region that is now part of Iraq.

These Jewish exiles were resettled in Babylon. Ezekiel belonged to a community established at a place called Tel Abib, by the "River" Chebar, which was actually an irrigation canal, drawing waters from the River Euphrates near the city of Babylon itself. The exiles built for themselves houses with mud bricks and settled there in a strange environment, not too far from the extraordinary capital city of the Emperor Nebuchadrezzar. It was in his fifth year as an exile in Tel Abib that Ezekiel had a profound religious experience. He was thirty years old at the time; if he had still been living in Jerusalem, it was the age at which he would have assumed the full responsibilities of priesthood. But instead he was called to the task of a prophet, of being a spokesman for God. For more than twenty years, he served as a prophet among the exiles. The last of his prophecies that can be dated with any certainty was given in 571 B.C., when he was in late middle-age. The date and location of his death are not known with any certainty.

There still exists a tomb in Iraq which is identified as the tomb of Ezekiel; it is situated at a place called al-Kifl, not far from the ruins of ancient Babylon. For many centuries, when there were still Jews living in Iraq, it was a place in which Jews gathered on special occasions for worship. In 1860, the tomb became a source of contention between the local Jews and Muslims. In an attempt to resolve the issue of ownership, the British Consul in Baghdad, J. M. Hyslop, wrote to his Ambassador in Constantinople, Sir H. L. Bulwer, that "the Jews declare that the tomb has been in their possession for upwards of 2,000 years and that their right to it has never before been questioned."

THE ESSENCE OF THE PROPHET'S MESSAGE

It is difficult, sometimes, to distinguish between the medium and the message, and certainly such a distinction is difficult to make in the prophetic ministry of Ezekiel. A prophet was a person who communicated God's word to the people of Israel. That word might refer to the present, past or future, but it would be wrong to think of confining the focus of prophecy to future events. Above all, the prophet addressed the divine word to his contemporaries, and it was relevant to them in their own time. Because prophecy involved the communication of the *word*, it commonly took the form of *speech*; many of the prophets were speakers and preachers. Yet there are other means of communicating knowledge to human beings, and in the prophetic ministry of Ezekiel there is perhaps more diversity in the mode of communication than is the case with any other biblical prophet.

Certainly, Ezekiel employed speech, but his words were rarely simple sermons. He recounted visions, expounded allegories, and propounded parables. And his words, both prosaic and poetic, were penetrated with symbolism and hidden meanings that lay beneath the surface of the words as such. But beyond speech, the actions of Ezekiel were extraordinary in their symbolism. The death of his wife was an event through which a part of the divine message was communicated. And during a period of dumbness, the prophet's silence cried more loudly than can human speech. When in a vision he ate a scroll (the ancient equivalent of a modern book), the account of his symbolic action was a powerful and effective method of communication.

There is thus enormous variety in the means by which Ezekiel fulfilled his responsibilities as a prophet. In a sense, all the varieties of prophetic experience seem to be packed into the life of this single prophet, so that his ministry is from one perspective the richest of any of the biblical prophets. But, on the other hand, the diversity of Ezekiel's religious experience has led some interpreters to doubt his mental health. A variety of psychoanalytic interpretations of the prophet have been proposed. For the most part, they are more informative with respect to the state of mind of the interpreter than of the "patient". While it is true that Ezekiel's character and experience were not totally normal, there is nevertheless considerable parallel between his experience and that of other prophets the world over. To diminish the value of his book on the basis of psychiatric suspicion would be to make a serious error.

The message itself cannot be summed up in a single sentence, but perhaps its most distinctive characteristic is the awareness expressed throughout the book of God's holiness. Ezekiel's sense of God was not that of a friendly neighbour who might be addressed on a first name basis. God was "other", vastly different from mere mortals in his power and purity. But despite the otherness of God, the essence of *religion* for Ezekiel (as for the other prophets) was to be found in the relationship between God and human beings. God's holiness required integrity in the human beings with whom he was to relate. Yet the prophet's analysis of human beings was bleak. They were evil, both individually and collectively; they shunned responsibility. Being evil, human beings could not hope for the continuity of relationship with God which was the very essence of Israel's religion. And yet, for all the negative analysis of the human condition, Ezekiel had a message of hope. It was not rooted in a liberal and optimistic view of mankind's potential for self-improvement; it was based, rather, in his vision of God and of the continuing mercy and forgiveness of God.

But there is more to Ezekiel's message; to grasp it, the modern reader of this ancient book must think constantly of the circumstances in which the message was delivered. The Jews of his time were faced with an enormous question; to put it in modern words, had their religion come to an end? Phrased so bluntly, it may sound foolish, especially with our knowledge of later history. Yet it was a real and awesome question at the time. The religion of the Hebrews had been linked intimately, before Ezekiel's time, to the existence of the state of Israel and the possession of the promised land. And yet those two foundations upon which the faith had been established were crumbling before their very eyes. Had their failure, and that of their ancestors, been so terrible that God had finally given up on his people? In such an age, and to such questions, the message of Ezekiel was particularly powerful. He spoke of doom and judgment, but ultimately his faith and message outstripped the reality of contemporary experience. Ultimately, there was hope. Even the disasters of those decades somehow had a purpose in God's plan. The events would somehow conspire to declare to the people that God was indeed the *Lord*. And so the final impression that is left after reading this extraordinary book is one of hope. It is not an unqualified and naive hope, but it is real nevertheless. And just as Ezekiel's message required a response from listeners in his own time, so too does it require a response from modern readers, if the hope is to remain alive in the twentieth century and beyond.

There is one further perspective that is pertinent to reading this ancient book. It was not written as a book in the modern sense; rather, it is a record of events and actions, sermons and sayings, that took place over many days and, indeed, many years. So it is an appropriate book to read, and reflect upon, in relatively short units, as they are presented in the interpretation that follows.

EZEKIEL

SETTING THE STAGE

Ezekiel 1:1–3

> ¹In the thirtieth year, in the fourth month, on the fifth day of the month, as I was among the exiles by the river Chebar, the heavens were opened, and I saw visions of God. ²On the fifth day of the month (it was the fifth year of the exile of King Jehoiachin), ³the word of the Lord came to Ezekiel the priest, the son of Buzi, in the land of the Chaldeans by the river Chebar; and the hand of the Lord was upon him there.

When we open a modern book and begin to read it, we usually find a title page, followed by a preface. The opening verses of Ezekiel's book serve both these purposes. If a longer title than the conventional English one were to be given, it would be: *The Word of the Lord to Ezekiel*. These words designate the very essence of prophecy and specify the person through whom God's word was to be communicated. And, like any good title page, the verses specify a date (about 593 B.C.) and a place in which the author was located. But the verses also contain a preface, written in the first person. "I was among the exiles", Ezekiel writes, when all this happened.

For all the brevity of these opening verses, they are packed with information about Ezekiel, all of it important in trying to understand the man and his message. Here is a man in exile; he has exchanged the fresh air of the highlands of Jerusalem for the damp and humid air around the Chebar Canal in Babylon. He used to know the privilege and position of a distinguished priestly family in Judah; now he must labour in Babylonian wastelands, trying to make them productive for a foreign power. As a young man, he had looked forward to assuming the full responsibilities of priesthood in this thirtieth year (see Num. 4:3); the reality of his thirtieth year was that of being cut off from the land in which the temple was located. Like a land-locked sailor, he could not perform the tasks for which he had been prepared.

So the book begins with one in exile, a man whose hopes and aspirations have been dashed and who cannot do the things for which he was educated. Such hope as remained was linked to the survival of a temple in a distant land, but that hope, too, survived only by a most tenuous thread. Better men would have despaired, but Ezekiel clung on and continued to hope. He was "by the river"—the words may mean no more than that the village in which he lived was located close to the river or canal. But it is possible that he was away from the village, in the place where the exiled community gathered to worship. Centuries later, it was the custom of Jewish exiles to gather by a river to worship (Acts 16:13). And while he was by the river, he had an extraordinary vision. The substance of the vision is described in the verses that follow, but it was the experience of the vision that set Ezekiel off onto a new path in life. The vision was his call; he was grasped by the Lord's "hand", by a power greater than himself, and propelled in a new direction. The man born to be a priest, but frustrated in his calling, was to become a prophet.

The beginning of the book is highly instructive of the manner in which God works. The exiles must have felt deserted and "cut off from the action", which was focused on the events in Jerusalem. What could a person do by the Chebar Canal? Indeed, who in Jerusalem had ever heard of the Chebar Canal? Yet there, in the lonely wasteland of human experience, the hand of God grasped a man and gave him a task to do. He was a young and disappointed man, perhaps not cut out for the task that was to be his. And yet the very fact of his new vocation was in itself a source of hope. The call to be a prophet implied some divine purpose, and even if that purpose were not clear at first, it was vastly more than the desolation with which Ezekiel had begun his life as an exile some five years earlier.

In a place and at a time when vision was lost, the vision came again. And it was not of Ezekiel's doing; the initiative in this extraordinary experience lay with God. Yet there is a sense in which the divine call was typical in its abnormality. Moses could hardly have anticipated the burning bush, nor Isaiah the temple vision; no more could Ezekiel have thought to see a vision of the opening heavens by the Chebar Canal. But though none could have expected the call, all were in some sense prepared. Though we can only speculate on Ezekiel's years in exile prior to his experience, one senses in his writings the survival of hope and the maintenance of faith. To such a one the call came. Grasped by a hand more powerful than himself, Ezekiel was to become a prophet.

EZEKIEL'S VISION

Ezekiel 1:4–28

⁴As I looked, behold, a stormy wind came out of the north, and a great cloud, with brightness round about it, and fire flashing forth continually, and in the midst of the fire, as it were gleaming bronze. ⁵And from the midst of it came the likeness of four living creatures. And this was their appearance: they had the form of men, ⁶but each had four faces, and each of them had four wings. ⁷Their legs were straight, and the soles of their feet were like the sole of a calf's foot; and they sparkled like burnished bronze. ⁸Under their wings on their four sides they had human hands. And the four had their faces and their wings thus: ⁹their wings touched one another; they went every one straight forward, without turning as they went. ¹⁰As for the likeness of their faces, each had the face of a man in front; the four had the face of a lion on the right side, the four had the face of an ox on the left side, and the four had the face of an eagle at the back. ¹¹Such were their faces. And their wings were spread out above; each creature had two wings, each of which touched the wing of another, while two covered their bodies. ¹²And each went straight forward; wherever the spirit would go, they went, without turning as they went. ¹³In the midst of the living creatures there was something that looked like burning coals of fire, like torches moving to and fro among the living creatures; and the fire was bright, and out of the fire went forth lightning. ¹⁴And the living creatures darted to and fro, like a flash of lightning.

¹⁵Now as I looked at the living creatures, I saw a wheel upon the earth beside the living creatures, one for each of the four of them. ¹⁶As for the appearance of the wheels and their construction: their appearance was like the gleaming of a chrysolite; and the four had the same likeness, their construction being as it were a wheel within a

wheel. [17]When they went, they went in any of their four directions without turning as they went. [18]The four wheels had rims and they had spokes; and their rims were full of eyes round about. [19]And when the living creatures went, the wheels went beside them; and when the living creatures rose from the earth, the wheels rose. [20]Wherever the spirit would go, they went, and the wheels rose along with them; for the spirit of the living creatures was in the wheels. [21]When those went, these went; and when those stood, these stood; and when those rose from the earth, the wheels rose along with them; for the spirit of the living creatures was in the wheels.

[22]Over the heads of the living creatures there was the likeness of a firmament, shining like crystal, spread out above their heads. [23]And under the firmament their wings were stretched out straight, one toward another; and each creature had two wings covering its body. [24]And when they went, I heard the sound of their wings like the sound of many waters, like the thunder of the Almighty, a sound of tumult like the sound of a host; when they stood still, they let down their wings. [25]And there came a voice from above the firmament over their heads; when they stood still, they let down their wings.

[26]And above the firmament over their heads there was the likeness of a throne, in appearance like sapphire; and seated above the likeness of a throne was a likeness as it were of a human form. [27]And upward from what had the appearance of his loins I saw as it were gleaming bronze, like the appearance of fire enclosed round about; and downward from what had the appearance of his loins I saw as it were the appearance of fire, and there was brightness round about him. [28]Like the appearance of the bow that is in the cloud on the day of rain, so was the appearance of the brightness round about.

Such was the appearance of the likeness of the glory of the Lord. And when I saw it, I fell upon my face, and I heard the voice of one speaking.

D. T. Suzuki began one of his books on Buddhism by writing: "Zen is indescribable." And yet the observation did not prevent him from composing several hundred pages in which he attempted to describe Zen. The dilemma is common to much of religious life and experience. There are things which ultimately defy the capacity of human speech for description, yet somehow they must be described and written. The vision of Ezekiel was like this. The vision was above all an experience, based initially not

upon speech, but upon sight and sound. We cannot share the
vision; we can only read the description, fully aware that the
limiting words cannot do justice to the awesome power of the
experience itself.

The vision begins in physical reality, and then transcends the
immediate environment. Ezekiel sees a storm coming towards
him from the north, accompanied by clouds and flashes of lightning. But as he watches the approaching storm clouds, it is as if
they are the curtains on a stage, suddenly drawn back to reveal a
heavenly scene, beyond the immediate curtain of earthly reality.
There were four strange creatures, combining the attributes of
humans, beasts, and heavenly beings. They were carrying an
extraordinary chariot-like vehicle on which was enthroned a
glorious being. And such was the power of the vision, that
Ezekiel fell on his face to the ground.

The primary purpose of the account of the vision is to convey to
the reader something of the overwhelming power of Ezekiel's
vision. It stunned him and prostrated him, because for all his
religious upbringing and theological training, nothing had prepared him for the vision of the living God. And so to inquire too
closely into the possible symbolism of the creatures' four faces, or
into the significance of the wheels, may be to miss the point. The
details are part of the total vision; the totality conveys to the
prophet the awareness of a dimension of reality and power that
were totally beyond his comprehension.

And yet there are a number of details in the vision that provide
some clue as to the force of its impact upon Ezekiel. The beings
bearing the divine chariot are inevitably reminiscent of the cher-
ubic figures that supported the ark of the covenant (1 Sam 4:4)
which was kept in the temple in Jerusalem. And the chariot-like
vehicle of the vision recalls that the ark itself was called a chariot
(1 Chron. 28:18). And suddenly, a part of the impact of the vision
on Ezekiel becomes clear. He was an exile, cut off not only from
his homeland, but also from the temple, the place in which the
presence of God was believed to be present in a particular way.
Where the temple was, there the ark was, and there the divine
presence could be known. But Ezekiel was in the Babylonian

wasteland, far from the focus of the divine presence. Yet here, in his vision, the symbols of God's presence appear. And so it became clear to Ezekiel that to be cut off from Jerusalem was not the same as being cut off from God. He perceived that the Lord could not be confined to a particular place; here, too, by the Chebar Canal, the Lord of heaven and earth could be experienced as a living being.

There are three points emerging from Ezekiel's visionary experience that are of enduring significance, extending beyond Ezekiel's period and place.

(i) The first concerns the nature of God. There is a sense in which Ezekiel could be called a *theologian* prior to his vision. That is, he came from a priestly family and had been prepared for divine service. He knew about God and had a sense of the nature and character of God fixed firmly in his mind. And yet, without being in any sense critical of Ezekiel's background, his theology was inadequate. The awareness of the inadequacy became apparent only in the vision, for although the vision was less than the reality of God, it totally overwhelmed the prophet's earlier understanding of God.

Not all are blessed with such a vision, yet an awareness of Ezekiel's vision is salutary. J. B. Phillips entitled one of his books *Your God is too Small*—the title encapsulates the danger of a pre-visionary theology, a view of God that is totally comprehensible, but much too small. If we fail to understand some of Ezekiel's vision, then paradoxically we have understood it in part! For its essence is that God is ultimately beyond our comprehension. In a way, the vision balances the second commandment. We are not to make images of God, and there is no simpler way of making an image than constructing a set of theological propositions. God is beyond all that; we get closer to grasping reality in the mysterious vision, but only when we realise that even the vision cannot fully comprehend the total majesty of the living God.

(ii) The brightness of God's presence seemed to Ezekiel to be like a "bow", or "like a rainbow in the clouds on a rainy day". The rainbow recalls the ancient covenant God made with humans following the flood: no more would the human race be destroyed.

Thus, in part, the rainbow penetrates the vision with a ray of hope for human beings, but more than that, it extends Ezekiel's understanding of the significance of the vision. As an exile, he was concerned for the future of his religion, for the survival of the covenant that went back to the days of Moses. Yet the rainbow alluded to an earlier covenant, to the time when God's commitment extended to all mankind.

For the Christian reader of the Old Testament, there is a breadth here to Ezekiel's vision. He was a Hebrew prophet, concerned with the destiny of the Hebrew people. Yet he sees a vision of God who cares not only for his chosen people, Israel, but also for the totality of the world. There are the seeds of hope in this. The vision extends, not only beyond that time and place, but also beyond the confines of Ezekiel's immediate faith; it points to a time when all creatures could worship the God known first to Israel.

(iii) Finally, we must not fail to learn from the *geography* of Ezekiel's vision. No less than Ezekiel, we tend to confine the experience of God to particular places and locations. It was one thing for the prophet to know of God's omnipresence; it was quite another thing to separate that knowledge from the deep-seated sense that God's presence was experienced in the temple in Jerusalem. And we too can confine God's presence to a particular place, whether it be a church, a city, or a country.

For Ezekiel, the experience of God's presence came in a foreign place, Babylon. But more than that, it was a place in which neither he nor his companions expected the divine presence. Being in Babylon somehow symbolised being cut off from God's presence. The vision that came in the clouds blowing down from the north reminds us forcibly that there is no place and no circumstances in which the experience of God may be denied. Perhaps it is even true that God's presence is known at the place and in the circumstances in which it is least expected. St Paul, many centuries later, expressed most powerfully the experience of Ezekiel, that nothing can separate a person from God. "For I am sure that neither death, nor life, nor angels, nor principalities, nor things present, nor things to come, nor powers, nor height, nor depth, nor anything else in all creation, will be able to separate us from the love of God in Christ Jesus our Lord" (Rom. 8:38–39).

EZEKIEL'S VOCATION

Ezekiel 2:1–7

[1] And he said to me, "Son of man, stand upon your feet, and I will speak with you." [2] And when he spoke to me, the Spirit entered into me and set me upon my feet; and I heard him speaking to me. [3] And he said to me, "Son of man, I send you to the people of Israel, to a nation of rebels, who have rebelled against me; they and their fathers have transgressed against me to this very day. [4] The people also are impudent and stubborn: I send you to them; and you shall say to them, 'Thus says the Lord God.' [5] And whether they hear or refuse to hear (for they are a rebellious house) they will know that there has been a prophet among them. [6] And you, son of man, be not afraid of them, nor be afraid of their words, though briers and thorns are with you and you sit upon scorpions; be not afraid of their words, nor be dismayed at their looks, for they are a rebellious house. [7] And you shall speak my words to them, whether they hear or refuse to hear; for they are a rebellious house."

"Not paralysis before him is required by God," wrote A. B. Davidson, "but reasonable service." As Ezekiel lay prostrate on the earth in the divine presence, he was among those who become aware of the mystery of God; but when God spoke, Ezekiel moved from among the mystics to join the ranks of the prophets. The vision of God that was granted to Ezekiel was not simply a profound experience, enriching the spiritual life; it was the context in which the call to service was delivered.

Perhaps Ezekiel would have preferred to remain on the ground, awed by the divine majesty. But suddenly Ezekiel was grasped by the *Spirit* (or perhaps by the *wind*: the Hebrew word may be translated by either term) and planted on his feet before God, who addressed him: "son of man"! We may be so accustomed to the New Testament usage of "son of man" that its force is lost here. The phrase, in this context, carries no messianic overtones; it stresses simply Ezekiel's status as a mortal human being. This is the beginning of all vocation: the immortal God addresses a mortal man.

The anatomy of Ezekiel's vocation is fascinating, for it provides a clue to the nature of all vocations. A vocation, whether in the ancient world or the modern, is not analogous to planning a career; quite different criteria are employed. There are three key points in Ezekiel's vocation worth noting.

(i) The initiative in vocation lies with God. It was God's initiative to approach, in visionary form, a person who could hardly have dreamed of becoming a prophet. It was God who spoke. And twice, he said to Ezekiel: "I send you" (verses 3, 4). The divine approach is crucial to vocation, for without it there is not the power to undertake the task. And so, though Ezekiel might be ill-prepared in a human sense for the rigours of a prophet's life, the divine approach was the basis of his graduation to the ranks of the prophets.

(ii) The message that the prophet was called to deliver, as it is condensed here, is curious. "Thus says the Lord God" (verse 4). It is like the preface to a book that consists only of blank pages. Yet, at the same time, this short statement condenses prophecy to its very essence. Prophecy is the declaration of God's word, and though the substance of that word is not yet made explicit, the principle is established. Ezekiel is to be God's spokesman. The words are very significant, not only because the substance of Ezekiel's ministry would be God's word, but also because that word carried its own authority.

As the living word was to Ezekiel's ministry, so Scripture has become in the contemporary Church, for it is the record of the word of God, both spoken and incarnate. And contemporary prophetic ministry is still the same: "thus says the Lord God". As in Ezekiel's time, so too today the word must be heard, and all vocations, in their variety of forms, are directed eventually to that end.

(iii) The third point about Ezekiel's call indicates more clearly than the others the distinction between a career and a vocation.

Ezekiel was promised no success; indeed, the injunction not to be afraid was almost a guarantee of frightening circumstances. He was to speak to his people, but was forewarned that they were a stubborn and impudent lot, unlikely to listen too attentively.

It is hardly a rosy picture that is painted for Ezekiel at the beginning of his new task. "Join the Navy and see the world", the slogans used to read. But a poster would read differently for prophets: "Join the prophets! Be cast among prickles and thorn-bushes! Sit on the scorpions!" (verse 6). It is hardly enticing. Yet one is not enticed to prophethood, but compelled. And the measure of Ezekiel's success would not be the public response to his message so much as his fulfilment of the divine commission. For the purpose of God, though it is not altogether easy to understand, was that "the people will know that there has been a prophet among them" (verse 5). The human response to the divine word cannot be predicted beforehand, and we should beware of those modern "evangelistic formulae" which feign to guarantee "success". The ultimate and true success of a calling will frequently remain unknown, even to the one who is called.

EATING THE SCROLL

Ezekiel 2:8–3:3

⁸"But you, son of man, hear what I say to you; be not rebellious like that rebellious house; open your mouth, and eat what I give you." ⁹And when I looked, behold, a hand was stretched out to me, and, lo, a written scroll was in it; ¹⁰and he spread it before me; and it had writing on the front and on the back, and there were written on it words of lamentation and mourning and woe.

¹And he said to me, "Son of man, eat what is offered to you; eat this scroll, and go, speak to the house of Israel." ²So I opened my mouth, and he gave me the scroll to eat. ³And he said to me, "Son of man, eat this scroll that I give you and fill your stomach with it." Then I ate it; and it was in my mouth as sweet as honey.

Ezekiel's vocation is not completed in the words of God commanding him to be a prophet to Israel. The young man, who so far has not spoken, is now commanded to act; his response to this immediate command will symbolise his response to the whole call of God delivered to him in the vision. Thus, these verses describe a kind of ordination service for the prophet; he is to act in a fashion that will symbolise the entire ministry to which he is called. Yet there are no friends and relatives at this ordination service; the entire action continues as a part of the vision.

"Eat what I give you," declares the voice of the awesome figure in the vision. No doubt Ezekiel was sufficiently terrified by the experience to eat whatever was placed in front of him, but the command is curious nevertheless. He was to eat a scroll, the ancient counterpart of the modern book. A scroll was constructed of parchment, or papyrus, in a long strip, wound around a central spindle. Some scrolls could be very long; one of the famous Dead Sea Scrolls, found at Qumran, measured approximately twenty-four feet in length. Normally, the writing on a scroll would be on one side of the paper only, but the scroll which Ezekiel was commanded to eat was unusual in that writing was on both sides. It was as if its divine author had so much to say that the conventional space was insufficient; the writing must be squeezed into every blank space!

The substance of this scroll is described as "words of lamentation and mourning and woe". The meaning is not so much that the message as such was mournful; rather, its effect on those who read, or heard, it would be to create misery and woe. A message of truth and joy can create misery in a liar; so too can the word of God make the ungodly mournful. And the purpose of the writing tightly packed onto this scroll is that it is to be addressed to the people of Israel.

It is difficult to know the extent to which Ezekiel's earlier experiences had shaped the substance and form of his vision. But it is worth recollecting that in the winter months of 603 B.C., when Ezekiel was a younger man and still a citizen of Jerusalem, a dramatic event had taken place. Jeremiah's prophecies had been written down on a scroll and read aloud in the temple. But King Jehoiakim, reacting negatively to the message on the scroll, had burned it piece by piece, and put out a bulletin for the arrest of its author (Jer. 36). Now Ezekiel was to take up a task similar to that of Jeremiah; he knew that Jeremiah's scroll had won him no favour, but he was being commanded to eat a scroll, so that it would become a part of him, the essence of his new ministry.

There are two aspects of Ezekiel's symbolic act that may continue to speak to us of the nature of vocation.

(i) Ezekiel was to be a prophet to a rebellious people, to people who refused to *obey* God, and so the first thing he was asked to do was *obey*. In obeying the command to eat, he immediately distinguished himself from the disobedient people to whom he was sent. And in his act of obedience, he discovered the taste of the scroll to be "sweet as honey". The same scroll that would taste so bitter to the house of Israel, tasted sweet on the new prophet's tongue. There is in all acts of obedience a sweet taste; obedience as such guarantees no freedom from pain, but it does bring the satisfaction of a life being fulfilled. When the psalmist wrote: "Taste and see that the Lord is good" (Ps. 34:8), he wrote as one who had suffered affliction, but trusted in divine deliverance.

(ii) We eat in order to live; food, when digested and absorbed by the body, provides the strength for the body to undertake its normal physical functions. And what food is for the body, the scroll was to be for Ezekiel's ministry. As the divine words were absorbed into his very being, they would be converted into the strength necessary for the fulfilment of the prophetic task. It is a reminder that any ministry requires strength and sustenance; for us, as for Ezekiel, that food and strength may come from the "consumption" of the word of God.

MINISTRY TO A STUBBORN PEOPLE

Ezekiel 3:4–15

4And he said to me, "Son of man, go, get you to the house of Israel, and speak with my words to them. 5For you are not sent to a people of foreign speech and a hard language, but to the house of Israel—6not to many peoples of foreign speech and a hard language, whose words you cannot understand. Surely, if I sent you to such, they would listen to you. [7]But the house of Israel will not listen to you; for they are not willing to listen to me; because all the house of Israel are of a hard forehead and of a stubborn heart. [8]Behold, I have made your face hard against their faces, and your forehead hard against their foreheads. [9]Like adamant harder than flint have I made your forehead; fear them not, nor be dismayed at their looks, for they are a rebellious house." [10]Moreover he said to me, "Son of man, all my words that I shall speak to you receive in your heart, and hear with your ears. [11]And go, get you to the exiles, to your people, and say to them, 'Thus says the Lord God'; whether they hear or refuse to hear."

[12]Then the Spirit lifted me up, and as the glory of the Lord arose from its place, I heard behind me the sound of a great earthquake; [13]it was the sound of the wings of the living creatures as they touched one another, and the sound of the wheels beside them, that sounded like a great earthquake. [14]The Spirit lifted me up and took me away, and I went in bitterness in the heat of my spirit, the hand of the Lord being strong upon me; [15]and I came to the exiles at Telabib, who dwelt by the river Chebar. And I sat there overwhelmed among them seven days.

As Ezekiel's vision and vocation draws towards a close, God again addresses Ezekiel; as before, he does not use his personal name, but calls him "son of man" (verses 4, 10), continuing to remind him of his mortality. God's last words to Ezekiel in the vision are not merely a repetition of earlier statements, but are designed to equip him for his task. He was to minister to a people who were incredibly stubborn, and so he too would be made hard and flint-like for the task. Suddenly, the prophet's name takes on significance; *Ezekiel* means "God hardens"! After equipping him for his task, the Spirit lifts him from the place of the vision, amid the phenomena of storm, and returns him to the community of exiles at Tel Abib. There Ezekiel was silent for a week, totally overwhelmed by his experience.

This final part of the vision provides further penetrating insight into the nature of vocation and ministry.

(i) Ezekiel is specifically hardened for his task (verses 8–9). Some interpreters have suggested that the prophet was by nature a tough and humourless man, and that he brought with him to his task all the baggage of his natural personality and character. But the opposite is more likely to be true. It is precisely because he was a sensitive man, not bull-headed by nature, that he had to be toughened for his task. And yet in the hardening of the prophet, we perceive his character being moulded like that of God. Though God loved his people, he sent them a terrible message; not to have done so would have been unloving. But the terrible message, entrusted to the new prophet, illuminates the suffering into which God's love for his people had drawn him. And, as Walther Zimmerli has put it, "the prophet sees himself set alongside God in an impressive solidarity of suffering." It was not unusual for prophets to suffer; what Ezekiel would experience had already been the lot of Jeremiah and others before him. But the point to be remembered in any suffering associated with ministry is that it is a participation in the suffering of God; that insight may not reduce the pain, but it does portray the privilege of suffering. And it does remind all servants of God that one of the many faces of love is that of agony and pain.

(ii) Ezekiel is also reminded, in this final preparation for prophethood, that he must continue to *listen* to the word of God. He has already eaten the scroll; in a sense, the divine word is already a part of his being. But the task of a prophet is not simply to deliver that which was once received. He must continue to hear the words that God would speak in the future (verse 10). The ministry to which he was called was thus not simply one of speaking and acting, but also one of perpetual listening. The same truth is perpetually true; unless we continue to listen, we cannot have any vital message to declare.

(iii) When Ezekiel was taken away from the place of vision, he says that he went "in bitterness" (verse 14). The words have been the source of considerable debate as to their precise significance, for at first they seem out of harmony with the immediate context. Yet, as one reflects on the experience of Ezekiel that had just ended, the words ring true of the aftermath of so much religious experience. From one perspective, the mountain-top experience is over and Ezekiel returns to the "heap" that is his home. (*Tel Abib* means "heap left by the flood" in Babylonian.) There cannot but be a sense of anticlimax, even bitterness, that the marvellous experience is over and exchanged once again for the gloomy reality of a life in exile. But there is more to the bitterness than this. It was one thing to be told in the vision to be a hard-hearted prophet to a stubborn people. But returning to the immediate reality of daily existence, Ezekiel saw the people to whom he must minister. They might indeed be stubborn, but they were his friends and only companions. Like him, they had experienced the agony of defeat and the emptiness of exile. To minister to a "people" would be one thing, but these people had faces he knew, a history he had shared and a life of desolate drudgery. Suddenly, his task seemed unkind, and a sense of bitterness overcame Ezekiel.

The experience of Ezekiel is typical at this point of most persons who are privileged at one point or another in life to see the vision. Having once soared up and seen beyond the immediate realities of human existence, it is not easy to return to the drabness of mortal life. For Ezekiel, as for many others, the temptation must have been strong to become a mystic, not a prophet. Yet he was called to be a prophet and that meant coming down from the mountain. And ultimately the test of any true vision is the recipient's ability to retain its power, even when the experience has passed.

COMMISSIONED AS A WATCHMAN

Ezekiel 3:16–21

16 And at the end of seven days, the word of the Lord came to me: 17"Son of man, I have made you a watchman for the house of Israel; whenever you hear a word from my mouth, you shall give them warning from me. 18If I say to the wicked, 'You shall surely die,' and you give him no warning, nor speak to warn the wicked from his wicked way, in order to save his life, that wicked man shall die in his

iniquity; but his blood I will require at your hand. ¹⁹But if you warn the wicked, and he does not turn from his wickedness, or from his wicked way, he shall die in his iniquity; but you will have saved your life. ²⁰Again, if a righteous man turns from his righteousness and commits iniquity, and I lay a stumbling block before him, he shall die; because you have not warned him, he shall die for his sin, and his righteous deeds which he has done shall not be remembered; but his blood I will require at your hand. ²¹Nevertheless if you warn the righteous man not to sin, and he does not sin, he shall surely live, because he took warning; and you will have saved your life.''

For one week after his awesome vision, Ezekiel remained in a state of near-shock in the company of his fellow exiles. And then, when the seven days had passed in reflection on the vision and vocation, God's word came to Ezekiel again. Already he was beginning to learn one lesson; a week earlier, he had been instructed to listen for the words of God (3:10), and now he was hearing the voice again, prefaced by the same reminder of his mortality, "son of man" (verse 17). The vision of the week before was not a delusion; it was the beginning of an experience that was to mark the remainder of Ezekiel's ministry. And fifty times, so we are told, God's word came to Ezekiel; for no other prophet is there a record of such sustained contact with the divine word, the very essence of prophecy.

The words that are now spoken to Ezekiel amplify still a further dimension of the ministry to which he is called; he is to be Israel's *watchman*. Later in his life and ministry, the prophet was to repeat these words, together with a parable, in one of his prophetic sermons to Israel (33:1–9). But now, the words are for his ears only; they open up a new and rather frightening aspect of the prophetic ministry, that of *responsibility*. (The parable as a whole is discussed in more detail at 33:1–9; here, only the implications for Ezekiel's vocation are considered.)

The prophet's role as a watchman illuminates various dimensions of the responsibility associated with ministry.

(i) Ezekiel's responsibility was inescapable and came with the prophetic task. When vocation is first encountered, it seems simple enough; it appears to be based on a relationship between two parties. God called, and Ezekiel responded; he could be judged by the faithfulness of his response. But having responded, the young man suddenly found himself responsible for the fate of multitudes. As a sentry is responsible for the lives of the soldiers in his camp, or a ship's captain is responsible for his crew and passengers, so too Ezekiel was to be responsible for the people of Israel. Vocation and responsibility went together; there could not be one without the other.

Of all the tasks a person may undertake, that of responsibility is the hardest to shoulder. There can be no shirking of the job, for that in itself would be irresponsible. Thus, when Ezekiel became the watchman of Israel, the lines of the remainder of his life were set; he could not live for himself alone, nor could he shrug off his responsibilities if those to whom he was sent were unresponsive to his call. Like it or not, he had assumed a responsibility that he would carry with him to the grave.

(ii) Though the prophet's assumption of responsibility was an awesome experience, it was also a reflection of God's love. Without the existence of a prophet, wicked persons could be judged by God for their evil acts and justly condemned; they had received the legacy of God's law and revelation and had failed to live in harmony with God. In terms of justice, there was no need for a prophet or watchman—an evil people could hardly plead the excuse of ignorance for their acts. Yet the fact that a watchman was appointed indicated that God did not operate by the mere requirements of law and justice. He desired to give them further warning, to make his people know what they should have known all along; this desire was rooted in love.

It is this perception that prophetic responsibility is rooted and grounded in divine love, that makes it possible to carry it. If one thinks only in egocentric terms, such responsibility seems more than any person should be asked to assume. Yet it is a form of love and, like so many of the faces of love, it may involve pain. But recognising the origin of such awesome responsibility in divine love provides also the key to discharging that responsibility. It is only when the prophet learns to love as God does, that responsibility becomes a privilege, not a burden.

(iii) Just as the strength to accept responsibility comes from the recognition of its roots in divine love, so too the enactment of responsibility in ministry must be an expression of love and concern for fellow human beings. Thus, *responsibility* and *duty* differ as to character, and the former is infinitely greater. There is a sense in which the office of watchman implied duties: wakefulness, alertness, speaking the word of warning, and so on. But duties can be fulfilled to the letter, with no involvement of the heart; the responsibility of the watchman involves entering into the compassion of God towards his people.

For the moment, Ezekiel is not required to make public his role as a watchman; he cannot share this dimension of his task. Only later does he reveal his role to his fellow exiles, and then it is in an attempt to make them see, not only the danger of the path in which they walk, but also God's concern that they turn back to the true path.

COMMISSIONED TO CONFINEMENT

Ezekiel 3:22–27

> [22] And the hand of the Lord was there upon me; and he said to me, "Arise, go forth into the plain, and there I will speak with you." [23] So I arose and went forth into the plain; and, lo, the glory of the Lord stood there, like the glory which I had seen by the river Chebar; and I fell on my face. [24] But the Spirit entered into me, and set me upon my feet; and he spoke with me and said to me, "Go, shut yourself within your house. [25] And you, O son of man, behold, cords will be placed upon you, and you shall be bound with them, so that you cannot go out among the people; [26] and I will make your tongue cleave to the roof of your mouth, so that you shall be dumb and unable to reprove them; for they are a rebellious house. [27] But when I speak with you, I will open your mouth, and you shall say to them, 'Thus says the Lord God'; he that will hear, let him hear; and he that will refuse to hear, let him refuse; for they are a rebellious house."

This short passage is puzzling in some of its details and has been the source of considerable debate among the commentators.

There are some who would interpret it as marking the beginning of Ezekiel's ministry as such, but it is probably better to read it as the conclusion of Ezekiel's commissioning, a theme which has dominated the first three chapters of the book. Later in the book, some of the dimensions of this description of the prophet's commission become clear; there are references to speechlessness and the return of speech in 24:27 and 29:21.

Ezekiel is compelled once again to leave his community and go out into the countryside. He goes to the *plain* (verse 23), but RSV's translation is a little misleading at this point. The Hebrew word should be translated *valley*; the only other context in which this word is used in the book is in Ezekiel's vision in the valley of the dry bones (37:1), and it is possible that this part of his commission takes place in the same location in which later he sees that vision. There in the valley, the young man again sees the vision of God's glory, in a form reminiscent of the experience which first set him on the path of prophethood. He falls on his face in awe, but once again is compelled to stand on his feet; he is to receive further instructions concerning the nature of the task that lies ahead of him.

The words that God addresses to Ezekiel indicate in a powerful manner a new dimension of his coming ministry. In his initial perception of the task, he has become aware primarily of his role as God's *spokesman*. He is to say: "Thus says the Lord God" (2:4). He is to cry out the watchman's warning. He has consumed God's scroll, so that the divine words are the driving force within him. But now Ezekiel perceives a further dimension of his ministry. There will be times when he is housebound and dumb; there will be times when he must go out among the people and speak.

The indication that Ezekiel would be bound with cords and rendered speechless is sometimes interpreted as a prophetic act as such. His inability to move and inability to speak would symbolise the manner in which an evil people had tied God by their actions and rendered him speechless. And the symbols of God's silence could be at least as terrifying as the substance of his speech. There is some merit in this interpretation and an extent to which it may be perceived later in aspects of Ezekiel's ministry.

But primarily the contrast between binding and freedom, and between dumbness and speech, illuminates the character of the prophetic office as such.

As a servant of God, the prophet is totally at his master's command. If he is told not to speak, that command would be as restricting as ropes tying him to a chair in his kitchen. But if he is told to speak, then God even opens his mouth (verse 27); he cannot restrain the words he must address to Israel. And so Ezekiel is finally beginning to understand all the implications of what he is being called to undertake. One cannot pin down precisely the length of the entire experience in which he became aware of his life's new calling. It was more than a week, and may even have extended over a few weeks. The experience was marked by vision, but the substance of the visions was constantly the call of God to obey and to serve. And in a very real sense, this extended experience of vocation was also a preparation and education for the task lying ahead. The overwhelming sense of God's glory and power would permeate the prophet's being and speech throughout his ministry.

The final words that God addresses to Ezekiel in this act of commissioning have a ring of freedom to them, but also of threat. "He that will hear, let him hear; and he that will refuse to hear, let him refuse" (verse 27). The words characterise the form of the divine address that Ezekiel was to deliver to Israel, and Jesus too was frequently to use these words in his ministry of teaching. The word was to be spoken, but no speech is complete without hearing. And with respect to the audience, it was not their auditory facility as such that was in question; rather, it was the facility to hear with understanding and with the intention of acting on the basis of understanding.

Thus, whenever one hears the divine word, whether through the ancient prophets, through the teaching of Jesus, or through some modern medium, one is placed in a situation of freedom. The physical act of hearing is in a sense involuntary; freedom is exercised in the response we make to that which we hear. The word thus comes to us with a respect for our persons; we are not bludgeoned into action, nor is the divine word like the electrical impulse that directs the actions of a robot. It comes to us and invites reaction; we are free to choose our response. But our freedom may be our salvation or our downfall. Aware of the responsibility involved in our freedom, we must listen with understanding, and understand with obedience.

THE SYMBOL OF JERUSALEM UNDER ATTACK

Ezekiel 4:1–3

> [1]"And you, O son of man, take a brick and lay it before you, and portray upon it a city, even Jerusalem; [2]and put siegeworks against it, and build a siege wall against it, and cast up a mound against it; set camps also against it, and plant battering rams against it round about. [3]And take an iron plate, and place it as an iron wall between you and the city; and set your face toward it, and let it be in a state of siege, and press the siege against it. This is a sign for the house of Israel."

In Chapter 4, the description of Ezekiel's ministry as such begins abruptly. The call and commission are complete; now the action must begin. And if Ezekiel had not been thoroughly prepared for his task, the first job he was given to do would have seemed very curious; "take a brick", God says to him! The prophetic ministry, as becomes so clear in the life of Ezekiel, involves more than preaching; he is to begin by being a map-maker and model-builder. But actions may speak as loudly as words. The actions that Ezekiel is now to undertake will communicate as forcibly as a sermon the divine message.

First, the prophet is instructed to take a brick and draw upon it a map of the city of Jerusalem. He would take a flat mud-brick, of the kind used in the construction of houses in Tel Abib, and while the mud was still soft, imprint the outline of Jerusalem's walls and key buildings on its surface. Then the brick would harden in the warm sun, fixing the map firmly upon its surface. (This act would not have been unusual in Babylon; archaeological discoveries in that region include a number of such bricks, bearing on their surfaces maps and architectural drawings.) Setting the brick down upon the ground, the prophet would then place around it models of the instruments of siege: towers, a siege-mound, military camps and battering rams. (The text is a little unclear; it is possible that these siege-works were to be included as a part of the map, but it is more likely that they were separate models, placed strategically around the brick with its map.) Then the prophet was to take an iron plate, of the large griddle-type used for baking bread; no doubt he would have used the one from his kitchen. The plate would have been wedged into the ground, alongside the map and model, in the form of an enormous wall (in proportion to the model!). Ezekiel himself took up a position behind the plate, sitting or lying down, gazing steadfastly at the map and model, but his view would have been impeded by the intervening plate.

One must suppose that this action took place just outside Ezekiel's house in Tel Abib. It must quickly have become the focus of attention, for the residents of Tel Abib, although they had certain freedoms, were in effect a community of prisoners-of-war. News of Ezekiel's strange action must have spread quickly through the community, and people would have come to watch. It would not have been too difficult to determine the meaning of the display. There was their beloved city, Jerusalem; the siege-works round about it indicated that it would again be besiged by an enormously powerful army. Thus far, Ezekiel's map and model were prophetic anticipations of the coming second siege of Jerusalem (it took place in 587 B.C.). But what was so disturbing about the display was the iron plate, with the prophet stationed behind it. The prophet represented God; the plate represented the division and separation between God and his holy city, the location in which his presence should be known with particular intimacy. Thus it became clear to the observers that the coming fate of Jerusalem was not unknown to God; indeed, indirectly the siege-works represented the actions of God against his own city. The steadfast gaze and the iron plate symbolised the divine anger; God's wrath was directed against the inhabitants of the supposedly holy city.

While the symbolic meaning of Ezekiel's action is clear, its meaning and relevance to the audience is not so immediately clear. At first impression, such a message should be delivered to the inhabitants of Jerusalem, the city in question, rather than to its desolate exiles in a remote Babylonian refugee camp. What could they learn from the prophetic action, other than the distressing fact that matters would soon get worse for Jerusalem than they already were?

The overall meaning of this action emerges both in the immediate context of exile and in the larger of the transformation taking place in Israel's religion. (a) In the immediate context of exile, the Jews had to cling to hope of some kind. The natural focus of such hope was the city of Jerusalem, from which they had been exiled; there, God's intimate presence had been known. But this source of hope was dashed by Ezekiel's action; if salvation were to be found, it would not be in Jerusalem, for God's face was steadfastly set against that city. (b) As it would gradually become clear in the prophet's unfolding ministry, the reason for God's wrath against his own city was the evil of its inhabitants. If there was any hope at all for the future, it would only be found in turning from evil, for evil brought only siege and destruction. The faith of the Jews was being weaned gradually from its attachment to a particular place; the prophet was calling for a commitment to God, unlinked to a city and transcending Tel Abib, that was rooted in repentance and righteousness.

There is thus in this opening action of Ezekiel's ministry a message of both darkness and light, of despair and of hope. It was a gloomy foreboding of future disaster for the beloved Jerusalem, but the very performance of the prophetic action contained the kernel of hope. There would be no need of such an action if God had finished with his people. Just as the coming destruction of Jerusalem was in part the result of their own past actions, so too God's future actions in the world would be the result in part of their present response to God. Every message of doom contains the seed of hope. Every announcement of judgment has implicit within it a call to repentance. If they would only hear the words pregnant within the prophetic action, a new map would unfold with a path for the future marked firmly upon it.

ACTIONS SYMBOLISING JUDGMENT

Ezekiel 4:4–8

> [4]"Then lie upon your left side, and I will lay the punishment of the house of Israel upon you; for the number of the days that you lie upon it, you shall bear their punishment. [5]For I assign to you a number of days, three hundred and ninety days, equal to the number of the years of their punishment; so long shall you bear the punishment of the house of Israel. [6]And when you have completed these, you shall lie down a second time, but on your right side, and bear the punishment of the house of Judah; forty days I assign you, a day for each year. [7]And you shall set your face toward the siege of Jerusalem, with your arm bared; and you shall prophesy against the city. [8]And, behold, I will put cords upon you, so that you cannot turn from one side to the other, till you have completed the days of your siege."

Of all the difficult passages in the Book of Ezekiel, this short text is one of the most complex. It is written in a terse, almost short-hand style, so that the precise details of some of the actions being described are left to the reader's imagination. And the numbers of days that are mentioned, not easy to interpret as they stand, are rendered still more complicated by the fact that the earliest Greek translation, the Septuagint, differs from the Hebrew text; where the Hebrew text reads 390 days (verse 5), the Greek text (followed by NEB) has 190 days. As a consequence, any interpretation of this passage must be tentative.

First, it is probable that the actions which Ezekiel was ordered to do should be interpreted as daily actions performed each day as part of a continuing ministry. Thus, when he is told to lie on his left side for 390 days, the sense is not that he was to remain totally motionless in that position, day and night, without so much as moving to prepare food and drink, or perform the necessary bodily functions. It is clear that there were other things to do, including actions and speech (verse 7), and the preparation of food and drink (verses 9–17). In other words, for a period of time each day (the precise time not being specified), Ezekiel was to lie on his side on the ground; presumably this would have been done in a public place, perhaps next to the prophet's map and models.

For 390 days, he was to lie on his left side each day, and then he was to lie on his right side for a further forty days. In addition, he was to set his face toward "the siege of Jerusalem", that is, toward the map of Jerusalem he had drawn on the mud brick, and one arm was to be bared as a sign of threat. This latter action was probably distinct from the former; a portion of each day would be spent lying on the side, and then the prophet would sit, or lie, gazing fixedly at the map and model, with arm bared as if for action. Thus, the primary focus of the ministry was in symbolic action, but there were also to be words, prophetic oracles directed against the city (verse 7). The binding with cords (verse 8) may describe his condition during the latter action; while gazing at the map of the city, he was to be bound and motionless, so that nothing could distract him from the object of his gaze.

To some extent, the interpretation of the actions is interspersed in the words describing them. As Ezekiel lay on his side, he symbolised the punishment of God that lay on Israel and Judah respectively. But the significance of the numbers is less clear, though the ratio is straightforward; one day in the prophet's symbolic actions represented one year in the history of the nations. The numbers 390 and 40 are probably rounded approximations, though their total is significant. 390 days/years may represent the period from the dedication of the temple in Solomon's time to its destruction in 587/6 B.C. 40 days/years, representing one generation, may symbolise either the exile itself, or the time from the destruction of the temple to the beginning of its restoration. But the total number of days/years, namely 430, no doubt was intended to parallel the years of the captivity in Egypt (Exod. 12:40). Yet it would be a mistake to take the numbers to be the central aspect of this symbolic action. For the audience at that time, the most evident aspect of the action would be that day after day, month after month, there was Ezekiel prostrate on his side on the ground, symbolising the weight of God's punishment on his people. It was the length and continuity of the actions that would carry such impact to the audience; only after the actions were completed would the numbers suddenly assume significance.

This continuous series of prophetic actions undertaken by the prophet, extending over a period of some fourteen months, contains two important insights; one pertains to the medium, namely Ezekiel, and the other to the message.

(i) From the very beginning of his ministry, Ezekiel was learning that the role of the prophet involved hardship and suffering. Quite apart from the physical discomfort, indeed pain, which his daily actions must have induced, he must also have been the target of a good deal of mockery and derision. He was fulfilling his orders, but his actions were not those of a normal person. We should probably be mistaken if we visualised Ezekiel's daily audience staring thoughtfully at his actions, attempting to discern their meaning; many would likely have laughed, suspecting that exile and the heat of the Babylonian sun had affected his mental stability. But Ezekiel, for his part, was learning that the servant of God must enter into the suffering of God.

(ii) The actions also contained a message. Although the verses describing them seem to be replete with doom, there is also a message of hope. It is to be found in the number of the total days that Ezekiel was to lie on his side: 430 days, representing 430 years. In the past, after 430 years in Egyptian servitude, there had been a glorious exodus, a liberation from bondage. The days that Ezekiel was to lie on his side were numbered; when the years which they symbolised were over, there was the hope of a second exodus and a new experience of God's liberating power. For those who had eyes to see and ears to understand, even the symbols of punishment could be transformed into hope.

One of the most powerful lessons communicated in the Book of Ezekiel is an understanding of the way in which darkness may be transformed into light, and despair into hope. For a people who had little hope, and whose only tangible anchor for fragile hope was soon to be destroyed, there came a more distant vision, for those who could see it, of God's liberation.

THE SYMBOLISM OF EZEKIEL'S DIET

Ezekiel 4:9–17

⁹"And you, take wheat and barley, beans and lentils, millet and spelt, and put them into a single vessel, and make bread of them. During the number of days that you lie upon your side, three hundred and ninety days, you shall eat it. ¹⁰And the food which you eat shall be by weight, twenty shekels a day; once a day you shall eat it. ¹¹And water you shall drink by measure, the sixth part of a hin; once a day you shall drink. ¹²And you shall eat it as a barley cake, baking it in their sight on human dung." ¹³And the Lord said, "Thus shall the people of Israel eat their bread unclean, among the nations whither I will drive them." ¹⁴Then I said, "Ah Lord God! behold, I have never defiled myself; from my youth up till now I have never eaten what died of itself or was torn by beasts, nor has foul flesh come into my mouth." ¹⁵Then he said to me, "See, I will let you have cow's dung instead of human dung, on which you may prepare your bread." ¹⁶Moreover he said to me, "Son of man, behold, I will break the staff of bread in Jerusalem; they shall eat bread by weight and with fearfulness; and they shall drink water by measure and in dismay. ¹⁷I will do this that they may lack bread and water, and look at one another in dismay, and waste away under their punishment."

The description of Ezekiel's diet supplements the actions described in the previous verses. Not only was the prophet to perform certain symbolic actions each day; even his diet was to be symbolic, conveying a message to those who observed the daily ritual in front of the prophet's house.

Each day, he was to make *bread* (verse 9); the Hebrew word may designate simply *food*, and the strange concoction Ezekiel was to cook was a kind of "bits-and-pieces bun", rather than simple bread. His daily ration of bread would weigh approximately eight ounces, and his ration of water was little more than a pint. We do not know whether this was the prophet's total daily diet, or whether it was simply the diet to be consumed during the daily public ministry, to be supplemented by more normal rations in the privacy of the home in the evening. If this little loaf and short drink were the total daily input, then we perceive again how the prophet's ministry involved hardship. But it is more probable that the diet should be considered strictly a part of the public ministry, to be supplemented at other times.

In the first instructions, Ezekiel was to cook the loaf on a fire fuelled by human excrement, but Ezekiel responded with dismay to this injunction. He was trained for priesthood and thus was particularly sensitive to any kind of ritual impurity; human excrement, according to the ancient Mosaic law, should be buried outside the settlement (Deut. 23:12–14). It was no doubt this ritual reaction, rather than the natural repugnance of cooking food on human dung, that provoked Ezekiel's outburst of horror at his instructions (verse 14). And so, as a concession, he was permitted to bake the bread on cow's dung. In ancient times, as in the modern Middle East, dried cow or camel dung, mixed with straw, was used for the cooking fire; in the absence of a supply of wood, it was an important commodity of daily existence. The bread was baked, either by being placed on the glowing fire, or on stones heated by the fire. But inevitably, in such a manner of baking, the cleanliness of the food cannot be absolutely guaranteed.

The prophet's restricted diet symbolises both siege and exile. It pointed to the shortage of food and drink that there would be in Jerusalem during the siege leading to its collapse. And the bread, made with such a mixture of cereals, was no gastronomic delight of the orient; it was a recipe for leftovers, indicating the short supply of staple foods, just as the short drink indicated the scarcity of water. Thus would God's people eat in siege, and thus would they eat in exile.

Ezekiel's diet, and the manner in which it was to be cooked, carry a two-fold message beyond the immediate symbolism of judgment.

(i) Far back in Israel's past, the wandering Hebrews had been sustained by God's manna in the wilderness; and yet the message of that divine feeding was that "man does not live by bread alone, but man lives by every utterance of the mouth of the Lord" (Deut. 8:3). And Jesus, too, quoted these ancient words in resisting the first of the temptations in the wilderness (Matt.

4:1–4). Just as, physically, one must eat to live, so too the spiritual life is dependent on partaking of the bread of life, the Word of God. But for ordinary humans, the first of these truths is more evident than the latter. Hunger will reduce the body to weakness and eventually death; but the well-fed and hungry alike may starve the soul and hardly be aware of what they are doing.

The prophet's symbolic diet reveals the reverse of this ancient truth. A people who for so long had ignored the bread of God's word, would eventually be reduced to emergency rations for the body. In a sense, the diet symbolised judgment; in a deeper sense, it contained a message, a reminder of the true starvation of the spiritual life which was the root cause of the physical crisis. There are some who fast, consciously to remind themselves of a deeper hunger and need. Ezekiel reminds us that God may send the fast, superficially as judgment, but more profoundly as a message of love.

(ii) The prophet's reaction of horror at the manner of baking he is instructed to employ provides a profound insight into God's nature. So far, in his prophetic ministry, Ezekiel has fulfilled his instructions without question, despite the hardship they involve. Now, he reacts in horror to the command to bake on human dung, and he receives a divine concession to bake with another fuel. Ezekiel is not just being fussy and unwilling to accept hardship in ministry; he demonstrates his willingness to suffer over and again throughout his life. His reaction stems from a lifetime of preparation for priesthood, and a profoundly based awareness of that which was ritually unclean. Thus his reaction to the command is not purely personal; it is rooted in an awareness of the purity required by his relationship to God. And thus, as an act of kindness, God changes the specification.

The incident is remarkable in a number of ways. While it gives some insight into Ezekiel's character, it is the insight pertaining to God that is more significant. The concession meant that something of the power of the symbolic message would be lost. Yet the message was modified for the sake of the messenger. For all the suffering he asked of his servant, God was not unfeeling; he was concerned for his messenger as well as for those to whom the message was sent. Ezekiel had no guarantee of such a concession in response to his outburst, but its receipt was an encouragement of love. And for all who would serve God, and accept the hardships which service brings, this little incident is a source of encouragement. We do not know that concessions will be made; but, when they are, their impact sheds light on the dark path that service may call us to tread.

THE SHEARING OF THE PROPHET'S HAIR

Ezekiel 5:1–4

[1]"And you, O son of man, take a sharp sword; use it as a barber's razor and pass it over your head and your beard; then take balances for weighing, and divide the hair. [2] A third part you shall burn in the fire in the midst of the city, when the days of the siege are completed; and a third part you shall take and strike with the sword round about the city; and a third part you shall scatter to the wind, and I will unsheathe the sword after them. [3] And you shall take from these a small number, and bind them in the skirts of your robe. [4] And of these again you shall take some, and cast them into the fire, and burn them in the fire; from there a fire will come forth into all the house of Israel."

The timing of the actions that Ezekiel is now instructed to perform is uncertain, though it is possible that they were to be done after the various symbolic actions described in Chapter 4. This prophecy has a double form. First, there are the actions as such (described in this passage), with their own implicit symbolism. There follows, in the verses immediately after, an oracle from God; the words of the oracle elaborate in greater detail the meaning of the symbolic actions.

Again, the prophet's actions must be envisaged as taking place in public view, with a crowd of watchful observers wondering what the crazy man was going to do next. Ezekiel took a sword and sharpened its heavy blade on a whetstone, preparing it for the unusually delicate task it must perform. Then, in full view of the onlookers, he began to shave the hairs from his head and jaw, collecting them all carefully into a pile in front of him. The hairy prophet they used to know gradually became a bald and clean-shaven man, the skin no doubt raw as a consequence of being sheared by so unwieldy a blade. Then the prophet took a balance, of the kind that a merchant would use, and carefully weighed out the hair into three equal heaps. The audience, by this time, no doubt found the whole scene to be hilarious; weighing hair is akin to using feathers for ballast!

The first pile of hair was burned in a fire beside the prophet. Then the second pile was chopped up by the sword, until the long tresses became short stubble. The third and final portion was tossed up into the air to be carried by the wind; the incongruity of the scene is completed by the picture of the prophet chasing the windblown hairs, striking at them with his flailing sword. But still the action was not complete. Crawling on the ground, the bald prophet recovered a few of the hairs scattered by the wind and tucked them into the folds of his garment. Returning to the side of his fire, he took some of the rescued hair from his garment and threw it into the fire to be burned. And then, standing baldly and boldly before his audience, he uttered an oracle, in which the meaning of the symbolic acts is clarified and proclaimed (below, verses 5–12).

But even before the proclamation of the oracle, the symbolism of the actions was there to be seen by those who had deeper perception. Shaving the head, among the Hebrews, could be a sign both of shame and of mourning. And the symbolism has elements of both, though shame predominates. As a dignified man would be shamed by having his head publicly shaved before a mocking audience, so too would a city be shamed by having its citizens evacuated. For what hair is to the head (I write as one "thin on top"), so citizens are to a city.

But there is more than shame and grief in the symbolism; the disposal of the three piles of hair is indicative of the fate of the city's citizens. The portion burned in the fire represented the citizens who would die in the hardship of the siege. That cut and flailed by the sword represented those who would die in the battle for the city. And the final portion, scattered by the wind, repre-sented those fleeing from the city in every direction after its fall.

But even of those who escaped, though some would survive, others would eventually perish from the hardships of their existence; even in exile, there would be no security.

In the symbolic actions, taken without the accompanying words, the message is one of unmitigated doom. There are occasions when evil has run so rampant, that only judgment can be foreseen. And though these symbolic actions do not represent the totality of Ezekiel's prophetic message, they do represent very accurately the gravity of his message. Disaster was coming!

Again, in this short passage, the impact of the message upon the messenger can be seen. We cannot imagine that Ezekiel found it easy to perform these strange actions, nor even to live with their hairless postlude. But the incident is instructive, a further reminder that the difficult message brings hardship to the messenger, and was surely no less painful to the One who sent it.

THE SHEARING OF JERUSALEM

Ezekiel 5:5–12

5"Thus says the Lord God: This is Jerusalem; I have set her in the centre of the nations, with countries round about her. 6And she has wickedly rebelled against my ordinances more than the nations, and against my statutes more than the countries round about her, by rejecting my ordinances and not walking in my statutes. 7Therefore thus says the Lord God: Because you are more turbulent than the nations that are round about you, and have not walked in my statutes or kept my ordinances, but have acted according to the ordinances of the nations that are round about you; 8therefore thus says the Lord God: Behold, I, even I, am against you; and I will execute judgments in the midst of you in the sight of the nations. 9And because of all your abominations I will do with you what I have never yet done, and the like of which I will never do again. 10Therefore fathers shall eat their sons in the midst of you, and sons shall eat their fathers; and I will execute judgments on you, and any of you who survive I will scatter to all the winds. 11Wherefore, as I live, says the Lord God, surely, because you have defiled my sanctuary with all your detestable things and with all your abominations, therefore I will cut you down; my eye will not spare, and I will have no pity. 12A third part of you shall die of pestilence and be consumed with famine in the midst of you; a third part shall fall by the sword round about you; and a third part I will scatter to all the winds and will unsheathe the sword after them."

After performing the symbolic actions described in the preceding verses, Ezekiel is now to declare the words of God to his audience. The words are intimately associated with the actions; they conclude with a specific interpretation of the significance of the actions, namely the disposal of the three piles of Ezekiel's hair (verse 12).

The reader of ancient history always has an advantage over the participants in the events of which he reads. We have known since 4:1 that Ezekiel's symbolic actions have pertained to Jerusalem. The map on the brick was a map of Jerusalem; the shaven head represented the denuding of Jerusalem. But, up to this point, Ezekiel has not declared openly the object of his symbolic actions. It should have been clear enough to those with eyes to see, but many did not want to see. They would have preferred to think of the symbolised city, and its impending judgment, as Babylon. But all such fake hopes and delusions are dashed with the first words of the oracle that Ezekiel declares: "This is Jerusalem!"

Again, one must imagine the scene. The speaker of these dramatic words offers a strange spectacle: his head is now bald and his jaw shaven of its traditional beard. And when he says, "This is Jerusalem", he refers in a manner to himself; this strange and sheared person you see standing before you represents the sorry estate to which Jerusalem is coming. His dreadful message is not of Babylon, the city of the hated enemy, but of their own beloved capital city.

But the oracle that the prophet declares goes beyond the symbolism of his actions. The actions declare only the judgment coming to Jerusalem; the words elaborate the reasons for that imminent judgment. Jerusalem has rejected God, and so will be rejected. The city set in the centre of the nations had failed miserably to fulfil its pivotal function. The city's sanctuary, which should have been the holiest of holy places, had become defiled and detestable. And therefore some awful words are declared on behalf of God by the prophet: "I, even I, am against you." Those who did not perceive the meaning of their history could have hoped that Jerusalem's only problem was that Babylon was against it; now, the terrible truth is declared that God was against Jerusalem.

A number of grave theological perspectives emerge from this oracle against Jerusalem.

(i) Jesus taught his disciples one of the most fundamental lessons of stewardship: "every one to whom much is given, of him will much be required" (Luke 12:48). The lesson applied equally to Jerusalem. It had been appointed the "centre of the nations". In it was located the sanctuary, the place where God's presence could be known in a particularly intimate fashion. Much had been given to Jerusalem and much was required, but it had failed to respond to its responsibilities.

Like Ezekiel's audience, we must be careful not to be deluded as to the point of the message. "This is Jerusalem"—the words brought home the message to the audience. But, from the Christian perspective, there is a sense in which each one of us is Jerusalem. We are God's temples (1 Cor. 3:16), and from those to whom much is given, much will be required.

(ii) In reading the Old Testament prophets, one may become so accustomed to prophecies of judgment and doom that their impact is blunted. Yet there are few more horrifying words in the Bible than those found here: "I, even I, am against you" (verse 8). Or again, "I will have no pity" (verse 11)—striking words from One whose nature it is to be compassionate! One only begins to grasp the gravity of the words when one imagines loving parents declaring the same statements to a child. If nothing else, these words proclaim the awesome seriousness of religion; it is not an easy matter, lightly assumed and casually discarded. It affects every dimension of life and must be treated with the utmost seriousness.

(iii) As always is the case, the message speaks of its sender, God; but it is the undertones of the words that are critical. At the superficial level, it is a frightening picture of God that emerges from this prophecy of doom, but behind the words, God's fuller nature may be seen.

One who has not deeply cared cannot deeply grieve. And one who has never penetrated the depths of love cannot perceive the force of hatred. Profound emotions always indicate one part of a polarity. The one who says "I am against you" is always the one who used to be so passionately for you. The one who proclaims "I will have no pity" is precisely the one who cannot ultimately quell the wellsprings of pity within. So the portrayal here of a passionate God inspires both hope and fear. If there were no such anger, there would be no preceding love. And the changes in the divine temperament are not the whimsical moods of a malevolent deity, but the reactions of a lover to the behaviour of those that are loved. And thus every prophetic portrayal of the wrath of God is in part a message of hope; the potential for changing the countenance of God lies within those to whom his wrath is revealed.

A REPROACH AMONG THE NATIONS

Ezekiel 5:13–17

13"Thus shall my anger spend itself, and I will vent my fury upon them and satisfy myself; and they shall know that I, the Lord, have spoken in my jealousy, when I spend my fury upon them. 14Moreover I will make you a desolation and an object of reproach among the nations round about you and in the sight of all that pass by. 15You shall be a reproach and a taunt, a warning and a horror, to the nations round about you, when I execute judgments on you in anger and fury, and with furious chastisements—I, the Lord, have spoken—16when I loose against you my deadly arrows of famine, arrows for destruction, which I will loose to destroy you, and when I bring more and more famine upon you, and break your staff of bread. 17I will send famine and wild beasts against you, and they will rob you of your children; pestilence and blood shall pass through you; and I will bring the sword upon you. I, the Lord, have spoken."

These verses bring to climax and conclusion the oracle of judgment that accompanied Ezekiel's symbolic act of shearing his head and beard. In part, they reinforce the preceding words, driving home the finality of the judgment; but in part, they elaborate still further a new stream in Ezekiel's message that grows broader as his ministry continues. It pertains to God's purpose for the nations of the world that surrounded the focal point of Jerusalem.

At first sight, the role of the foreign nations in this passage is that of the executors of God's judgment. They will carry out the actions culminating in defeat. And to the surrounding nations, Jerusalem would become a "reproach and a taunt, a warning and a horror" (verse 15). But we do not see the full impact of Ezekiel's message until we set it against the historical backdrop of the position that God's chosen people should have had amongst the foreign nations of the world. What was their appointed position?

According to the ancient covenant with Abraham, through his descendants, all the nations of the world should have been blessed (Gen. 22:18). According to the stipulations of the Sinai Covenant, Israel was to have become a "kingdom of priests and a holy nation" (Exod. 19:6). That is to say, Israel's election as the chosen people of God had been for a purpose, and the purpose had been intimately related to the nations of the world. Through Israel, as a nation, all other countries should have perceived the righteousness of God in this world; they should have learned from what they saw. Israel was to have been God's beacon amidst the dark travail of nations.

But none of this had happened. The true tragedy of Ezekiel's day was not the coming destruction of Jerusalem and its nation, but the nation's failure to fulfil its high calling. The evil of the chosen people, so constantly condemned in the prophetic words, was even greater than at first it appeared to be. What they had done was bad enough; what they had failed to do was that for which they had been called into existence.

Against this general background, we perceive how Ezekiel's theology introduces a new twist. If Israel would not be a light to the nations, it could be a reproach to the nations. And the irony of the insight is that the nations could receive the same message, the one originally intended in Israel's election and high calling. If Israel had fulfilled its calling, it would have revealed the righteousness and justice of God. But equally in failure, the message could go out; the awful judgment on Judah and Jerusalem would declare no less the righteousness and justice of God in his dealing with the nations of the world.

Thus we begin to perceive how the message of God will somehow go out, even if the messenger failed. It was designed to be communicated through a righteous and prosperous nation, but it could be conveyed through a nation in ruins. But equally, it becomes clear that the message of the prophet is addressed ultimately to two audiences, and each audience in turn impacts upon the other.

(i) First and foremost, the prophet is addressing the chosen people. But the circumstances of his audience are such that they tend to introversion and egocentricity. "Why is this happening to me? What have I done?" Such self-centred reflection in a sense compounds the sin that brought the judgment. There should be a dawning realisation of the failure of responsibility, of the disservice done to the nations through having failed to fulfil the calling. Thus, gradually the prophet seeks to broaden the horizons of his immediate audience. They must not merely lament in a selfish fashion, but must perceive also the unfilled needs of the nations lying beyond.

(ii) But in addition, the message of the prophet is being broadened. Though he does not literally address the nations, or even his captors, at this point, it becomes increasingly clear that in Ezekiel's understanding of the scheme of things, Israel's God is also in some fashion the God of all the nations. Though this perspective is implicit in much of the biblical narrative, in Ezekiel it becomes more clear than in other places. And so, though we may belong to a people other than Israel, the ancient prophet's message is not without relevance to us; we begin to see the world of the Gentiles being brought into focus.

A MESSAGE TO THE MOUNTAINS

Ezekiel 6:1–7

[1]The word of the Lord came to me: [2]"Son of man, set your face toward the mountains of Israel, and prophesy against them, [3]and say, You mountains of Israel, hear the word of the Lord God! Thus says the Lord God to the mountains and the hills, to the ravines and the valleys: Behold, I, even I, will bring a sword upon you, and I will destroy your high places. [4]Your altars shall become desolate, and your incense altars shall be broken; and I will cast down your slain before your idols. [5]And I will lay the dead bodies of the people of Israel before their idols; and I will scatter your bones round about your altars. [6]Wherever you dwell your cities shall be waste and your high places ruined, so that your altars will be waste and ruined, your idols broken and destroyed, your incense altars cut down, and your works wiped out. [7]And the slain shall fall in the midst of you, and you shall know that I am the Lord."

The whole of Chapter 6 contains a message to the "mountains of Israel", but the message falls into three parts; the first seven verses constitute the first part of the message. Although the words are addressed to the mountainous land, they clearly incorporate the citizens of that land; both the nation and its inhabitants are lumped together in this prophecy of Ezekiel amidst the exiles. And the focus of this message has broadened beyond that of the previous messages; whereas formerly Ezekiel had directed his words and actions primarily against Jerusalem, now it is the whole land that comes within his purview.

At first sight, the message seems rather harsh on the mountains and hills, the ravines and valleys; one can hardly blame the land itself for the atrocities performed on its surface. And yet, when one reflects on the words in the context of ancient religious thought, one begins to perceive the power of the polemic. The ancient religions of the Near East did not view the world merely as inanimate substance; it was believed to be alive with divine power. And the hills and valleys of the land were pockmarked with the shrines and altars of the ancient fertility faith, so that the masters and mistresses of nature's power could be worshipped on their own terrain.

When the Hebrews had first settled in the land, they had converted some of the ancient pagan shrines into the service of their true religion; on many a hilltop and in country shrines, genuine worship had been offered. But the power of the native religions, and their insidious attractions, had reasserted themselves over the centuries. The true worship of the God of Israel had become fused with that of Baal and the goddesses of nature. These semi-pagan shrines scattered through the hilly countryside of the promised land had flourished, and neither the efforts of King Hezekiah nor those of King Josiah had been successful in eliminating their base appeal. It was the false fellowship on the hilltops that had contributed in part to the terrible decline of true faith in the promised land; not only had the people desecrated the true sanctuary of Jerusalem, but they had popularised the false sanctuaries of the countryside.

And so the mountains and their shrines are roundly condemned in these prophetic declarations issued in the presence of a people living now on the plain. Their altars would become desolate, their supposedly holy places desecrated by the bodies of their dead worshippers being cast upon them. And through it all, God's purpose would be achieved: the false deities of mountain and ravine would know that the only true god was the Lord (verse 7).

In these prophetic words, Ezekiel is developing the substance of his message; he declares not merely judgment, but some of the roots which bear the fruit of judgment. And two points emerge which are pertinent to the continuity of true religion at all times and in all places.

(i) The first point is the danger of *syncretism*, or the fusing of elements of foreign religion into the true religion handed down from past generations. The threat of syncretism may come from a variety of directions; in Israel's case, it had started with a noble goal. When the Hebrews had settled in the promised land, they brought their faith with them; it seemed reasonable enough to take over the old shrines of the land and dedicate them to a new and holy purpose. But there was always risk in such endeavour, like playing with fire. And gradually the innate power of the old faiths reasserted itself, like a latent virus suddenly revitalised to affect the whole body.

In any century, past or present, the danger of syncretism is present, and its approach is always subtle. A faith must always seek the pulse of its own generation, in order to know the means by which to communicate its truth. But the ethos of an age may carry within it the seeds of its own destruction. The formidable challenge to any living religion is to discover the means whereby the ways of the world may be converted into the worship of God, without being converted by them.

(ii) Ezekiel's prophetic words also remind us of the ever-present attraction of nature religion. At root, the problem of the unfaithful Hebrews was that they did not really believe that their God was Lord of Nature. He was indeed the Lord of History, but everyone else in the Near East recognised the need of seeking the assistance of gods and goddesses of nature and the powers of fertility and potency. The one who began to worship nature's forces no longer fully believed in a God of Creation. It was a loss of spiritual nerve which prompted a redirection of faith, and the new and false direction appeared to be supported by all kinds of "empirical" evidence.

The tendency to worship nature, in conscious or sometimes unconscious forms, is present no less in our own century than in Ezekiel's. But apart from the false religion to which it leads, such redirection also leads to a blurring of one of the most fundamental insights of the Old Testament. The world of nature is not animate, imbued with its own divine power; it is substance, the work of the Creator's hand, pointing beyond itself to the one upon whom all existence depends. To worship nature in any form is misguided. The power of a painting points beyond itself to the painter. The emotive force of great music points back to composer and performer. No less does the majesty of the mountains reflect on the Creator, and to worship the object is to do it disservice.

THE THERAPY OF MEMORY

Ezekiel 6:8–10

> [8]"Yet I will leave some of you alive. When you have among the nations some who escape the sword, and when you are scattered through the countries, [9]then those of you who escape will remember me among the nations where they are carried captive, when I have broken their wanton heart which has departed from me, and blinded their eyes which turn wantonly after their idols; and they will be loathsome in their own sight for the evils which they have committed, for all their abominations. [10]And they shall know that I am the Lord; I have not said in vain that I would do this evil to them."

Suddenly, the midst of this prophecy of darkness, there dawns a ray of light. It is now the people of the promised land, not its mountains, who are addressed. And the light is this: amid all the bloodshed and slaughter of judgment, there are to be some people who will survive. The survivors will return eventually to a true knowledge of God, and the therapeutic path of their return is instructive; it has three stages.

(i) The therapy begins with *memory* (verse 9). Memory, in the biblical perspective, is more than simply the capacity of the mind to recall facts and information; it involves also understanding. In the conception of some people, human memory is rather like a computerised filing system; data from the past can be recalled at the console operator's command. But such a computer has no *perception*, and *perception* is crucial to the biblical understanding of memory. For truly to remember is first to recall the facts, and second to understand them. Historical memory goes beyond the recollection of the sequence and dates of events, but understands the relationship between them and the reasons for their occurrence. Personal memory recalls not only the events of an individual's life, but also the reasons lying behind the successes and the failures. True memory is a branch of wisdom.

From the vicissitudes of captivity, the Jews would remember, not only their past history, but also their God. And they would recognise the causes of the disaster in which they found themselves, and also the fact that former forgetfulness had been a contributing factor to their fall. Their rediscovery of memory would be a return to the foundations of their faith. The great sermon of Moses, delivered to the Hebrews prior to their entry into the promised land, had hammered home the importance of memory, if they were to survive (Deut. 8). And having been forgotten, the lessons of memory would have to be learned again in a foreign land.

In Ezekiel's prophecy, the blunted stimuli of memory are to be revitalised in the experience of judgment. But the process of vital memory, however activated, is vital to any healthy spiritual life. What we have become may be to a large extent the consequence of our experience of life; what we may become depends in large part upon our memory and understanding of that experience. And not least important, as Ezekiel makes so clear, is that central in our memory must be the knowledge of the experience of God.

(ii) When the therapeutic process of memory had begun, there developed the second stage in the path to health, namely *horror*: "they will be loathsome in their own sight..." (verse 9). Cut off from all the blessings of a former life, and broken hearted at their present plight, the people would recognise with horror the cause of their predicament. It was not the flukes of fortune or tricks of history that had brought them to where they were; it was their own evil and abominable deeds that had cast them from their homes to captivity in the earth's remote corners. Memory, in other words, creates an awareness both of the sins of the past and of their consequences. And there can be no genuine progress on the path to health until this recognition has been reached. Without such recognition, the folly and blindness of the past could simply be repeated. Recognising the past and its failure was an integral part of the educational role of memory in the process of restoration.

But the self-loathing which came from an awareness of past deeds was more than an introverted, self-centred condition. The past had involved failing themselves, but failing others also. Yet above it all, the worst failure had been that before God. The ingratitude and lack of love in the years gone by reared their ugly heads, creating such a sense of worthlessness, that no hope could rise above the shame. Yet there was a purpose in this rock-bottom experience of horror; only after this horrifying insight had been grasped would it be possible to start making some upward progress on the path to health.

(iii) The final stage in the therapy involved *recognition*: at last, they would "know that I am the Lord" (verse 10). What should have been known all along would finally become clear at the end of a painful process.

This theme of the recognition of the Lord is a central one in the entire Book of Ezekiel, and no less central in this chapter. Thrice it is mentioned, and thrice the different ways of achieving such knowledge are illuminated. (a) The mountains would recognise the Lord from the dead carcases of idol-worshippers strewn on their slopes (verse 7); in death, God's lordship could be seen. (b) The remnant of exiles would recognise it after the painful process of therapy through which they passed (verse 10). (c) And Israel as a whole would learn of God's Lordship through the desolation of its land (verse 14). But all these avenues of recognition were painful and all were rooted in forgetfulness; better to remember the truth early in life and retain it throughout.

THE DANCE OF DEATH

Ezekiel 6:11–14

[11]Thus says the Lord God: "Clap your hands, and stamp your foot, and say, Alas! because of all the evil abominations of the house of Israel; for they shall fall by the sword, by famine, and by pestilence. [12]He that is far off shall die of pestilence; and he that is near shall fall by the sword; and he that is left and is preserved shall die of famine. Thus I will spend my fury upon them. [13]And you shall know that I am the Lord, when their slain lie among their idols round about their altars, upon every high hill, on all the mountain tops, under every green tree, and under every leafy oak, wherever they offered pleasing odour to all their idols. [14]And I will stretch out my hand against them, and make the land desolate and waste, throughout all their habitations, from the wilderness to Riblah. Then they will know that I am the Lord."

The darkness of judgment with which this message to the mountains began was penetrated briefly by the light of hope; a remnant would survive and return to a true knowledge of God. But now, in the conclusion of the oracle, the clouds darken again; it closes with the ominous threat of further judgment. While hope for a few is present, it must not create false hope, and delusions that things would go well after all are shattered by these closing words of the chapter.

When the oracle began, Ezekiel had been instructed to "set his face toward the mountains" (6:2), a symbolic position accompanying his words. But the concluding words are to be accompanied by more dramatic symbolic gestures and actions. As he speaks these words, the prophet is to clap his hands and stamp his feet upon the ground, as if grasped by the grief of the death dance. To an extent, the actions may symbolise taunt and mockery, but more than that, they communicate the mortal danger and grief of the accompanying words. The prophet cannot stand still and dispassionately declare the sentence of death on multitudes by pestilence, sword, and famine. His body is jerked into agitated action by the substance of the sentence he speaks.

And the words are indeed terrible. Whereas earlier, the prophet had addressed the mountains, informing them of their forthcoming desecration from the dead bodies piled upon them, now he addresses the people themselves. They would die because of their evil. And the message was not without irony. The purpose of the judgment was so that the people would "know that I am the Lord" (verses 13, 14), but who would be left alive to know it? The truth dawns gradually that death brings its own kind of knowledge.

Faced with such a dreadful passage as this, one is tempted to ask (and the question arises over and again in reading the Prophets): what kind of God would do these terrible things to his people? Is he some kind of heartless monster? Yet the question is misconstrued, for the actions of God are conditioned by the word *because* (verse 11), indicating the human cause of God's terrible declaration of judgment. It is always important to remember certain fundamentals in reading these prophecies of judgment.

(i) The divine sentences of judgment reflect the very opposite of God's will and intention for his people. He willed only love and blessing, as is so clear in the covenant documents that are foundational to Israel's faith. Yet human beings were endowed with will and a certain freedom. Without these attributes there could be no real love or true relationship with God. Yet the attributes which made possible a relationship with God held also the possibility of disaster. In that sense, the fruits of judgment in Ezekiel's prophecy trace their roots to the parable of Adam and Eve.

(ii) Thus, though coming doom is presented as the judgment of God, it is in a very real sense of human making. We cannot attribute all misfortune to past deeds, as the Book of Job makes so abundantly plain. But the fact that much suffering remains rooted in mystery should not blind us to our own human capacity to create our own kind of hell. One can never say: "Because I am suffering, I must have done something terribly wicked." On the other hand, the Book of Ezekiel makes it plain that there is more than an element of truth in the converse of that statement. The dedicated and rigorous pursuit of evil brings eventually its own evil returns, and the results are not always limited to the perpetrators. Ezekiel preached not only to a wicked generation, but to the latest in a long line of wicked generations, and there was little mystery attached to the origin of the disasters declared so clearly in his prophetic preaching.

THE TEMPEST OF DESTRUCTION

Ezekiel 7:1–27

> [1]The word of the Lord came to me: [2]"And you, O son of man, thus says the Lord God to the land of Israel: An end! The end has come upon the four corners of the land. [3]Now the end is upon you, and I will let loose my anger upon you, and will judge you according to your ways; and I will punish you for all your abominations. [4]And my eye will not spare you, nor will I have pity; but I will punish you for your ways, while your abominations are in your midst. Then you will know that I am the Lord.

⁵"Thus says the Lord God: Disaster after disaster! Behold, it comes. ⁶An end has come, the end has come; it has awakened against you. Behold, it comes. ⁷Your doom has come to you, O inhabitants of the land; the time has come, the day is near, a day of tumult, and not of joyful shouting upon the mountains. ⁸Now I will soon pour out my wrath upon you, and spend my anger against you, and judge you according to your ways; and I will punish you for all your abominations. ⁹And my eye will not spare, nor will I have pity; I will punish you according to your ways, while your abominations are in your midst. Then you will know that I am the Lord, who smite.

¹⁰"Behold the day! Behold, it comes! Your doom has come, injustice has blossomed, pride has budded. ¹¹Violence has grown up into a rod of wickedness; none of them shall remain, nor their abundance, nor their wealth; neither shall their be pre-eminence among them. ¹²The time has come, the day draws near. Let not the buyer rejoice, nor the seller mourn, for wrath is upon all their multitude. ¹³For the seller shall not return to what he has sold, while they live. For wrath is upon all their multitude; it shall not turn back; and because of his iniquity, none can maintain his life.

¹⁴"They have blown the trumpet and made all ready; but none goes to battle, for my wrath is upon all their multitude. ¹⁵The sword is without, pestilence and famine are within; he that is in the field dies by the sword; and him that is in the city famine and pestilence devour. ¹⁶And if any survivors escape, they will be on the mountains, like doves of the valleys, all of them moaning, every one over his iniquity. ¹⁷All hands are feeble, and all knees weak as water. ¹⁸They gird themselves with sackcloth, and horror covers them; shame is upon all faces, and baldness on all their heads. ¹⁹They cast their silver into the streets, and their gold is like an unclean thing; their silver and gold are not able to deliver them in the day of the wrath of the Lord; they cannot satisfy their hunger or fill their stomachs with it. For it was the stumbling block of their iniquity. ²⁰Their beautiful ornament they used for vainglory, and they made their abominable images and their detestable things of it; therefore I will make it an unclean thing to them. ²¹And I will give it into the hands of foreigners for a prey, and to the wicked of the earth for a spoil; and they shall profane it. ²²I will turn my face from them, that they may profane my precious place; robbers shall enter and profane it, ²³and make a desolation.

"Because the land is full of bloody crimes and the city is full of violence, ²⁴I will bring the worst of the nations to take possession of their houses; I will put an end to their proud might, and their holy places shall be profaned. ²⁵When anguish comes, they will seek peace, but there shall be none. ²⁶Disaster comes upon disaster, rumour follows rumour; they seek a vision from the prophet, but the law perishes from the priest, and counsel from the elders. ²⁷The king mourns, the prince is wrapped in despair, and the hands of the people of the land are palsied by terror. According to their way I will do to them, and according to their own judgments I will judge them; and they shall know that I am the Lord."

This melancholy message develops further the theme of judgment on the homeland which was the substance of the preceding chapter; but now the prophet is seized by a greater sense of urgency. "An end!" he declares, and as he continues to speak, it is as if he is becoming more and more aware of the imminence of the end. Over and again, he asserts that it is coming, as if he were a meteorologist observing the havoc of a tempest destroying all around him and drawing closer to the place where he stands. But as is so often the case in the declaration of judgment, the coming disasters are not the whimsical actions of a capricious deity; they are rooted in human sin. And interspersed within the body of the judgment, there may be seen the anatomy of evil, the actions evoked by the judgment which in themselves point to its origin. For human sin brought on the disaster that the prophet now declares; and the disaster, creating panic in the people, brings out their true nature. Faced with doom, they turn not to their true defender, but rather to sources of human strength upon which they have come to depend; and these actions, in turn, illuminate the reasons for the judgment.

(i) *Pride* and *pomposity* had become the hallmarks of their society, and also one of the grounds for that society's judgment. For pride was a plant that flowered into judgment (verse 10), and judgment, when it came, would eliminate pride and pre-eminence (verse 11). The proud thought they could weather the storm, until their ship began to sink and they recognised the truth.

The attitude of pride, with its attributes of pomp and the desire for pre-eminence, were fundamentally opposed to the attitude required of God's covenant people. "Beware lest you say in your heart, 'My power and the might of my hand have gotten me this wealth' " (Deut. 8:17); and yet in Israel's history, this ancient caveat had constantly been cast aside. What is required of us all is the recognition that what we are and what we have become are the gifts of God; there should be gratitude, not pride. But the judgment of the proud, here announced, brought home powerfully the ultimate dependence of human beings upon God, in their inability to stand alone on the day of trial.

(ii) Pride was followed closely by *self-confidence in human strength*. In the past, when disaster had threatened the land, the army had been summoned and the danger averted. And so, faced with a new threat, the people would blow the trumpet and make ready for war (verse 14), thinking thereby to stave off defeat once again. But they had forgotten that the Lord was their true warrior (Exod. 15:3); there was no point in blowing the trumpet to summon the army when the enemy was God, for their army was then without arms. The trumpet would blast, but none would march to battle (verse 14).

Once again, the response to coming judgment brings out its roots. The spontaneous reaction to threat was to turn to that old standby, the army; that reaction, rooted in a long history of self-confidence, and lack of confidence in God, illustrated one of the reasons why judgment was coming. If they consistently refused to depend upon God, then the ruin of judgment would illustrate the folly of depending on any one else. Only when this overweening self-confidence had been demolished might it be possible to plant the seed once again of the true source in which all human confidence must be placed.

(iii) Another of the grounds of human confidence was *wealth*. Silver and gold, the symbols of wealth and its power, may provide a person with considerable influence and security in society. And so the hoarding of silver and gold create the confidence of insurance and assurance of security. But in a time of judgment, the false fellowship of financial support would be shown for what it was; money would be cast into the streets, like slops into the sewage ditch. For when the true test came, financial security collapsed as does a house of cards (verse 19).

The symbolism of this denunciation of the security of wealth is no less powerful today than it was in Ezekiel's time. There are many forms of money in our world, some of which are even labelled "securities". But, in times of international crisis, it is usually the price of gold that goes up first in the world markets. It is somehow the most enduring symbol of security. But Ezekiel's point is not to criticise wealth as such; rather it is a matter of perspective. If there is no food to buy, silver will not satisfy hunger; if a sword is penetrating your abdomen, gold will lose its offer of security. It is *dependence* on wealth that is condemned, and the delusion of money's security that is shattered.

(iv) Even the *temple* would be destroyed (verses 20–22), and in this declaration, that last illusion of security is eliminated. For the citizens of Jerusalem thought that they would ultimately be safe from foreign enemies, even if all was not well with their society. It was inconceivable that God would allow his own temple to be pillaged by the pagans. And this was the most subtle of all forms of false confidence, the confidence in religious security. The subtlety lay in the element of truth that permeated the confidence; God would indeed protect his sanctuary from foreign invaders. But the danger lay within, not with the enemy; the evil of the people had already desecrated the sanctuary, so that there was nothing left worth protecting.

The temple, the people's final resort of confidence in a time of trial, illustrated the hypocrisy of their religion. The temple existed so that the presence of God might be known in a special manner in the midst of the chosen people; when the presence was gone, the temple was little more than a husk of the real thing. And so those who had never bothered to use the temple for its true purpose, turned to it at last for the wrong reason. But then it was too late; the presence of God could not be found there for, as the prophet declares on behalf of God, "I will turn my face from them" (verse 22).

To summarise this bleak oracle of judgment, it speaks not only of a coming end, but also of the false faith which not only invited such an end, but would fail to offer salvation when the end came. Neither human pride, the might of the army, the power of wealth, nor even the security of a long-neglected temple, could turn aside the coming end. Like King Canute facing the advancing waters, they would be unable to turn back the tide of judgment.

THE VISION OF JERUSALEM

Ezekiel 8:1–6

> ¹In the sixth year, in the sixth month, on the fifth day of the month, as I sat in my house, with the elders of Judah sitting before me, the hand of the Lord God fell there upon me. ²Then I beheld, and, lo, a form that had the appearance of a man; below what appeared to be his loins it was fire, and above his loins it was like the the appearance of brightness, like gleaming bronze. ³He put forth the form of a hand, and took me by a lock of my head; and the Spirit lifted me up between earth and heaven, and brought me in visions of God to Jerusalem, to the entrance to the gateway of the inner court that faces north, where was the seat of the image of jealousy, which provokes to jealousy. ⁴And behold, the glory of the God of Israel was there, like the vision that I saw in the plain.
>
> ⁵Then he said to me, "Son of man, lift up your eyes now in the direction of the north." So I lifted up my eyes towards the north, and behold, north of the altar gate, in the entrance, was this image of jealousy. ⁶And he said to me, "Son of man, do you see what they are doing, the great abominations that the house of Israel are committing here, to drive me far from my sanctuary? But you will see still greater abominations."

The date, with which this passage begins, introduces a new and significant vision in Ezekiel's ministry; in September, 592 B.C., some fourteen months after the initial vision, Ezekiel received this extraordinarily powerful vision which is described in Chapters 8–11.

Ezekiel was sitting in his house and the elders, or leaders, of the exiled community came to see him. It is probable that they visited him for a purpose; recognising him now to be a prophet, they came to consult him on the future of their beloved city, Jerusalem. Their request was not simply rooted in curiosity, nor were they desirous merely of keeping up with the news; their own future as exiles rested on the future of their land and capital city. They could remain exiles only so long as there was a place to which they could return; if that were gone, they would be no longer exiles, but stateless persons with no permanent home.

As the elders sit before the prophet, awaiting a response, he is gripped by the power of a profound religious experience. It is not known how long the experience extended, but when Ezekiel "returned" from his vision to normality, he related the details of what he had seen to his audience (11:24–25). Thus the prophet's vision was a part of his prophetic ministry; what he saw was to be described to his fellow exiles, so that in the description they could hear again the prophetic word of judgment.

In the vision, a heavenly being appeared to Ezekiel and took hold of him by the hairs of his head. Then the Spirit of God transported him, still in the state of visionary experience, and set him down in Jerusalem. Just as in our dreams we may experience other places while never moving from our beds, so too does Ezekiel; physically, he is bound to the reality of exile in Babylon, but in his dream, he becomes a visitor in the holy city that was once his home.

Ezekiel finds himself standing in the outer court of the temple in Jerusalem, at a spot close to the northern entrance to the inner court; it was through this entrance that the king and royal family passed into the inner court to worship. Standing there, he is aware of the awesome glory of God, just as he had been in his first vision on the plain. But he is instructed to look towards the north and there he sees something else—it is the "image of jealousy" (verse 5). Any image would provoke the divine "jealousy", but it is probable that this Hebrew expression should be translated "Image of Lust". As such, it would refer to the image of Asherah, the Canaanite goddess of love. Such an image had been placed in the temple in the past (2 Kings 21:7), and though removed in Josiah's reformation, it may well have reappeared in the last sad days of the temple's history prior to its destruction. While Ezekiel is looking at this reprehensible image, he hears the divine voice again, saying that the abominable acts of Israel are driving God out of his own house.

There are three striking features of this first instalment of Ezekiel's great vision.

(i) Two things were present where there should only be one. The glory of God was there, but so was the image of a false deity, and immediately there is a sense of the incongruous. As mercury and water will not mix, no more would the worship of Israel's God mix with that of other gods.

From a biblical perspective, a true temple has room for only one god. If two are present, one or other will leave. If a false god remains the true God will leave; if the true God is to remain, the false god must be removed. This is as true for church as it is for temple; and it is equally true of the person whose body may be a temple for God. Better to remove the false presence, than have the true presence depart.

(ii) When Ezekiel saw the image in the temple, he perceived immediately that the first of the Ten Commandments was being broken; that commandment prohibited the recognition of any gods other than the Lord. The first commandment expressed the fundamental principle of Israel's faith, that of absolute commitment and faithfulness to the God of Israel. When that commandment is broken, the entire foundations of the faith are undermined. Thus, one is already forewarned that things will get worse as the vision progresses, for when the first commandment has gone the remainder will quickly follow.

(iii) The third point involves the recognition of the profound pathos of this first part of the vision. God says to Ezekiel that his people are driving him out of his own sanctuary (verse 6). The anger will grow later, but for the moment the tone is that of grief. The people are driving God from his temple, and in doing so demonstrate that they have forgotten entirely the very reason for the temple's existence.

There is the same pathos to be seen in those persons who by their actions drive God out of their lives. For as the temple built of wood and stone was designed to house the divine presence, so too is the temple made of flesh and blood. But the evacuation of the divine presence (for which the temple was constructed) opens the doors to other presences, which pervert the purpose of the original structure.

THE ART OF IDOLATRY

Ezekiel 8:7–13

> [7]And he brought me to the door of the court; and when I looked, behold, there was a hole in the wall. [8]Then said he to me, "Son of man, dig in the wall"; and when I dug in the wall, lo, there was a door. [9]And he said to me, "Go in, and see the vile abominations that they are committing here." [10]So I went in and saw; and there, portrayed upon the wall round about, were all kinds of creeping things, and loathsome beasts, and all the idols of the house of Israel. [11]And before them stood seventy men of the elders of the house of Israel, with Ja-azaniah the son of Shaphan standing among them. Each had his censer in his hand, and the smoke of the cloud of incense went up. [12]Then he said to me, "Son of man, have you seen what the elders of the house of Israel are doing in the dark, every man in his room of pictures? For they say, 'The Lord does not see us, the Lord has forsaken the land.'" [13]He said also to me, "You will see still greater abominations which they commit."

Now the action of the vision progresses to a second stage. Ezekiel is led to the door of the inner court, which was not a simple gate, but a massive structure. In the stonework of the wall around the door, he sees a hole or a gap. At this point in the narrative, most English translations are a little misleading. Verse 8 should be translated: "Then he said to me: 'Son of man, examine the wall closely.' And when I examined the wall, lo, there was a door!" The door was a secret entrance to an inner chamber, accessible through a gap in the stonework, but not readily visible to those who did not know it was there; its presence was revealed only to Ezekiel's close examination of the structure.

Ezekiel then entered the secret room, and an extraordinary sight met his eyes. The walls of the room were decorated with the paintings, or reliefs, of all kinds of creatures; there were insects, reptiles and vermin, most of them considered unclean for purposes of consumption under Israel's dietary laws. But it was not the art on the walls that evoked the prophet's horror; rather, it was the art of idolatry that the inhabitants of the room were practising. Seventy of Israel's leading citizens were there, offering their worship and incense to the inanimate murals decorating the room. And in the midst of this scene of debased religion was a man of good family and distinction, Ja-azaniah; his father, Shaphan, had played a leading role in Josiah's great reform of the faith (2 Kings 22:3–20). Ja-azaniah's presence there in the secret room indicated how sadly Israel's faith had fallen since the days of Josiah's reformation.

Ezekiel stood observing this strange scene of false religious practice being undertaken within the supposedly sacred precinct of the temple; as he stood there, the divine voice addressed him again. There is irony in the words; to paraphrase them: "Look what they're doing—and they think they can't be seen!" But the secret worshippers have a reason of their own for their deviant practice; they think that their Lord has forsaken their country.

This second stage in the prophet's vision of Jerusalem illustrates a number of important points with respect to the state of religion in the capital city.

(i) *The nation's leadership was actively engaged in the pursuit of evil.* When the integrity of a nation's leadership is lost, there is no hope for its people. "If a ruler himself is upright, all will go well without orders," Confucius wrote. "But if he himself is not upright, even though he gives orders, they will not be obeyed" (from the *Analects*).

Ezekiel saw in his vision that the elders of Jerusalem had lost the faith; afterwards, he would report his vision to the elders of the exile, seated before him. The message would not be lost on them. On the one hand, it would be a message of despair: if Jerusalem's leadership were lost, what hope could there be for the survival of the city? On the other hand, the message contained a challenge: if the elders at home had failed in their responsibility, how much more did the future now depend on the elders in exile!

(ii) *The root of the elders' sin was loss of faith.* This becomes clear upon examination of the curious practice in which they were engaged. Why were they worshipping in secret? In times of spiritual health, the answer would be obvious: such idolatry was prohibited in Israel and in the temple. But it is already clear from the first part of the prophet's vision that the worship of the temple had become sadly debased; a pagan altar had been set up in the temple's outer court. So why, with a public altar outside, was there *secret worship* of other false gods inside? Probably, there were two forms of false religion present. The open altar outside represented the public false cult, that akin to the religion of neighbouring Canaan. But the leaders of the land had not lost their nationalistic spirit, even if they had lost their faith; they still sought deliverance from the enemy, Babylon. But in seeking that deliverance, they turned to Egypt; they were engaged in secret in the worship of Egypt's gods. And thus there is further terrible irony in the scene. After the Exodus from Egyptian slavery, seventy elders had participated in the making of the covenant (Exod. 24:1, 9). Now, threatened by slavery once again, seventy elders of another age turned back to Egypt, of all places, in seeking salvation.

Thus, the secret scene of seventy sinners represents a loss of the sense of liberation; fearing slavery again, they turned back to their old slave-masters, not to the God who delivered them from slavery. The life of liberation called for continuing faith in the great Liberator. But the tragedy of so much of human existence is that, faced with new bondage, there is a loss of courage and a voluntary return to the old forms of slavery.

(iii) The elders suffered from the *delusion of secrecy*. They thought they could act without being seen, and though primarily their secrecy was directed towards their people, at a deeper level it was an attempt to remain secret from God. Yet Ezekiel is standing there, and God is with him, observing the action.

There are no secrets from God. To act as if there were is the height of folly. For human life is conducted on a stage like the interrogation room of a modern police department; the insiders cannot see out, but the observers can see and hear all that goes on inside the room. All speech and behaviour should be conducted with an awareness that ultimately there are no secrets from God.

SACRAL WEEPING AND SUN WORSHIP

Ezekiel 8:14–18

> ¹⁴Then he brought me to the entrance of the north gate of the house of
> the Lord; and behold, there sat women weeping for Tammuz. ¹⁵Then
> he said to me, "Have you seen this, O son of man? You will see still
> greater abominations than these."
>
> ¹⁶And he brought me into the inner court of the house of the Lord;
> and behold, at the door of the temple of the Lord, between the porch
> and the altar, were about twenty-five men, with their backs to the
> temple of the Lord, and their faces toward the east, worshipping the
> sun toward the east. ¹⁷Then he said to me, "Have you seen this, O son
> of man? Is it too slight a thing for the house of Judah to commit the
> abominations which they commit here, that they should fill the land
> with violence, and provoke me further to anger? Lo, they put the
> branch to their nose. ¹⁸Therefore I will deal in wrath; my eye will not
> spare, nor will I have pity; and though they cry in my ears with a loud
> voice, I will not hear them."

Ezekiel's vision continues and, like a visitor on a guided tour of
the temple, he is now conducted by his divine guide to observe
two more serious scenes in the temple precinct. Each scene
demonstrates still further the terrible estate into which worship in
the Jerusalem temple has sunk.

(i) *Sacral weeping* (verses 14–15). In the entrance of the north
gate to the most sacred temple areas, the prophet observed a
group of women who were sitting on the ground and weeping.
They were not possessed with simple human grief, but were
engaged in one of the sacral acts associated with the Babylonian
god Tammuz. Not a great deal is known of Tammuz. In the oldest
Mesopotamian texts (in which he is called Dumuzi), he is referred
to as a shepherd-god. But in the Babylonian period in which
Ezekiel lived, he was both a fertility-god and god of the underworld. His death in the months of summer could be observed in
the world of nature, as the land dried up and plants died; in the
absence of his vital power, vegetation ceased to flourish. But in
spring, Tammuz came to life again, and with his resurrection,
new life burst forth from the ground to bring the freshness of

springtime. Thus, the role of Tammuz in the religion of Babylon was essentially similar to that of Baal in Palestine, or Osiris in Egypt. He was a fertility god, upon whose health the world of nature depended.

The weeping women that Ezekiel saw were engaged in the summer ritual, mourning the demise of Tammuz and seeking his return the following spring. And the place of their forbidden worship illuminates their loss of faith: at the entrance to God's sacred sanctuary, they wept for another god. But their sin was not only lack of faith; they betrayed also a fundamental lack of understanding of Israel's God. The God of Israel was above all the *Living God*; this was no less true in the fresh growth of spring than the dry drought of summer. But the women worshipped a dying god! To believe in a living God is to trust in one who is alive, regardless of the evidence of nature and circumstance. At all times and in all places, in both human life and human death, God is and was alive. Weeping for Tammuz was a waste of tears.

(ii) *Sun worshipping* (verses 16–18). For the fourth scene in his vision, Ezekiel was conducted into the inner court of the temple. Entering by the north gate, he could see the altar in front of him, and lying to his right was the entry to the holy sanctuary, the building in which the "holiest of holies" was situated. Between the altar and the porch of the inner sanctuary, he observed a group of twenty-five men; they stood together, their backs to the sacred sanctuary, facing towards the east where the morning sun arose. And they were engaged in worship. Whether they were worshipping the sun as such, or whether they worshipped the sun as a symbol of God, cannot be known for certain; if it was the latter, they were breaking the second commandment, believing that a part of the created order could be an image of the true God.

This fourth scene adds still further to the horror of Ezekiel's vision. His eyes were riveted to the spot where the priests should have been standing, facing towards the *west*, or God's sanctuary; they should have been weeping (not, like the women, for Tammuz); rather praying for God's mercy on his people (Joel 2:17). But the men in the vision, who were almost certainly priests, were facing the wrong way; instead of beseeching God's mercy in tears, they turned their expectant faces to the morning sunlight, hoping that would dispel the gloom of their existence.

The four scenes with which this great vision begins, taken together, form a comprehensive condemnation of Israel's worship. All were involved, with no exceptions. The idol of Asherah at the north gate indicated the popular worship of the people. The secret room of sacrilegious murals demonstrated the distinctive failure of the nation's leaders, the elders. The weeping women illustrated the loss of faith in the Living God. And, in the midst of it all, even the priests were turning backwards in their misdirected attempts at worship. And not only were all the people engaged in this folly; they were without discrimination in their choice of idols. The idol of Asherah represented the religion of Canaan; the secret murals were drawn from the religion of Egypt. The weeping women turned to a god of Babylon, while the priests worshipped the sun, whose cult was practised in almost every nation of the ancient Near East.

To Ezekiel and his few faithful companions in exile, the vision must have been a devastating blow. If there was any hope for them, it might seem to lie in Jerusalem; and if there was any hope for Jerusalem, it lay only in the continuity of true and proper worship in the temple. And the vision seemed to indicate clearly enough that there was no hope—for the temple, for Jerusalem, and so even for the exiles. God would no longer hear the cry of his people (verse 18). But there are two aspects of this part of the vision that deserve particular attention.

(a) *The focus of the vision is the failure of worship*. It is not sin in general that is condemned, but the failure to worship God. All too easily, religion can be reduced to matters of morality, so that good and evil are limited in meaning to ethical and unethical acts. But worship, and the failure to worship, were matters of equal gravity in ancient Israel. All human beings are summoned to worship their Maker; not to do so, or to do so wrongly, is to miss a part of the meaning of our existence. Thus it becomes evil and a ground of judgment.

(b) *Failure in worship leads to failure in morality*. Although the condemnation is of the failure in worship, this in turn cannot become divorced from morality. Israel's failure had resulted in a land filled with violence (verse 17), for worship and morality are intimately interrelated. This interrelationship is hard to grasp and hard to explain. What we do is deeply rooted in what we are, and what we are is shaped by our understanding of ourselves and of God. The one who worships, knows God, and begins to know the relationship between God and human beings. And so worship, in addition to being a fundamental expression of the relationship between a person and God, also shapes the character of the person as such. Thus, when we cease to worship, we lose our understanding, which in turn may be followed quickly by the loss of morality.

SLAUGHTER IN THE CITY

Ezekiel 9:1–11

¹Then he cried in my ears with a loud voice, saying, "Draw near, you executioners of the city, each with his destroying weapon in his hand." ²And lo, six men came from the direction of the upper gate, which faces north, every man with his weapon for slaughter in his hand, and with them was a man clothed in linen, with a writing case at his side. And they went in and stood beside the bronze altar.

³Now the glory of the God of Israel had gone up from the cherubim on which it rested to the threshold of the house; and he called to the man clothed in linen, who had the writing case at his side. ⁴And the Lord said to him, "Go through the city, through Jerusalem, and put a mark upon the foreheads of the men who sigh and groan over all the abominations that are committed in it." ⁵And to the others he said in my hearing, "Pass through the city after him, and smite; your eye shall not spare, and you shall show no pity; ⁶slay old men outright, young men and maidens, little children and women, but touch no one upon whom is the mark. And begin at my sanctuary." So they began with the elders who were before the house. ⁷Then he said to them, "Defile the house, and fill the courts with the slain. Go forth." So they went forth, and smote in the city. ⁸And while they were smiting, and I was left alone, I fell upon my face, and cried, "Ah Lord God! wilt thou destroy all that remains of Israel in the outpouring of thy wrath upon Jerusalem?"

⁹Then he said to me, "The guilt of the house of Israel and Judah is

exceedingly great; the land is full of blood, and the city full of injustice; for they say, 'The Lord has forsaken the land, and the Lord does not see.' ¹⁰As for me, my eye will not spare, nor will I have pity, but I will requite their deeds upon their heads."

¹¹And lo, the man clothed in linen, with the writing case at his side, brought back word, saying, "I have done as thou didst command me."

As the vision continues, a new and more horrifying scene unfolds before the prophet's eyes. The four preceding parts of the vision had revealed the total breakdown in the worship of the temple; now, the divine reaction to the failure in worship is revealed. And, as in the opening part of the vision, the movement had been from the outer part of the temple to the inner court, now the direction is reversed: judgment would begin at the heart of the temple and move outwards towards the city. The prophet, still accompanied by God as his Guide, watches the events; they resemble a scene from a dramatic tragedy enacted upon a stage.

With a loud voice, God summoned the executioners, and six "men" (they are angels, or "divine beings") came filing into the inner court of the temple, following the same route that the prophet himself had used a little earlier. As the six men lined up like a small squad of elite troops alongside the bronze altar, another man came and joined them. The six slaughterers carried their weapons of destruction, but the seventh man was quite different in appearance: he wore a white linen tunic, of the kind that a priest might wear. And instead of a weapon, the seventh man carried a writing case; it was a wooden box, containing quill pens, ink, a small knife and probably some sheets of parchment.

Then God addressed the man dressed in linen, who appeared to be the squad leader. He was to go through the city of Jerusalem; wherever he found a person who was not engaged in evil, but who was deeply exercised by the crimes being committed in the city, he was to put a mark upon that person's forehead. And the six slaughterers were then instructed to follow him through the city; any person—male or female, young or old—who did not have the mark, was to be executed upon the spot. So the judgment began, starting with the nation's leaders who had failed so miserably in their task.

Ezekiel sees the slaughter begin in front of him, and then the scribe and the slaughterers leave the inner court and begin their journey through the city, to carry out their terrible task. And suddenly, Ezekiel has an awful thought. What if the total population were killed? Would that not mean an end to God's work in this world? Horrified by the thought, he falls on his face before God and tries to pray. But he does not receive much encouragement from his intercession; sin as appalling as that of Jerusalem invites judgment. Yet as Ezekiel lies prostrate on his face before God, the seventh man returns, still carrying his writing case. He declares that he has fulfilled his orders, and though his words are not specific, there is an element of hope in them; surely some people must have been marked and escaped judgment!

This scene of slaughter in the city is essentially one of darkness, yet there are a few beams of light that penetrate the gloom.

(i) The form the judgment takes is an indication of doom. The seventh man is to mark the heads of the innocent, and then the six destroyers are to kill the unmarked. And inevitably the scene recalls the first Passover and the escape from Egypt. On that night, too, the angel of death had made his rounds, but the purpose was that of liberation and the birth of a nation. Now the march of death's six angels marked not the beginning, but the end of a nation. Therein lay the sense of finality. This did not seem to be a simple judgment, but a judgment to end all judgments; what had been begun centuries ago in love, was now to be ended in wrath. This is the darkness of the scene, but there are rays of light.

(ii) The prophet intercedes, and as such he is engaged fully in his prophetic ministry. For the prophet is no mere megaphone, through whom God's words may be amplified for the people. He also prays and intercedes on behalf of those whom he serves, as Moses and others had done before him. And his intercession is spontaneous, flowing from the heart; his deepest feelings are expressed in these words addressed to God.

Ezekiel's intercession is instructive for all who would intercede. It is a spontaneous prayer, rooted not only in compassion, but also in a vision of God's work in this world and its possible failure if the slaughter were to proceed. From a certain perspective, it might appear an ill-considered prayer; the people to be judged fully deserved their sentence and God had every right to carry it out. But still, in compassion, Ezekiel interceded, and his compassion was rooted in the knowledge of God. And he did not appear to receive much encouragement in response to his intercession; God clearly declared that he would not have pity. It is only with the benefit of a knowledge of later history that we can perceive Ezekiel's intercession in its true light. The judgment did take place, but some were spared; God's greater purpose for the world was not eliminated. There was indeed a response to the prophet's intercession, though Ezekiel did not know it at the time. This is the first ray of light in the dark scene. It is latent in the seventh man's writing case—if none were to be spared, he would not have needed it!

(iii) But for the Christian reader of the account of Ezekiel's vision, there is a further ray of light; it was not seen by the prophet, nor by those who heard the substance of his vision. It becomes clear only in the light of the New Testament.

The seventh man was to put a *mark* on the foreheads of those to be spared (v. 4). The Hebrew word translated *mark* is *taw*, the last letter of the Hebrew alphabet, which was written in the 6th century B.C. in the form of an X, a slanting cross. And perhaps the writer of the Book of Revelation had Ezekiel in mind, when he described the faithful standing on Mount Zion with the Lamb (Rev. 14:1). The names of the Lamb and his Father were written on the foreheads of the faithful, and the sign X, in Greek script, is the first letter of the name *Christ*. Without delving into the complexities of St John's vision, there is clearly continuity with that of Ezekiel. In the midst of judgment, a remnant continues, and the continuity of the remnant is to be found in the mercy of God, which was to be given its ultimate expression in the person of Jesus, the *Christ*.

THE SCATTERING OF BURNING COALS

Ezekiel 10:1–8

[1]Then I looked, and behold, on the firmament that was over the heads

of the cherubim there appeared above them something like a sapphire, in form resembling a throne. ²And he said to the man clothed in linen, "Go in among the whirling wheels underneath the cherubim; fill your hands with burning coals from between the cherubim, and scatter them over the city."

And he went in before my eyes. ³Now the cherubim were standing on the south side of the house, when the man went in; and a cloud filled the inner court. ⁴And the glory of the Lord went up from the cherubim to the threshold of the house; and the house was filled with the cloud, and the court was full of the brightness of the glory of the Lord. ⁵And the sound of the wings of the cherubim was heard as far as the outer court, like the voice of God Almighty when he speaks.

⁶And when he commanded the man clothed in linen, "Take fire from between the whirling wheels, from between the cherubim," he went in and stood beside a wheel. ⁷And a cherub stretched forth his hand from between the cherubim to the fire that was between the cherubim, and took some of it, and put it into the hands of the man clothed in linen, who took it and went out. ⁸The cherubim appeared to have the form of a human hand under their wings.

This section of the account of Ezekiel's great vision in Jerusalem is extremely difficult to interpret with clarity. Verses 1–8 seem clearly to continue the theme of judgment that dominated Chapter 9; then, the account of events is continued fairly coherently in Chapter 11. But in the latter half of Chapter 10, and to an extent in the verses now being considered, there is a repetition of some of the basic features of Ezekiel's great vision as described in Chapter 1. Whether Ezekiel's disciples and editors have inserted it into the Jerusalem vision, or whether it is integral to this new vision, must remain somewhat uncertain.

In 10:1–8, the vision of judgment continues, though in the context of the prophet's re-emerging awareness of God's glory and his heavenly throne. The Lord is no longer simply Ezekiel's Guide, standing beside him in the temple, providing a running commentary on the events taking place; now he is more centrally involved in the events as such. The perspective of the vision has changed radically, as may so easily happen in the world of dreaming. The key figures are God, the "seventh man" (from the preceding portion of the vision), and the *cherubim*, or divine beings, who are in attendance at the throne of God.

God addresses the seventh man; he is still clothed in linen, but has set aside his writing case, for it will be unnecessary in the task that is now to be assigned to him. He is instructed to go beneath the throne supported by the cherubim and to take a handful of burning coals from the brazier; the coals are to be scattered over the city of Jerusalem. The action is difficult to describe accurately; the throne and its accompanying beings appear to be moving, perhaps from the inner sanctuary out towards the inner court. The seventh man goes and stands beside one of the wheels of the heavenly chariot-throne, and one of the cherubim takes some burning coals and places them in his hand. Then the seventh man leaves, carrying the coals, and Ezekiel can no longer see him; but the narrative strongly suggests that he has left the temple area to carry out his task of scattering burning coals on the evil city of Jerusalem.

There are two new perspectives which emerge in this scene of the vision.

(i) *The judgment of God cannot be distinguished from the glory of God.* The burning coals that threaten such severe destruction to the city of Jerusalem are the same burning coals that are a part of the glory and purity of God's throne.

This pregnant theme of purity and punishment is common in much of the literature of religion. The Iranian prophet Zarathustra, perhaps a contemporary of Ezekiel, wrote of a flood of molten metal coming on the day of judgment; it would wash around the feet of the righteous, purifying them like warm milk, but would scorch and destroy the unrighteous in their impurity. A similar tension is present in Ezekiel's vision: the holy city of Jerusalem should have had nothing to fear from the coals of God, unless it were no longer holy. But the coals that could have purified were threatening, precisely because there was such flammable impurity throughout the city.

God's burning purity may hold either threat or promise. To those that seek to walk in God's way, the coals of God may purify and heal, as Isaiah discovered in his great vision of God in the temple (Isa. 6:6). But the same coals may consume the impure, as the inhabitants of Sodom and Gomorrah had discovered to their cost (Gen. 19:24). The tragedy of Jerusalem was that it was going the way of those sinful cities of the Dead Sea valley.

(ii) *The judgment of God marked the departure of God.* Although the vision is complex at this point, there is clearly movement of the chariot-throne of God, a movement which is to accelerate as the vision continues in the remainder of this chapter and Chapter 11. And, upon reflection, it becomes clear that the movement of God is more ominous than the judgment represented by the burning coals. For the judgment of a God who is present, however terrible, is surely preferable to the absence of God.

The prophet is thus beginning to develop a theme which is not easy to grasp. The doom of the prophet's oracles clouds so much of his ministry, that it is hard to conceive of a situation worse than judgmental doom. But active judgment at least implies the presence of God; the absence of God is the ultimate horror. And this first step in God's evacuation of his temple is forced upon him. He does not want to move, but is evicted by an evil people.

The ultimate privilege of religion is the presence of God, however elusive. The most awful loss is the removal of that presence. But Ezekiel makes it clear that the divine presence is not lost without cause, but only as the consequence of the steadfast pursuit of evil.

THE VISION OF THE PLAIN RENEWED

Ezekiel 10:9–22

9And I looked, and behold, there were four wheels beside the cherubim, one beside each cherub; and the appearance of the wheels was like sparkling chrysolite. 10And as for their appearance, the four had the same likeness, as if a wheel were within a wheel. 11When they went, they went in any of their four directions without turning as they went, but in whatever direction the front wheel faced the others followed without turning as they went. [12]And their rims, and their spokes, and the wheels were full of eyes round about—the wheels that the four of them had. [13]As for the wheels, they were called in my hearing the whirling wheels. [14]And every one had four faces: the first face was the face of the cherub, and the second face was the face of a man, and the third the face of a lion, and the fourth the face of an eagle.

[15]And the cherubim mounted up. These were the living creatures that I saw by the river Chebar. [16]And when the cherubim went, the wheels went beside them; and when the cherubim lifted up their wings to mount up from the earth, the wheels did not turn from beside them. [17]When they stood still, these stood still, and when they mounted up, these mounted up with them; for the spirit of the living creatures was in them.

[18]Then the glory of the Lord went forth from the threshold of the house, and stood over the cherubim. [19]And the cherubim lifted up their wings and mounted up from the earth in my sight as they went forth, with the wheels beside them; and they stood at the door of the east gate of the house of the Lord; and the glory of the God of Israel was over them.

[20]These were the living creatures that I saw underneath the God of Israel by the river Chebar; and I knew that they were cherubim. [21]Each had four faces, and each four wings, and underneath their wings the semblance of human hands. [22]And as for the likeness of their faces, they were the very faces whose appearance I had seen by the river Chebar. They went every one straight forward.

The vision of Ezekiel, which up to this point had moved smoothly from scene to scene, suddenly seems to stall, as the writer describes in detail the chariot throne and its accompanying cherubim. Much of the description is repetitive, recalling in particular the details of Chapter 1:15–28. And so, inevitably, there has been much debate amongst the scholars as to whether these verses are integral to the vision of Jerusalem, or whether they represent an editorial reworking, in which some of the verses of Chapter 1 have been inserted into the present context. Whatever the solution to this complex literary problem, we should not fail to appreciate the effect of these verses on the narrative context as a whole. At the beginning of Chapter 10, a movement begins towards climax; the movement is that of the throne of God *out* of the temple of God. And the effect of this sudden lengthy description, with its whirling wheels and multitude of faces, is to build up the tension and delay the climax of the vision as a whole. But whether this is a literary device, or integral to the vision as such, remains uncertain.

There is one element of novelty in this portion of the text. In the vision of Chapter 1, the heavenly throne was accompanied by *living creatures*; but twice, in this context, the prophet goes out of his way to stress that the *living creatures* of the first vision were none other than the *cherubim* of the present vision. Perhaps, in his first vision, Ezekiel could not have believed that the creatures were the *cherubim*, for the latter were intimately associated with the temple decoration and the Ark of the Covenant itself. But now, in the vision in Jerusalem, it is clear that they are the cherubim. It may perhaps be stretching a point unduly, but there appears to be a certain irony in the narrative. On the Babylonian plain, the creatures that belonged to the temple *brought* the throne of God to the exiled Ezekiel; here, in their Jerusalem "home", they are engaged in *taking* the throne of God from the temple. There is already an anticipation here of a theme to be introduced in Chapter 11: though leaving the temple, God may yet work through his people in exile. And thus, this otherwise verbose portion of the description of the vision not only increases tension, but also introduces an element of hope.

DEATH AT THE TEMPLE GATE

Ezekiel 11:1–13

[1]The Spirit lifted me up, and brought me to the east gate of the house of the Lord, which faces east. And behold, at the door of the gateway there were twenty-five men; and I saw among them Ja-azaniah the son of Azzur, and Pelatiah the son of Benaiah, princes of the people. [2]And he said to me, "Son of man, these are the men who devise iniquity and who give wicked counsel in this city; [3]who say, 'The time is not near to build houses; this city is the cauldron, and we are the flesh.' [4]Therefore prophesy against them, prophesy, O son of man."

⁵And the Spirit of the Lord fell upon me, and he said to me, "Say, Thus says the Lord: So you think, O house of Israel; for I know the things that come into your mind. ⁶You have multiplied your slain in this city, and have filled its streets with the slain. ⁷Therefore thus says the Lord God: Your slain whom you have laid in the midst of it, they are the flesh, and this city is the cauldron; but you shall be brought forth out of the midst of it. ⁸You have feared the sword; and I will bring the sword upon you, says the Lord God. ⁹And I will bring you forth out of the midst of it, and give you into the hands of foreigners, and execute judgments upon you. ¹⁰You shall fall by the sword; I will judge you at the border of Israel; and you shall know that I am the Lord. ¹¹This city shall not be your cauldron, nor shall you be the flesh in the midst of it; I will judge you at the border of Israel; ¹²and you shall know that I am the Lord; for you have not walked in my statutes, nor executed my ordinances, but have acted according to the ordinances of the nations that are round about you."

¹³And it came to pass, while I was prophesying, that Pelatiah the son of Benaiah died. Then I fell down upon my face, and cried with a loud voice, and said, "Ah Lord God! wilt thou make a full end of the remnant of Israel?"

At the beginning of Ezekiel's vision, he moved gradually into the temple area, starting at the north gate and moving towards the inner court; now, as the vision draws gradually to a close, his movement (like that of his divine Guide) is outwards. Still in a state of visionary trance, he is set down at the east gate of the temple, in a large, open area used for meetings and public assemblies. There, the prophet sees a group of twenty-five men, engaged in a meeting. Two of them he recognises by name: Jaazaniah (the name is common and this is not the same person as the man named in 8:11) and Pelatiah. They are "princes of the people", in effect ministers of state, and their meeting is thus an assembly of the national council ruling Judah and Jerusalem, under delegated authority.

The agenda of their meeting is not entirely clear, for the translation of their words (verse 3) is subject to debate. The note indicating an alternative translation in RSV is probably more accurate; this turns the first phrase into a question; but the best meaning of the text may be preserved in the old Greek translation of the Old Testament, the Septuagint: "Have not the houses been rebuilt recently?" That is to say, the meeting is a self-congratulatory one. The twenty-five members of the government have come to review the progress of their work. A lot of damage had been done to their city in Nebuchadrezzar's first invasion, but their "housing and works programme" had been successful in restoring buildings and bringing back the city to its former state of good repair. And so the committee members smugly cite an old proverb: "The city is the cauldron, and we are the flesh." In effect, they were the "meat", the truly substantial and influential persons in the city, establishing their positions by means of effective building programmes.

But in the vision, the smug satisfaction of the group is suddenly overshadowed by the prophetic words that Ezekiel is instructed to utter. There is no reason to believe that the council of twenty-five could hear the prophetic declaration, for Ezekiel and God are unseen observers. The declaration shatters the delusions of the princely leaders. They pride themselves on successful building programmes, but fail to see that they have caused the blood of the innocent to run in Jerusalem's streets. And so, in the prophecy, their pompous proverb is reversed. The city is still the cauldron, but it is the slain who are the "meat", the best of the city's citizens; indeed, the princely twenty-five would be taken out of the city altogether, for judgment, and would have no continuing part in it. Meeting after meeting, they had moved and approved statutes and bylaws for the civic plans, but had forgotten the bylaws of God. Hence, their judgment must inevitably come, and it would come on the borders of their land, far from the city in which they took such false pride.

And then, a dramatic turn in events took place, still in the vision. There are two levels of activity, going on concurrently, but without interrelationship: the council were enacting their business (unaware of the prophet's unseen presence) and Ezekiel was prophesying. But the two levels suddenly interrelate, for as the prophet is speaking, one of the council's ministers suddenly drops dead, as if from a massive heart attack. Ezekiel reacts with horror, falling down on his face; the sudden death of Pelatiah, occurring during his declaration of coming judgment, seems to indicate to Ezekiel that the coming judgment will totally eliminate God's people and purpose in this world. No doubt Pelatiah's death really took place, and a part of Ezekiel's trance included the capacity that is referred to nowadays as *clairvoyance*. The report of the vision to the exiles, followed later by the news bulletin of Pelatiah's actual death, must have caused considerable consternation in Tel Abib.

What is particularly striking in this scene from Ezekiel's vision is the anatomy of blindness, as it is dissected in the council meeting of Jerusalem's leaders. The city had been in a shambles after the events of 597 B.C., and new leaders of the city had rightly seen that something must be done. But what they had done was to deal with the surface manifestations of the crisis; they had not looked for the underlying causes. They rebuilt the houses, but did not really ask why they had been destroyed in the first place.

Such blindness is not uncommon. When riots break out, it is one thing to crush the riot, but it is altogether more important to seek the roots of the riots and seek to cure that ill. Or when cancerous growths appear on the body's skin, it is one thing to treat the skin, but unless more radical treatment is undertaken for the physical condition culminating in the dermatological manifestation, the surface treatment will be wasted. So to rebuild the houses of the holy city, but not to address the unholiness that led to their collapse, was folly of the first order.

And what was true of Jerusalem's council may be equally true of kirk sessions, synods and vestries the world over. A building programme is not always the solution to a state of disrepair. What is needed first is the recognition of the roots of disaster, so that the moral and spiritual house may first be rebuilt. The rest of the programme of restoration should then follow more naturally.

A MISSION FOR THOSE IN EXILE

Ezekiel 11:14–25

¹⁴And the word of the Lord came to me: ¹⁵"Son of man, your

brethren, even your brethren, your fellow exiles, the whole house of Israel, all of them, are those of whom the inhabitants of Jerusalem have said, 'They have gone far from the Lord; to us this land is given for a possession.' [16]Therefore say, 'Thus says the Lord God: Though I removed them far off among the nations, and though I scattered them among the countries, yet I have been a sanctuary to them for a while in the countries where they have gone.' [17]Therefore say, 'Thus says the Lord God: I will gather you from the peoples, and assemble you out of the countries where you have been scattered, and I will give you the land of Israel.' [18]And when they come there, they will remove from it all its detestable things and all its abominations. [19]And I will give them one heart, and put a new spirit within them; I will take the stony heart out of their flesh and give them a heart of flesh, [20]that they may walk in my statutes and keep my ordinances and obey them; and they shall be my people, and I will be their God. [21]But as for those whose heart goes after their detestable things and their abominations, I will requite their deeds upon their own heads, says the Lord God."

[22]Then the cherubim lifted up their wings, with the wheels beside them; and the glory of the God of Israel was over them. [23]And the glory of the Lord went up from the midst of the city, and stood upon the mountain which is on the east side of the city. [24]And the Spirit lifted me up and brought me in the vision by the Spirit of God into Chaldea, to the exiles. Then the vision that I had seen went up from me. [25]And I told the exiles all the things that the Lord had showed me.

The account of the vision now comes to a close; when it is over, Ezekiel recovers consciousness from his trance-like condition and reports all that he has seen to the fellow exiles sitting with him. The last part of what he must recount is of particular importance to his fellow exiles. Thus, while some scholars may be correct in their view that several of the verses now being considered represent insertions in the text from a later period in Ezekiel's ministry (note particularly the similarity between verses 19–20 and Chapter 36:26–27), nevertheless the general substance of this passage must be integral to the prophet's great vision of Jerusalem. Only then does the vision as a whole really make sense as a part of Ezekiel's prophetic ministry to the exiles, as we shall see in a moment.

In essence, the final words of God to the prophet link what has been seen and said of Jerusalem to the exiles at Tel Abib in Babylon. The surviving citizens of Jerusalem had already written off the exiles in their thinking and actions; they perceived themselves to be the true heirs of the holy city. But God has a different message to declare to the exiles. Though they have been scattered among many nations, yet would they be regathered and repossess the land. After an inner transformation, effected by God, there would be in effect a new exodus and a new establishment of the faith in the promised land. This was the promise of God, but even as the promise was declared, the wheels of justice were still in motion; the glory and throne of God departed from the temple and its city, to rest on the hill lying to the east of the city. Already, it seemed the future of the city lay not with its surviving inhabitants but with those exiled from it.

The concluding part of the vision is particularly instructive with respect to both the prophet, and the two groups of persons involved, the citizens and the exiles.

(i) The prophet has his hope restored at the last moment, just as he must have thought that there was to be no redeeming ray of hope at all in his visionary visit to Jerusalem.

Immediately preceding this scene in the vision, Ezekiel had cried out in despair, when Pelatiah had dropped dead in the midst of the council's deliberations. The reason for his reaction lay partly in the meaning of the council member's name: *Pelatiah* means "the Lord causes a remnant to escape", so that his death appeared to remove even the possibility of a surviving remnant. But now, in the last words addressed to him in the vision, Ezekiel sees slender hope. Though nothing could avert the judgment of Jerusalem, his ministry was not only the declaration of doom; there remained a task to be undertaken, and the exiles to whom he must report his vision would be responsible in part for carrying out that task.

Some would view the task of the prophet as totally hopeless. ("At the end of the tunnel, there is a light—it is a train coming towards me!") Such is not the case, for there is always a fragment of hope. ("At the end of the tunnel, there really is a light, albeit far away!")

(ii) The citizens of Jerusalem, with whom the future should have rested, had compounded their errors and lost their opportunity. In 597 B.C., many of their fellows had gone into exile, but they had survived. Instead of being grateful for being spared, they had been proud. With so many distinguished men and women absent in exile, they had seized the opportunity to grasp power for themselves. And in their driving ambition, demonstrated in the grasping of selfish opportunity, they lost the opportunity of a lifetime to bring back their city to its true place in history.

Great opportunities come to all people from time to time, but they cannot be grasped unless they are seen. And there is nothing so blinding to the presence of honest opportunity, as the obsession with ambition and the search for selfish opportunity. What might have happened in the history of Jerusalem, *if only* its citizens and leaders had seen the last opportunity that was given to them between 597 and 587 B.C.? We shall never know, though we may guess that much of the course of its history would have been changed. So too shall we never know the answer to the *"what if?"* questions in our own lives, if we allow the opportunities to pass by untouched.

(iii) And so it was upon the exiles that the future now depended. Thinking themselves to be useless, they had looked to others in far off Jerusalem to provide a source of hope. But the tables were being turned. If there was hope to be found, it lay within them, not in the empty hands of others far away. The citizens of Jerusalem had already written off the exiles as irrelevant to the future of their city. Indeed, the exiles themselves thought that there was nothing they could do. But now they were learning that the weak of this world were the ones through whom God would work. And such new hope was not without its attendant anxiety, for it involved awesome responsibility.

Yet the message of the prophet to his fellow exiles carried with it a potent promise, to be developed still further later in his ministry. The future now lay with those in exile, yet it was plain for all to see that they did not have in themselves the strength to undertake the task. The enabling power would be provided by

God in the gift of a new spirit and a new heart (see further 36:26). The doomed citizens of the city had built by themselves, and their buildings would soon come toppling down. The exiles, in their mission, would have to learn to build in a new way, employing the strength coming from their new and God-given heart and spirit.

EXILED FROM THOSE IN EXILE

Ezekiel 12:1–16

¹The word of the Lord came to me: ²"Son of man, you dwell in the midst of a rebellious house, who have eyes to see, but see not, who have ears to hear, but hear not; ³for they are a rebellious house. Therefore, son of man, prepare for yourself an exile's baggage, and go into exile by day in their sight; you shall go like an exile from your place to another place in their sight. Perhaps they will understand, though they are a rebellious house. ⁴You shall bring out your baggage by day in their sight, as baggage for exile; and you shall go forth yourself at evening in their sight, as men do who must go into exile. ⁵Dig through the wall in their sight, and go out through it. ⁶In their sight you shall lift the baggage upon your shoulder, and carry it out in the dark; you shall cover your face, that you may not see the land; for I have made you a sign for the house of Israel."

⁷And I did as I was commanded. I brought out my baggage by day, as baggage for exile, and in the evening I dug through the wall with my own hands; I went forth in the dark, carrying my outfit upon my shoulder in their sight.

⁸In the morning the word of the Lord came to me: ⁹"Son of man, has not the house of Israel, the rebellious house, said to you, 'What are you doing?' ¹⁰Say to them, 'Thus says the Lord God: This oracle concerns the prince in Jerusalem and all the house of Israel who are in it.' ¹¹Say, 'I am a sign for you: as I have done, so shall it be done to them; they shall go into exile, into captivity.' ¹²And the prince who is among them shall lift his baggage upon his shoulder in the dark, and shall go forth; he shall dig through the wall and go out through it; he shall cover his face, that he may not see the land with his eyes. ¹³And I will spread my net over him, and he shall be taken in my snare; and I will bring him to Babylon in the land of the Chaldeans, yet he shall not see it; and he shall die there. ¹⁴And I will scatter toward every wind all who are

round about him, his helpers and all his troops; and I will unsheathe the sword after them. [15]And they shall know that I am the Lord, when I disperse them among the nations and scatter them through the countries. [16]But I will let a few of them escape from the sword, from famine and pestilence, that they may confess all their abominations among the nations where they go, and may know that I am the Lord."

With this enacted parable of exile, a new phase of Ezekiel's life and ministry appears to begin, though the substance of Chapters 12–24 is still concerned primarily with Jerusalem and its coming fall.

The prophet is instructed first to perform certain actions; then the actions are to be followed by words of interpretation. Thus, the message he is now to bring to his people will be both seen and heard; by one means or another, there is a possibility that his audience will understand the meaning of the message. Ezekiel was first to prepare an "exile's bag". It would contain at once all a person's earthly possessions, but also only the bare necessities of survival: some personal items, clothes, food, perhaps a cloak that could be used as a blanket, and minimal cooking implements. The bag would be placed by the door of his house. In the evening, with fellow exiles watching in curiosity, he would dig a hole through the mud-brick wall (either of his house, or perhaps of a low retaining wall surrounding the refugee encampment), and depart from the encampment with his bag on his shoulder. As he left, he would cover his face, as if to hide from his sight a last look at the land from which he was departing. And then he would disappear from the audience's range of sight, into the quickly falling darkness.

The audience would have the evening and the night to reflect on Ezekiel's latest antics and wonder what he was up to now. They had become accustomed to his enacted parables, and so had a problem to solve: what was the meaning of this newest drama? In the morning, the prophet returned to the encampment and declared to the exiles the interpretation of what he had done. His actions were a sign of what would happen to the "prince in Jerusalem" (presumably Zedekiah: 2 Kings 25:4) and the other inhabitants of the city. They would leave the city through its breached wall, destined for exile; a few would survive, but many would perish.

A number of instructive features emerge from this enacted parable and its interpretation.

(i) *The ministry of judgment retains the hope of repentance.* "Perhaps they will understand," God says to Ezekiel, though recognising fully the perverse and rebellious nature of the prophet's audience. The fact that the prophet's ministry continues at all is based on this "perhaps"; people seem to be so blind and deaf, but perhaps if something is said and done often enough, someone will understand. And so it becomes clear again that the continuing declaration of judgment is in fact a sign of grace. The warning of impending judgment always leaves open the possibility of repentance.

(ii) *The parable compels reflection for its correct understanding.* When we read this account with the benefit of hindsight, we cannot easily enter the dilemma of interpretation confronting the initial observers of the enacted parable. Consider their dilemma on the evening of the parable. The prophet packs up his belongings and departs at dusk from the encampment; what did it mean? The most obvious meaning to those refugees surviving by hope was that the exile was about to end! As Ezekiel packed and left, so too would they soon leave, setting out again on the road to Jerusalem. But if such were their interpretation, hope was dashed the morning after, when Ezekiel declared the true sense of what he had done.

Like many parables, it offers two meanings, the one carnal and the other spiritual. Desperate hope wanted to make the parable positive; spiritual insight would have revealed that its thrust must be negative. Hence the prophet's stress on those "who have eyes to see, but see not", a theme reiterated in the ministry of Jesus. The parable compels reflection, if its true sense is to be discerned. Equally, it contains a warning of the dangers of imposing our own desires and wishes upon the word of God.

(iii) *The purpose of parable and judgment is to declare God's Lordship.* In the interpretation, it is stressed again, as so often elsewhere in Ezekiel's ministry, that judgment has a goal, namely the creation of awareness in those that are judged "that I am the Lord" (verses 15 and 16). The purpose makes the judgment positive and worth while. To live life without the knowledge that God is the Lord is to miss the entire point of human existence. And so the judgment may ultimately be seen as an act of mercy: if the truth cannot be learned in peace, then it must be learned in judgment—but either is preferable to not learning the truth at all.

DINING IN THE TWILIGHT OF DOOM

Ezekiel 12:17–20

> [17]Moreover the word of the Lord came to me: [18]"Son of man, eat your bread with quaking, and drink water with trembling and with fearfulness; [19]and say of the people of the land, Thus says the Lord God concerning the inhabitants of Jerusalem in the land of Israel: They shall eat their bread with fearfulness, and drink water in dismay, because their land will be stripped of all it contains, on account of the violence of all those who dwell in it. [20]And the inhabited cities shall be laid waste, and the land shall become a desolation; and you shall know that I am the Lord."

In this simple, but dramatically enacted parable, a further fearful message is conveyed to the exiles by the prophet. At the divine command, Ezekiel was to eat bread and drink water, while quaking as if in mortal terror. From what we know of Ezekiel's life and ministry, the quaking may not have required much skill in acting; in his state of exhaustion and ill-health, the trembling hands and shaking body may have become a part of Ezekiel's daily existence. This physical frailty was now to become part of an enacted meal, eaten in public, as a further parable of God's coming judgment. One can visualise the scene: the prophet's hand would be shaking so that water spilled before reaching his lips and the bread was fumbled at the mouth. By his actions, he was demonstrating to his audience the fearful condition of the inhabitants of Jerusalem, who would dine in trembling in the twilight of their city's doom.

The power of this parable emerges from some of the fine points of its substance.

(i) *The judgment was rooted in the former actions of those judged.* Jacques Ellul, a distinguished French lawyer and theologian, has described the "laws of violence", of which one of the most fundamental is this: "Violence begets violence—*nothing else*" (*Violence*, 1969, p. 100). Central to the parable is *trembling*, caused by the fear of coming *violence*; and yet, as the prophet's explanation makes clear, the only reason for violence coming to the inhabitants of Jerusalem was that they had already exercised violence within the city. Those who had caused others to quake with fear were to experience trembling themselves. For acts of violence are like seeds planted in the ground; they bring forth in the future their own harvest of violence. And all those who exercise the power and threat of violence may come to reap their own harvest in fear and trembling.

(ii) *Even in crisis, human beings may fail to see their real source of life.* Although the most dramatic aspect of the enacted parable was the prophet's trembling fear, the most fundamental activity of the parable was eating and drinking. Most basically, a person eats and drinks in order to stay alive, and even on the eve of destruction, the city's inhabitants naturally would continue to eat and drink in order to keep their bodies functioning. Faced with death, they continue to feed the living body; there is no suggestion of fasting and penitence, or controlling the body's appetites in an attempt to avert disaster.

Yet there may have been a deeper message to the exiles living in Babylon. They were resident in a land which had spawned one of the most ancient of human sayings, a proverb that continues to flourish in the twentieth century. "Eat, drink and be merry, for this is man's sole purpose"—the words were first spoken to Gilgamesh, a hero of ancient Babylonia, by a barmaid he encountered in his quest to understand human existence. But there is an irony in this. Gilgamesh, the pagan, had heard the words in a noble quest for life's meaning, and he did not listen to them; to the citizens of Jerusalem, at home and in exile, the parable of eating and drinking in despair was a consequence of their own evil, not counsel from God.

All must eat and drink. But as Moses said (Deut. 8:3), and as Jesus was also to say (Matt. 4:4), "Man does not live by bread alone." Those who eat the bread of violence cannot also eat the bread of life, and so eventually must eat the bread of trembling, in fear of life itself.

(iii) *There is strength in the weakness of ministry*. Not the least incongruous feature of this enacted parable is the portrait of a weak and trembling prophet. He spills his water and messes his mouth; he was not an impressive sight to his audience of exiles. And though in part he was acting a parable, in part no doubt he was so gripped with the horror of his message that the fumbling feeding was quite naturally done.

Had Ezekiel been a seminary student of homiletics, he would doubtless have failed the course on this performance. The prophet-preacher must surely be dynamic and strong, inspiring his audience. He must surely draw them by a positive personality, not appal them by trembling theatrics. No! The most fundamental requirement of any prophet is obedience to the divine command. And if that command involves the demonstration of frailty, it should never be forgotten that divine strength can be communicated in human weakness.

THE REVERSAL OF ANCIENT PROVERBS

Ezekiel 12:21–28

21And the word of the Lord came to me: 22"Son of man, what is this proverb that you have about the land of Israel, saying, 'The days grow long, and every vision comes to naught'? 23Tell them therefore, 'Thus says the Lord God: I will put an end to this proverb, and they shall no more use it as a proverb in Israel.' But say to them, The days are at hand, and the fulfilment of every vision. 24For there shall be no more any false vision or flattering divination within the house of Israel. 25But I the Lord will speak the word which I will speak, and it will be performed. It will no longer be delayed, but in your days, O rebellious house, I will speak the word and perform it, says the Lord God."

26Again the word of the Lord came to me: 27"Son of man, behold, they of the house of Israel say, 'The vision that he sees is for many days

hence, and he prophesies of times far off.' ²⁸Therefore say to them,
Thus says the Lord God: None of my words will be delayed any longer,
but the word which I speak will be performed, says the Lord God.''

In the ministry of any prophet, resistance is to be expected from
the audience, and if the message is an unpalatable one of doom,
the resistance will be all the more steadfast. Given the substance
of Ezekiel's prophetic preaching, it is not surprising that there
was resistance to his message. But Ezekiel was not the first
prophet to minister to Israel; many had preceded him, both true
and false, and the people over many generations had developed
certain standard responses to the dramatic preaching of the
prophets. What had once been simple responses became, with
the passage of time, popular sayings or proverbs. Whenever some
messenger of doom came onto the scene, his message could be
sloughed off with the conventional responses.

In this short passage, it is implied that there was resistance to
the prophet's ministry; the exiles may have listened to him, but
they did not take him too seriously. The prophet's enactment of
parables and his declarations of imminent disaster were met by
the audience with the same old proverbs and clever answers that
their ancestors had used. And so now the prophet is instructed to
take a more aggressive approach in his ministry. Rather than
simply acting out and speaking the divine declarations, he is to
take up the responses of his people and undermine their hard-
hearted lines of defence.

The conversion of the two ancient proverbs is in itself instructive, but equally illuminating is the implication of this short
passage for understanding both the prophet and his audience.

(i) *The first proverb: prophecy is never fulfilled.* The English
translation of the proverb (verse 22) does not quite catch the
terseness and brevity of the Hebrew text. To paraphrase it:
"Time passes and nothing happens!" The audience's response, in
other words, was that it was unnecessary to take seriously the
declarations of the prophets. They were always warning of terrible disasters, and nothing ever happened. And, as with most
defensive responses, there was an element of truth in it; many

things had been prophesied (and who was to distinguish between true and false prophets?) that had not come to pass. There are two distinct elements to this first defensive proverb. (a) There is the element of *time*. A prophet says something will happen, but as time goes by, nothing does happen. (b) Hence, there is the implication of *falsity*; if nothing seemed to happen, the prophecy could not be true.

Thus, Ezekiel's new prophecy takes a distinctive twist; it reverses the defence mechanisms of his audience. The reversed version of the proverb may be paraphrased: "Time's up and everything is going to happen!" The audience could still claim that this prophecy was no different from the others, but as in the next two or three years it became evidently true, culminating in the defeat of Jerusalem, their response would take on the hollow ring they once attributed to prophecies. The scene is like an anticipation of the day of judgment. "There's no such day," the people cried, but the echo would return to them on the actual day of their judgment.

(ii) *The second proverb: fulfilment is far in the future.* The second response to prophetic preaching is somewhat more cautious; it would appeal to those who like butter on both sides of their bread. Instead of implying that prophecies are not true, those who used the second response indicated that the fulfilment of prophecies lay far in the future (verse 27); there was therefore little need to be worried about them in the present. Let future generations worry! And so the prophet reverses this one too: it will happen now, in your own time.

Thus, in two declarations, the prophet undermines the defences of the intransigent exiles. God's word is not false, as will be demonstrated in its fulfilment. Nor is it distant, as will so quickly become clear. But there is tragedy in all this: the divine response to human resistance hastens the disaster. More precisely, the human resistance to the divine word precipitates the end, thereby reducing the opportunity for repentance which was implicit in the word in the first place.

(iii) *The people's defence demonstrated their blindness.* There is an awful irony in the people's proverbs, which illustrates their fundamental blindness to the acts of God in relation to their personal history. "Time passes, and nothing happens," they said, in reaction to the prophet's preaching. Yet it had already happened to them! They were in exile. It is like a prisoner sending a letter to the judge from his prison cell: "You are always threatening to put me in prison, but you'll never do it!" Of all people, the exiles should have known the folly of protesting that prophecy would not come true, or would happen only in the distant future. The end was already upon them, if they only had the eyes to perceive it.

And yet for us, the modern readers of the ancient text, it is always easier to perceive blindness in others than in ourselves. The prophetic word is always coming to us, and we naturally respond as did the exiles. "It won't happen, not in my lifetime, in any case!" Such a response only brings closer that which we wish to delay. There must always be recognition of the fact that the prophetic word of judgment is actually a word of grace. To respond immediately releases hope; to delay permanently invites disaster.

(iv) *The prophet's message illustrates the difficulty of his task.* As we read Ezekiel, or the books of the other prophets, we must always keep their audiences in mind if we are to understand the true difficulty of prophetic ministry. Ezekiel's message was not welcomed, nor did his people respond enthusiastically to the divine word. They trotted out the old answers to prophetic preaching that had been in vogue for generations. And the old answers, albeit excuses, were not without merit, for Ezekiel knew full well that every generation had had its false prophets who called in question the credibility of prophecy as a whole.

We can only speculate on Ezekiel's own uncertainties. How did he know that his own prophecies were true? How could he be sure, even as he reversed the popular proverbs, that he was right? Any normal human would undergo agonies of torment and doubt in such circumstances. But for Ezekiel, the truth of his words went back to the overwhelming reality of his vision and vocation. He had encountered the Living God. He had not chosen a career, but had been compelled into fulfilling a task. And thus the truth of his words rested in his knowledge of the One who spoke them. But Ezekiel's experience is a reminder of the constant need of the servant of God to remain close to the One whom he serves; to listen too long to those who were his people could seriously undermine the strength of his conviction.

LITTLE FOXES, WHITEWASHED WALLS, AND FALSE PROPHETS

Ezekiel 13:1–16

¹The word of the Lord came to me: ²"Son of man, prophesy against the prophets of Israel, prophesy and say to those who prophesy out of their own minds: 'Hear the word of the Lord!' ³Thus says the Lord God, Woe to the foolish prophets who follow their own spirit, and have seen nothing! ⁴Your prophets have been like foxes among ruins, O Israel. ⁵You have not gone up into the breaches, or built up a wall for the house of Israel, that it might stand in battle in the day of the Lord. ⁶They have spoken falsehood and divined a lie; they say, 'Says the Lord,' when the Lord has not sent them, and yet they expect him to fulfil their word. ⁷Have you not seen a delusive vision, and uttered a lying divination, whenever you have said, 'Says the Lord,' although I have not spoken?"

⁸Therefore thus says the Lord God: "Because you have uttered delusions and seen lies, therefore behold, I am against you, says the Lord God. ⁹My hand will be against the prophets who see delusive visions and who give lying divinations; they shall not be in the council of my people, nor be enrolled in the register of the house of Israel, nor shall they enter the land of Israel; and you shall know that I am the Lord God. ¹⁰ Because, yea, because they have misled my people, saying, 'Peace,' when there is no peace; and because, when the people build a wall, these prophets daub it with whitewash; ¹¹say to those who daub it with whitewash that it shall fall! There will be a deluge of rain, great hailstones will fall, and a stormy wind break out; ¹²and when the wall falls, will it not be said to you, 'Where is the daubing with which you daubed it?' ¹³Therefore thus says the Lord God: I will make a stormy wind break out in my wrath; and there shall be a deluge of rain in my anger, and great hailstones in wrath to destroy it. ¹⁴And I will break down the wall that you have daubed with whitewash, and bring it

down to the ground, so that its foundation will be laid bare; when it falls, you shall perish in the midst of it; and you shall know that I am the Lord. ¹⁵Thus will I spend my wrath upon the wall, and upon those who have daubed it with whitewash; and I will say to you, The wall is no more, nor those who daubed it, ¹⁶the prophets of Israel who prophesied concerning Jerusalem and saw visions of peace for her, when there was no peace, says the Lord God."

Not least of the difficulties faced by Ezekiel in his ministry was the influence exerted by false prophets. Their lying words and vacant visions lulled the people into a false sense of security and made his own task vastly more difficult. It would have been hard enough to have been Israel's sole prophet, but to be a lone prophet of truth among the many religious bandits of his day was to complicate considerably his prophetic ministry. How would the people be able to distinguish truth from falsity among the multitude of messages? Now God's word comes to Ezekiel again, and he is directed to declare an oracle against the false prophets.

In one sense, the persons whom he describes are not false; Ezekiel calls them the "prophets of Israel", and no doubt they had been granted the title officially. Their sophistry lay in their message, its deception the more dangerous precisely because it was delivered by a recognised person. And so it is the message and motives that are condemned, rather than the office as such, in these powerful oracular statements. The prophet uses two illustrations to press home his critique of the prophets of falsehood.

(a) *Little foxes*. They are like little foxes that live in the ruins of a deserted and desolate city. The simile is not at once clear to modern urban dwellers and indeed has elicited scholarly explanations of extraordinary obscurity. But the essence is clear enough: the prophets are like the smaller beasts of prey, finding their own comfortable little nest of security in the ruins left by others. They inhabit the ruins and make a living there, but to rebuild the ruins is beyond their powers. Of such a kind were the false prophets. They acted like the real thing, prefacing their pronouncements with "Says the Lord" (verse 6); but really they were beasts of prey, seeking only carrion and comfort for themselves, contributing nothing to the desolate wilderness in which they lived. And so, because of their lies and deceptions, a terrible judgment is pronounced (verses 8–9): God was against the false prophets, and would cut them off eventually from their own people and land.

(b) *Whitewashed walls.* The second illustration of the falsehood of the lying prophets is developed in the metaphor of the white-washed wall. They were like masons that constructed a shoddy wall from dry stones, neither fitting them well nor cementing them together, but taking care to cover the defects with brilliant whitewash. They constructed shabby weakness, but covered the whole with the whitewashed veneer of strength. Yet it was a false strength. It pleased those who wanted to see strength, but it would not stand the test of storm. The prophets are condemned for constructing illusion, deliberately and consciously, for their own ends. Their people desperately wanted a message of peace, so they gave it to them, preferring to declare the happy lie than the terrible truth. But the illusory world of false prophetic preaching would collapse under the pressure of divine judgment, and the prophets themselves would wane with their wall.

Ezekiel's critique is so picturesque and powerful, that it is easy to join with him in the solemn condemnation of false prophecy, but in so doing we must be careful not to be blind to the insidious nature of that which is condemned. For the disease afflicts not only false prophets in all ages, but also their willing audiences.

(i) *The false prophets took the easy way.* They were, by profession, genuine prophets; they lost their vocation the moment they became deaf to God's words and prefixed their own pompous preaching with "Thus saith the Lord". And the temptation to which they succumbed is one that faces prophets and preachers in every age. God's word is not always palatable, nor does it always evoke favourable reactions from an audience. Indeed, there are times when a misplaced sense of compassion suggests a message of peace and comfort, though the substance of the message is false. And having lied once, the lie became easier, as it always does; false prophecy is a grand deception, but may reap a lucrative and comfortable living.

There is no easy way in either prophecy or preaching. It is not that the message must always be harsh. But the message must be genuinely from the Lord; the prophet cannot afford to become deaf to the divine word that he is to communicate to his people.

(ii) *False prophets require willing audiences.* The evil of the "successful" preaching of the false prophets cannot be laid entirely at their feet, for there is a degree of complicity in such a ministry. Their message of falsehood was the easy way only because the lies they declared were exactly what the people wanted to hear. In times of calamity, such as those of the last months of Jerusalem's freedom and the early months of exile, the people would rather be comforted than told the truth of their plight. Better a message of "peace" with its future hope, than judgment with its bleak despair.

It is a human preference to be sheltered from those truths that reveal the evil within us; far better to bolster the inner delusion of innocence, especially if that bolstering is done by a prophet or preacher. The condemnation of false prophets, in other words, is equally a condemnation of false congregations. The true listener, as much as the true preacher, must be prepared to hear the word of God, whether it bring comfort or pain.

(iii) *False prophecy is ultimately futile.* False prophecy is like a religious form of addiction. It dulls the senses, blinds the eyes, and creates its own fantastic hallucinations. But it is not real and its ultimate futility is never so clear as when the drug is removed and the focus on reality is regained amidst the agony of withdrawal. And this is the lot of all false prophecy and preaching.

THE DAUGHTERS OF DECEPTION

Ezekiel 13:17–23

[17]"And you, son of man, set your face against the daughters of your people, who prophesy out of their own minds; prophesy against them [18]and say, Thus says the Lord God: Woe to the women who sew magic bands upon all wrists, and make veils for the heads of persons of every stature, in the hunt for souls! Will you hunt down souls belonging to my

people, and and keep other souls alive for your profit? ¹⁹ You have profaned me among my people for handfuls of barley and for pieces of bread, putting to death persons who should not die and keeping alive persons who should not live, by your lies to my people, who listen to lies.

²⁰"Wherefore thus says the Lord God: Behold, I am against your magic bands with which you hunt the souls, and I will tear them from your arms; and I will let the souls that you hunt go free like birds. ²¹Your veils also I will tear off, and deliver my people out of your hand, and they shall be no more in your hand as prey; and you shall know that I am the Lord. ²²Because you have disheartened the righteous falsely, although I have not disheartened him, and you have encouraged the wicked, that he should not turn from his wicked way to save his life; ²³ therefore you shall no more see delusive visions nor practise divination; I will deliver my people out of your hand. Then you will know that I am the Lord."

Ezekiel's oracle against false prophets is followed now by an oracle against the prophetesses, the "daughters of the people" (verse 17), who had become in reality daughters of deception. There had been distinguished prophetesses in Israel's history (Miriam, Deborah, Huldah, and others), but the women described here are those who, like the false prophets, had prostituted their calling to selfish ends.

The prophetesses had turned to the magic arts as a source of income and power. The precise nature of their magic remains unclear. The magic bands they sewed on clients' wrists were doubtless supposed to ward off evil and sickness. The veils that covered the head and upper body of customers were used in magic rituals. But all their magical rituals were fundamentally evil. Magic, by definition, is to harness (or attempt to harness) the divine power for one's own selfish ends. And while some magic had the relatively harmless goal of seeking self-protection (the wrist-bands may have been sorts of amulets), much of it was directed as a form of evil against others. Personal goals and ambitions were sought at the expense of the "souls" of others, whose lives became merely obstacles in the drive towards selfish ambition and achievement. So when people thought that magic would eliminate a competitor or enemy, they resorted to the witches who claimed to be prophetesses; they paid for the services rendered to their lust and hate.

Whatever the particular manifestations were that the magic assumed, at root the fundamental evil was the breaking of the third commandment: "You shall not take the name of the Lord your God in vain" (Deut. 5:11). This is one of the most misunderstood commandments of the Decalogue: its purpose is not the prohibition of blasphemy, but rather the prohibition of the misuse of the divine name in magical practices. For as magic was the attempt to harness divine power for personal gain, so too it was believed that the power could be used by spells and incantations in which the divine name was employed. Thus, not least of the sins of magic was the fact that it "profaned" God (verse 19), by linking his name to practices and goals that were entirely alien to the divine will. The false prophetesses attempted to sell what they did not own, the power that lay dormant in the personal name of God that had been revealed to Israel. It was, in every sense, an abuse of the privilege of relationship that God had granted to his people in the covenant. And so, in Ezekiel's oracle, God declares that the magical practices will be terminated and that his people will be liberated from the hands of the witches.

At first sight, this critique of ancient magic seems remote and distant from our modern world, but such is not the case.

(i) *Magic has a perpetual appeal.* In many ways, the modern world has been liberated from the fear and influence of magic, but it still exists. In some contemporary societies, it still holds powerful influence over the hearts and minds of men and women. And even in the Western world, it continues to thrive, though largely in the shadows of modern society. But magic, in one form or another, will always be with us, for it appears to offer power to the powerless and a weapon by which to achieve our selfish and sinful goals. And as with the false prophets, so too the prophetesses prospered only because of their multitude of clients. There were always those who wanted special protection, or the injury of an enemy, and they would pay for it handsomely. And for those who never practise the black arts, there are the inner longings to have such powers and to use them for the perpetration of evil. In thought and in practice, the possibility of gaining a handle to super-human power and using it to personal advantage is devilishly enticing. And especially is this so in times of trouble and danger, such as the times in which Ezekiel and his contemporaries lived. It is a form of evil barely held at bay by the veneer of civilisation, and ever ready to return to the central position in society that once it held.

(ii) *Magic may penetrate prayer.* It is too easy to limit magic to the black arts. Central to the practice of magic was the use of the divine name, for it was thought that the name was the lever by which the divine power could be released for personal use. And there are multitudes of Christians who engage in a form of magic, totally unaware of what they are doing. They call it prayer, but in practice it is magic. For the privilege of prayer is given in God's name, and our prayers end "in the name". But prayer, like magic, can be reduced to a technique whose goal is simply to harness the divine power for selfish ends. Instead of fellowship and communication with God, it can become little more than a "shopping list", in which we declare the things we need for the day and which, by divine power, we hope to acquire. When our prayer becomes such, then we "profane" God like the ancient prophetesses, for "handfuls of barley and for pieces of bread".

(iii) *The return to magic is the loss of freedom.* It is almost impossible for us, in the twentieth century, to conceive the massive liberation that was granted to Israel in the law prohibiting magic. For not only was the evil practice banned, but concurrently the people were freed from the curse and fear of living in a society where others might constantly be seeking their ill through magic spells and rites. The wax dolls, the voodoo spells, the incantations and dark rituals, all combined to form a netherworld of terror and anxiety. But that, in Israel, was banned; they lived in a freedom not known to any other Near Eastern nation in biblical times. Yet the false prophetesses sought to change all that. At a time when Israel was about to lose its national independence, these purveyors of magic sought to sell the nation's soul into slavery. But Ezekiel's oracle contains not only the condemnation of magic and divination, but also a promise, good for any generation: "I will deliver my people out of your hand. Then you will know that I am the Lord" (verse 23).

THE IDOLS OF THE ELDERS

Ezekiel 14:1–11

> [1]Then came certain of the elders of Israel to me, and sat before me. [2]And the word of the Lord came to me: [3]"Son of man, these men have taken their idols into their hearts, and set the stumbling block of their iniquity before their faces; should I let myself be inquired of at all by them? [4]Therefore speak to them, and say to them, Thus says the Lord God: Any man of the house of Israel who takes his idols into his heart and sets the stumbling block of his iniquity before his face, and yet comes to the prophet, I the Lord will answer him myself because of the multitude of his idols, [5]that I may lay hold of the hearts of the house of Israel, who are all estranged from me through their idols.
>
> [6]"Therefore say to the house of Israel, Thus says the Lord God: Repent and turn away from your idols; and turn away your faces from all your abominations. [7]For any one of the house of Israel, or of the strangers that sojourn in Israel, who separates himself from me, taking his idols into his heart and putting the stumbling block of his iniquity before his face, and yet comes to a prophet to inquire for himself of me, I the Lord will answer him myself; [8]and I will set my face against that man, I will make him a sign and a byword and cut him off from the midst of my people; and you shall know that I am the Lord. [9]And if the prophet be deceived and speak a word, I, the Lord, have deceived that prophet, and I will stretch out my hand against him, and will destroy him from the midst of my people Israel. [10]And they shall bear their punishment—the punishment of the prophet and the punishment of the inquirer shall be alike—[11]that the house of Israel may go no more astray from me, nor defile themselves any more with all their transgressions, but that they may be my people and I may be their God, says the Lord God."

Ezekiel describes here a scene from his life as a prophet. Some people come to visit him, as they would frequently have done during the years in exile. They visit him because he is a prophet;

one of the tasks of the prophet was to take the prayers and inquiries of the people to God and seek from him some response. Ezekiel's visitors are *elders*, or representatives of the leaders of the exiled community, and they have come to him with a particular question to be addressed to God. We are not told what was the substance of the question; it may have concerned the future of Jerusalem, if the incident described here took place before the downfall of the city. And their question may have had something to do with their leadership and their constant attempt to cope with the questions of their people: How much longer were they to remain as exiles in this foreign land?

The substance of the question is not really important, for the divine response to the elders addresses their spiritual condition, not their temporal inquiry. God perceives, as no doubt Ezekiel does, that though the elders have come to seek God's word, their question is but the veneer of an orthodox faith. The elders had their idols, kept in secret no doubt, but worshipped nevertheless. They were guilty of breaking the first commandment, but still did not hesitate to hedge their bets, and to seek God's guidance in addition to that of their closet deities. And so God's response to Ezekiel is to indicate that such men deserved no response at all to their inquiry. But he responds anyway, addressing them directly. And yet here, as elsewhere in the Old Testament, the response of God does not address the question spoken aloud; it probes beneath the surface to the deeper needs and sins of the inquirer.

The words that God speaks to the elders are terrible in their solemnity; they carry the tone of law and the sonority of legal sentence. There is a call to repentance from the evils of idolatry, but the weight of the message is judgment. If a person turns away from God to seek idolatrous aid, God in turn will avert his face from that person. When the idolater turns aside, it is sin; when God turns aside, it is death. Yet the solemnity of this proclamation of divine judgment cannot suppress its final goal, which is salvation. For the judgment, in all its severity, is not merely the reward reaped for evil deeds; more than that, its purpose is to turn from evil and restore a knowledge of God and the true faith.

As is so often the case with Ezekiel's ministry, the prophet's words probe like x-rays the anatomy of the human condition.

(i) The blindness of the elders is exposed. They were in exile, and if they had understood any of the prophet's message, they would surely have known that exile was in part a consequence of human sin. Indeed, idolatry in Israel was one of the evils that had culminated in God's judgment. Yet here they were in exile, still indulging in the evils that had brought them there. They were like a criminal imprisoned for murder, who then in prison kills a fellow convict—and wonders why he cannot be released from his cell. Yet expressing the blindness in such a stark simile may not alert us to how common and subtle such blindness may be. The elders wanted, perhaps subconsciously, to cover every possibility of safety; their faith in God, so they thought, could be usefully supplemented by a little worship of the local gods, some of whom might offer assistance. And the totality of their blindness is indicated by the fact that they were apparently not the least bit uneasy in coming to Ezekiel for God's help, thinking their idolatrous practices were unknown to God.

Yet the sin of the elders is merely archetypal of a common human blindness. We live our own lives, pursue our own idols, but—if the need arises—we do not hesitate to seek God's help, blithely unaware of the radical inconsistency of such behaviour. And there is a certain irony in such moral and spiritual blindness; with time, it breeds the sublime conviction that God, too, is blind, and sees only what we want him to see. The words of God to the elders revealed all too clearly that God was not blind, and his words removed the hypocritical scales of moral blindness in human beings.

(ii) The ignorance of prayer is exposed. The elders had a question: it was to be addressed to God, as a prayer requiring an answer. And their action takes us back to one of the oldest questions of the religious life: Does God answer prayer? The biblical answer is clearly "yes"; but the answer may not coincide with the petition. The elders asked a question: persons of such spiritual depravity had no right to be answered at all, as God's words to Ezekiel make clear (verse 3). Yet God answers anyway: he does not answer the question they asked, but answers the question they should have asked and needed to know. The answer was extremely uncomfortable to the elders, to put it mildly; they came seeking a little comfort, and heard what amounted to a sentence of death. Yet there was mercy to be found in the fact that God answered at all. If only they would hear and understand his response, and then turn from their evil, then the answer to their first question would emerge. For every evil of exile was rooted in human sin, and the answer of God to the elders' prayer diagnosed clearly that the rot had not been removed.

(iii) There was a risk in the prophetic office. One of the surprising features in the substance of God's declaration is the manner in which not only inquirers, but also prophets, run the risk of divine judgment. It would have been all too easy for Ezekiel, seeking to avoid unpleasantness and confrontation, to give an assuring and comforting response to the question of the elders. He could have overlooked their idolatry and pointed hopefully (and falsely) to better times in the future. But the prophetic office carried with it responsibility. Only the upright could honestly inquire; and only the truth could be given to any inquirer. Ezekiel walked a tight-rope; to fail in his task would be to join the ranks of those to whom the message of judgment was addressed.

But the dilemma for every servant of God is real. There is a misplaced sense of compassion within us that would make us prefer to say the comforting words, rather than declare the truth. Yet ultimately there is no compassion in hiding the truth. For truthfulness may bring out the awful nature of evil, but a cure can be sought when the diagnosis is known. Veiling the truth with comforting platitudes permits the inner disease to fester, until at last it brings its own form of death.

NOAH, DANIEL, AND JOB

Ezekiel 14:12–23

> [12]And the word of the Lord came to me: [13]"Son of man, when a land sins against me by acting faithlessly, and I stretch out my hand against it, and break its staff of bread and send famine upon it, and cut off from it man and beast, [14]even if these three men, Noah, Daniel, and Job,

were in it, they would deliver but their own lives by their righteousness, says the Lord God. [15]If I cause wild beasts to pass through the
land, and they ravage it, and it be made desolate, so that no man may
pass through because of the beasts; [16]even if these three men were in it,
as I live, says the Lord God, they would deliver neither sons nor
daughters; they alone would be delivered, but the land would be
desolate. [17]Or if I bring a sword upon that land, and say, Let a sword
go through the land; and I cut off from it man and beast; [18]though these
three men were in it, as I live, says the Lord God, they would deliver
neither sons nor daughters, but they alone would be delivered. [19]Or if I
send a pestilence into that land, and pour out my wrath upon it with
blood, to cut off from it man and beast; [20]even if Noah, Daniel, and
Job were in it, as I live, says the Lord God, they would deliver neither
son nor daughter; they would deliver but their own lives by their
righteousness.

[21]"For thus says the Lord God: How much more when I send upon
Jerusalem my four sore acts of judgment, sword, famine, evil beasts,
and pestilence, to cut off from it man and beast! [22]Yet, if there should
be left in it any survivors to lead out sons and daughters, when they
come forth to you, and you see their ways and their doings, you will be
consoled for the evil that I have brought upon Jerusalem, for all that I
have brought upon it. [23]They will console you, when you see their ways
and their doings; and you shall know that I have not done without
cause all that I have done in it, says the Lord God."

For the modern reader of the Book of Ezekiel, a part of the
difficulty in understanding the force of its message lies in our
ignorance of the background and circumstances pertaining to
each part of the book. The substance of the divine declaration
contained in these verses seems reasonably clear, but the purpose
of the message must be understood in the context of certain
events taking place in the exiled community. We must suppose
that certain heretical views were being disseminated amongst the
exiles and were growing in popularity; they probably originated
with the false prophets, who have already been the target of
Ezekiel's criticism (13:1–16). This oracle, addressed to Ezekiel
by God, is designed to demolish one particular falsehood, namely
that the city of Jerusalem would be spared from final disaster
because of the remnant of righteous people that existed amidst its

population. The view was not only false, but dangerous; for it awakened false hopes and, at the same time, dulled the moral sensibility of the people as to the real gravity of the times in which they lived.

The words of God state in simple terms a principle, and then elaborate it with a fourfold illustration, repeating over and again the basic principle. The principle is this: if a nation persists in its sin, then it will not be delivered from judgment, even if three of the world's most righteous men were amongst its citizens. The fourfold elaboration does not change one whit the principle; it merely varies the nature of the judgment (famine, desolation, war, and pestilence), to drive home the point that there can be no escape. And the land referred to in the general statement could be any land (indeed, a foreign country is implied); the principles of divine justice extend to all human beings.

The universality of the principle is exemplified by the three righteous persons who are employed as models of integrity; none were Israelites. Noah, known in the biblical Flood story, is also known in a variety of other ancient texts; under the name Utnapishtim, he is referred to in the Babylonian version of the flood story as a righteous man who escapes judgment. Daniel is not the biblical hero of that name, but rather an heroic figure referred to in the literature of Phoenicia and Syria. In an ancient text (approximately 13th century B.C.) from Ugarit, on the coast of Syria, we may read of upright *Danel* and his encounter with grief. And Job is known from the prologue and epilogue of the book of that name; he is not there referred to as an Israelite, but he is presented as an upright man of integrity. All these men are known as universal examples of righteousness; yet, even if three such heroes of integrity inhabited a persistently evil nation, they could not avert the onset of judgment. They would be delivered from the judgment, but their righteousness would not serve in a redemptory fashion to save their land.

And such would be the case, Ezekiel declares, with Jerusalem (here representing the nation of Judah). There may indeed have been some righteous persons left in Jerusalem, but they could not turn back the awful tide of judgment that the nation's sin had released. But then, Ezekiel's judgment has a sting in its tail. There may indeed be survivors from the coming horrors of Jerusalem's downfall, but they would not be upright men like the gentiles Job, Daniel and Noah. When those in exile saw the survivors, they would be "consoled" (verse 22) that Jerusalem had been judged; they would not be honest men plucked from the burning, but samples of the dead wood that had burned so easily.

Thus, the prophet is addressing here a nation and its morality; no nation can survive, if it doggedly persists in its commitment to crime and evil. And in the last resort, the survival of a remnant of righteous persons in the heart of the nation cannot halt a national slide to destruction. For a while, the righteous are like children, their fingers plugging the holes in the dike, desperately holding back the flood of destruction. But eventually, there are more holes than fingers, and the floods pour through, wreaking damage in their path. Such would be Jerusalem's fate.

Although Ezekiel was addressing the fate of the nation, his words were aimed at those in exile. They continued to cling forlornly to the hope that somehow Jerusalem would survive, for surely Jerusalem was not like other nations. In so hoping, they clung to the weak straws of a hope that there was still a future, and avoided facing not only the reality of their situation, but also the reason for their situation. As an alcoholic is tied to his future by drink, yet continues to imbibe for the hope that it brings of better days ahead, so too Ezekiel's companions in exile persisted in delusion, afraid to let go of false dreams and see the reality of where they stood.

The prophet spoke to exiles in Babylon, cut off from their promised land. Yet his message extends across the centuries to the present, seeking an audience with all who are exiles. It is a message which would destroy the delusion that somehow everything will work out all right, that somehow the universal principle does not apply to us. The underlying premise of the message is that it is better to know the unhappy truth, than to be comforted by the happy delusion. For when the truth is known, namely that evil always leads to destruction and is not averted by the righteousness of other humans, then at last an honest search for salvation can begin. But the New Testament takes us further, and adds a new insight to the heroes Daniel, Noah and Job. They, by their righteousness, could not rescue a nation. Yet it is central to the Christian Gospel that one man, Jesus, could, by his righteousness, rescue a world. But there are two differences from Ezekiel's message. To avert the fate of the world, Jesus accepted it for himself; he did not escape the judgment, as did the heroes of old. But ultimately, the achievement of Jesus in changing the future requires that men and women first be freed from the delusion of Ezekiel's contemporaries, that somehow everything would work out all right in the end, regardless of what they did or did not do.

THE WOOD OF THE VINE: A PARABLE

Ezekiel 15:1–8

> [1]And the word of the Lord came to me: [2]"Son of man, how does the wood of the vine surpass any wood, the vine branch which is among the trees of the forest? [3]Is wood taken from it to make anything? Do men take a peg from it to hang any vessel on? [4]Lo, it is given to the fire for fuel; when the fire has consumed both ends of it, and the middle of it is charred, is it useful for anything? [5]Behold, when it was whole, it was used for nothing; how much less, when the fire has consumed it and it is charred, can it ever be used for anything! [6]Therefore thus says the Lord God: Like the wood of the vine among the trees of the forest, which I have given to the fire for fuel, so will I give up the inhabitants of Jerusalem. [7]And I will set my face against them; though they escape from the fire, the fire shall yet consume them; and you will know that I am the Lord, when I set my face against them. [8]And I will make the land desolate, because they have acted faithlessly, says the Lord God."

Again, Ezekiel is given words by God to declare to his companions in exile. He is to declare to them a parable about the wood of the vine. The purpose of the parable was not simply to teach, as was the common function of parables in ancient Israel; it was to serve as a vehicle for the proclamation of the prophetic message. And, as is the case with most parables, this parable has a surface simplicity which hides an inner depth and more profound meaning.

At its surface level, the parable can be paraphrased and amplified as follows:

> Think of all the different kinds of trees there are in the forest. And think of the wood that they provide. Is the wood of the vine better than any of the other types of wood that can be found in the forest? There are hardwoods: you can use them to make pegs, furnishings for the home, on which to hang kitchen utensils, or even clothes. But you wouldn't use the wood of the vine to do that. And then there is cedar, a fine wood for construction and furniture, but you wouldn't use the wood of the vine for that. No, the only thing vine wood is good for is burning; it'll keep you warm for a moment or two, and then it is gone.
>
> And if a bit of vine has been burned at both ends, but some is left in the embers of the fire in the morning, that bit is still no good. So when you make the fire again in the evening, you put the vine wood back and give it another chance to burn.
>
> The wood of the vine is good for nothing, only burning.

That, so it may seem, is the parable. But at first it seems a little weak. So what, if vine is only good for burning? Who ever claimed that vine, as wood, was good for anything else? So you begin to think about it for a while, as Ezekiel's audience must have done. Some woods are good for nothing, growing in the forest; but cut down the tree, and you can construct an excellent peg. But the vine is not like that; cut, it is nothing, but growing, the vine can do what no other tree can do, namely produce a harvest of grapes. And from grapes, wine can be made.

Now we are getting closer to the force of the parable, but still we will not grasp its thrust unless we recall one of the primary metaphors that was used to describe Israel in Old Testament times. Israel was like a vine, taken from Egypt and planted in the promised land, where it grew and flourished and was fruitful (see Ps. 80:8–11). The Israelites thought of themselves in the metaphor of a flourishing vine, but Ezekiel's parable turned the metaphor on its tail. And his audience, as they reflected on the parable, would gradually begin to discern its force.

What was a vine good for? Only one thing—it produced fruit. As wood, it was useless. But if a vine ceased to produce fruit, there was no point in leaving its roots in the ground; it would be far better to cut it down and burn it, for there was no other profitable purpose to which it could be put. And Israel was to have produced fruit, it was to have been God's holy nation, his particular people, a testimony to all the world of the righteousness of God. There was no other reason for its time of flourishing in the past. Israel had not pioneered the mathematical skills of the Babylonians or the architectural skills of the Egyptians; its sole *raison d'être* was to bear witness in the world to the true God. And when it failed to do that, then (like the wood of the vine) it was good only for burning.

And so the parable is one of the failure of function. God had given Israel a task to undertake, but she had failed to fulfil it. And the "burning of the wood" would soon be seen in the destruction of Jerusalem; if a few twigs were to escape the fire, they too would be eventually burned, as good for nothing else. Having failed to fulfil the high calling of God, there was no alternative calling to which Israel could turn, no other skill to which she could turn her hand. The end had almost come, such is the force of Ezekiel's grim parable. The only bright spark amid the smoky gloom is the single assurance that the few who survived would know that God was the Lord (verse 7).

The ancient parable continues to apply to the church, as it did to Israel in centuries long past. Like Israel, the church has a single mission: it is to convey the love of God to the world. Love is in the roots of the church, just as it must be in the fruits of the church. For the members of the church must love God, the first commandment; and they must love one another, the second commandment. Only then can love flow through the church in the fulfilment of its mission to the world. But there is a constant tendency for the church to forget that it is a vine; it seeks instead to become an oak or a cedar. It exchanges the mission of love for a multitude of worldly pursuits, all honest enough in themselves, but not the purpose for the church's existence. And when it has failed in its function, it is good for nothing else.

But it is always too easy to criticise an institution, yet fail to see the parallels in the lives of individual persons, indeed in our own lives. For we each have a calling, the ministry of love; it may be exercised in a multitude of different ministries, yet its central concern remains the same. But we, like Israel, may be side-tracked from our calling. Ambition may become the focal point of our lives, or luxury, or money, or power, or the various forms of evil. Some side-tracks seem innocent enough and some are patently sinful, yet all become wrong in that they have led away from the first calling, namely to love. And like the wood of the vine, we can make ourselves useless; failing to provide fruit, we can always be bundled for firewood.

It is a solemn parable, and like the later parables of Jesus, it invites careful thought and reflection, so that its essence may penetrate our innermost beings.

A LOVE STORY

Ezekiel 16:1–14

[1]Again the word of the Lord came to me: [2]"Son of man, make known to Jerusalem her abominations, [3]and say, Thus says the Lord God to Jerusalem: Your origin and your birth are of the land of the Canaanites; your father was an Amorite, and your mother a Hittite. [4]And as for your birth, on the day you were born your navel string was not cut, nor were you washed with water to cleanse you, nor rubbed with salt, nor swathed with bands. [5]No eye pitied you, to do any of these things to you out of compassion for you; but you were cast out on the open field, for you were abhorred, on the day that you were born.

[6]"And when I passed by you, and saw you weltering in your blood, I said to you in your blood, 'Live, [7]and grow up iike a plant of the field.' And you grew up and became tall and arrived at full maidenhood; your breasts were formed, and your hair had grown; yet you were naked and bare.

[8]"When I passed by you again and looked upon you, behold, you were at the age for love; and I spread my skirt over you, and covered your nakedness: yea, I plighted my troth to you and entered into a

covenant with you, says the Lord God, and you became mine. ⁹Then I bathed you with water and washed off your blood from you, and anointed you with oil. ¹⁰I clothed you also with embroidered cloth and shod you with leather, I swathed you in fine linen and covered you with silk. ¹¹And I decked you with ornaments, and put bracelets on your arms, and a chain on your neck. ¹²And I put a ring on your nose, and earrings in your ears, and a beautiful crown upon your head. ¹³Thus you were decked with gold and silver; and your raiment was of fine linen, and silk, and embroidered cloth; you ate fine flour and honey and oil. You grew exceedingly beautiful, and came to regal estate. ¹⁴And your renown went forth among the nations because of your beauty, for it was perfect through the splendour which I had bestowed upon you, says the Lord God."

The prophet Ezekiel employed a variety of means to communicate to his people the divine message. Sometimes he spoke and sometimes he enacted his message; his words contained the strange descriptions of his dreams, but also the harsh declarations of coming judgment. Now, Ezekiel turns to the story as a means of communicating God's words to those in exile; as the chapter develops, his gift as a story-teller becomes evident. The whole of this long chapter is taken up with the story and its interpretation; it probably began as a simple story addressed by Ezekiel to his companions, with an equally straightforward application. But over time, the interpretation of the story has been amplified and reworked, whether by Ezekiel or his disciples we cannot be sure, so that Chapter 16, in its present form, is extremely long and complex. But the chapter begins simply enough with the first part of the story; it is not explicitly interpreted, though its meaning is clear enough. It is a love story.

In its external form, the story is addressed to Jerusalem (verse 2), and it is told as if it were the first part of an address delivered in court. In the opening verses, it tells of love; only later do we see that the love was spurned and so we begin to sense that the words are addressed to a court as if in the proceedings of a divorce suit. But although the words are formally addressed to Jerusalem, they apply equally to Ezekiel's audience in exile, who were former citizens of the city of Jerusalem.

The story is a simple one. A girl-child was born to parents of mixed ethnic background in the land of Canaan, but the child was not wanted and was not loved. Instead of the usual cleansing and care normally afforded to the newborn, this child was left to die. Still stained with the blood of birth, the navel string uncut, the child was abandoned in the countryside, a practice which, tragically, was not uncommon in various parts of the ancient Near East.

But a passer-by saw the child on the verge of death; in the story, the passer-by is none other than God himself, though in the original story, it would have been a young man, or prince. Moved by love, he would not let her die. He commands her to "Live" (verse 6), a word which brings with it the provision and power of living. And so the unloved and unwanted child, with the full provision of the prince (implied, but not specified), begins to grow and comes to full maturity. And then, many years later, the prince comes by again, to see the one for whom he has made provision over many years. When first he had seen her, he was moved by that kind of love which is compassion and pity; now, as he sees her in maturity and beauty, he loves her in a different way. The two are married (the word *covenant*, in verse 8, is used of marriage contracts, as well as of the covenant religion of Israel). And where, on the first encounter, the prince had made provision for the child's survival, now on the second encounter, he richly provides her with the gifts of a bride. The foundling child, dying in a field, has become a beautiful queen, famous throughout all the world for her beauty.

Although the principal prophetic message is attached to the new part of the story, the opening scene is informative in itself.

(i) The whole story is rooted in God's love. It concerns the city of Jerusalem, yet in a sense it pertains to the chosen people as a whole, who are the citizens of that city. And what is immediately clear is that God's love is not conditioned by external factors. The child was of a mixed background, not loved even by those who should have been drawn by the natural parental bonds of love, but God loved the child anyway. The prophet embodies the ancient mystery of Israel's calling: Israel was not chosen for any inherent merit or extraordinary capacities, but only because God first loved (Deut. 7:7–9). But the story also exemplifies the fact that God loved not only the unloved, but also the unlovely; the child, messy in its birth blood, was loved nevertheless. And in these simple points of Ezekiel's story, we are reminded of the nature and origins of God's love; love is not deserved, is not elicited by external beauty, cannot be bought or required. It lies in the heart of the lover, and the compassion within the heart that is not blinded by external ugliness.

And as Israel's story is rooted in the mystery of God's love, so too is the story of the church. It exists not for any merit of its own, but because God loved first; indeed, without the love of God, it would have no existence. And thus the meaning of the continuing existence of the church may only be found in that which first called it into existence, namely love.

(ii) The story also illustrates the manner in which the unlovely, on becoming the recipient of love, may grow gradually towards loveliness. And, in the maturity of beauty, the first love may grow to a deeper level. At first, the helpless child in the story could only be loved; she had not the capacity to return that love. Later, as she became beautiful, she also developed the capacity to return love, and thereby to enrich the entire relationship of love that had grown gradually over the years.

This too had been the experience of Israel, just as it has been the experience of the church. To be the object of love brings out a beauty from within that was not at first perceived, and further, the growth in love and beauty may be accompanied by a growth in the capacity to return love and to explore its deepest dimensions of relationship.

Such should be the path of all true love stories, but beauty brings its own perils, and this story is not yet complete.

LOVE GONE ASTRAY

Ezekiel 16:15–34

[15]"But you trusted in your beauty, and played the harlot because of your renown, and lavished your harlotries on any passer-by. [16]You

took some of your garments, and made for yourself gaily decked shrines, and on them played the harlot; the like has never been, nor ever shall be. ¹⁷You also took your fair jewels of my gold and of my silver, which I had given you, and made for yourself images of men, and with them played the harlot; ¹⁸and you took your embroidered garments to cover them, and set my oil and my incense before them. ¹⁹Also my bread which I gave you—I fed you with fine flour and oil and honey—you set before them for a pleasing odour, says the Lord God. ²⁰And you took your sons and your daughters, whom you had borne to me, and these you sacrificed to them to be devoured. Were your harlotries so small a matter ²¹that you slaughtered my children and delivered them up as an offering by fire to them? ²²And in all your abominations and your harlotries you did not remember the days of your youth, when you were naked and bare, weltering in your blood.

²³"And after all your wickedness (woe, woe to you! says the Lord God), ²⁴you built yourself a vaulted chamber, and made yourself a lofty place in every square; ²⁵at the head of every street you built your lofty place and prostituted your beauty, offering yourself to any passer-by, and multiplying your harlotry. ²⁶You also played the harlot with the Egyptians, your lustful neighbours, multiplying your harlotry, to provoke me to anger. ²⁷Behold, therefore, I stretched out my hand against you, and diminished your alloted portion, and delivered you to the greed of your enemies, the daughters of the Philistines, who were ashamed of your lewd behaviour. ²⁸You played the harlot also with the Assyrians, because you were insatiable; yea, you played the harlot with them, and still you were not satisfied. ²⁹You multiplied your harlotry also with the trading land of Chaldea; and even with this you were not satisfied.

³⁰"How lovesick is your heart, says the Lord God, seeing you did all these things, the deeds of a brazen harlot; ³¹building your vaulted chamber at the head of every street, and making your lofty place in every square. Yet you were not like a harlot, because you scorned hire. ³²Adulterous wife, who receives strangers instead of her husband! ³³Men give gifts to all harlots; but you gave your gifts to all your lovers, bribing them to come to you from every side for your harlotries. ³⁴So you were different from other women in your harlotries: none solicited you to play the harlot; and you gave hire, while no hire was given to you; therefore you were different."

The story that started on such an idyllic note now turns sour.

What began as a demonstration of the loftier forms of love is now continued in a panorama of love's abuse. And as the prophet continues with his theme, the story gradually becomes fused with its interpretation; the actions of the beautiful princess are still present, but more and more Jerusalem and its sins begin to dominate the prophet's narrative.

The unloved child who had experienced love from a passing prince is now mature, and her natural beauty has flowered with her coming of age. But beauty has brought its own peril: whereas in her destitute childhood, she had no strength, now she has influence and power to use or abuse as she will. She abused her new-found strength, and began to act like a prostitute; her behaviour was not rooted in the desperation of destitution, but in the lust and pride that had become integral to her character. We are provided with no psychoanalytic reasons for the curious twist in personality, or for the way in which the one who had known only love's beauty had learned so quickly its perversion. Rather, we are treated to a catalogue of love's abuse, its self-seeking lusts and awful public shame. And the dreadful account of the woman's downward slide towards degradation has a double thrust to it. On the one hand, it is a tragedy: one who had everything somehow lost it all through a terrible twist of character. But the story is not all tragedy, but also a tale of grief, for when she turned her love aside, the woman inevitably also brought grief to the one who loved her. The prince, who pitied her as a child and loved her as a woman, observes the tragic decline; he has lost her companionship and knows now only the consolation of grief. And the story-teller presses home the hurt that is involved. The gifts the prince had given her, in token of love, were converted into the pathetic images of her false lovers (verse 17).

And yet, as the story is continued, it is weaker in its primary purpose and the underlying message becomes more explicit. For the deeper love story concerns Jerusalem, the holy city and its inhabitants; and the true decline, amplified in this portion of Ezekiel's narrative, was the decline and fall of that holy city. And when one reflects on the story in the light of that city's history, the appropriateness of the terrible imagery of the story becomes apparent. For the true religion of the God of Israel had gradually been exchanged over the years for false faiths and unholy alliances. The shrine of the one true God had been abandoned for the local houses of the fertility gods and goddesses, where the sexual activity of the "worshippers" was undertaken in the hope of securing the beneficence of the deities of earth and crop. The holy city that should have been the sole bride of the One God had become instead a prostitute to the nations. And that story too had a double theme: it was a tragedy for Jerusalem and a source of grief to Jerusalem's God.

The prophet's story and judgmental theme concerned Jerusalem and its fate in his own time. Yet it is a story with universal themes, not bound by time or culture, and the most universal of these are to be found in the anatomy of evil as it is presented here. It is to be found in the character and actions of the woman in the story, though it may be typical of all men and women everywhere by whom the true vision of love has been lost.

(i) The root of evil in this story is *forgetfulness*, at first sight an innocent enough failing, but one that culminated in disaster. In all her actions, she did not "remember the days of youth" (verse 22); if she had done so, the story might have been otherwise. Memory is crucial to a healthy life; forgetfulness is dangerous. For love is a response to prior love, and the person that forgets love cannot respond properly to it. In the story, the woman forgot her entire past—the destitution of childhood that had been removed by love and the loneliness of young adulthood that had been filled by love. Her problem was not *amnesia* in any medical sense; it was not the facts she forgot, but the meaning of the facts of her life. She did not remember that the mosaic of her earlier life was a picture of love. And, having forgotten, she turned aside to abuse the greatest capacity that she had, the capacity to love. And insofar as the story is told of Jerusalem, the city's failure to remember was a failure to have learned one of the most basic lessons of faith and history. In the days of Israel's childhood, the people had been warned: *remember* God's goodness and do not *forget* all that he has done (Deut. 8:2–20).

In the life of faith, memory is essential; forgetfulness comes before the fall. For if we forget all that God has done in love, then our own love will be misdirected; rather than responding in love to all the experience of love in every day of past life, we will turn aside to the abuse of love. And as with Israel, so with us, the problem is not amnesia in a technical sense; it is rather a form of spiritual forgetfulness. And the close companion of forgetfulness is ingratitude; failing to remember past acts of love, we are no longer grateful for them. But there is a form of therapy. Memory, like the body, requires exercise from time to time. And the decline of forgetfulness can be averted if, on occasion, we exercise the memory by recalling past mercies. It is reflection on God's mercies, meditation on all former and present acts of God's love, that may instil in us a sense of thankfulness and direct our own love on its proper course.

(ii) Forgetfulness, when left unchecked, leads quickly to *pride*. "You trusted in your own beauty," Ezekiel says of the woman in his story. She could only do that because she had forgotten the source of her life and beauty. But once she trusted in her own beauty, the proper priorities of her life were reversed. True beauty is not self-conscious, but finds its fulness in the love of another; pride vaunts its own image of beauty and seeks not to give, but only to receive the adulation of others. And so this woman lavished her favours on any passer-by who would give her a moment of praise. But her world had now only one focal point—herself; anyone that fed her growing ego would be given some moments of her time, but the casually granted interludes of companionship denied her the richness of any true relationship.

Pride is a form of evil in that it perverts the fundamental meaning of human life. We are created for relationships—for a relationship of love with God and with our fellow human beings. But true love consists in seeing beauty in others and in responding to it; it is not to be found by gazing in the mirror. For pride, with its centre in the self, eventually creates its own impotence: so obsessed may we become with ourselves that we cannot respond to others. Memory, if fully restored, will help to parry pride. As we recall that we have no beauty other than that given to us by

God, so we may recapture the humility that seeks to discern only beauty in others.

(iii) Forgetfulness and pride culminate in a life of *evil*. Dragged gradually downwards by the obsession with self, the woman in the story is portrayed eventually as a tragi-comic figure, going to ridiculous lengths to satisfy her lusts. She became the lewd laughing-stock of the world, where once she had been famous for her beauty. Stripped over time of all the inhibitions of honest behaviour, she became dedicated to the practice of evil. Not a little unkindly, the prophet portrays her as worse than a prostitute; she will not even take money for her favours, but pays with gifts those that will serve her.

The lowest point of the decline to evil is presented as a warning. It started simply enough with the seed of forgetfulness; that seed grew to the bud of pride. And pride eventually blossomed into the flower of evil, lurid in its colours and laughable in its excesses. But those who are caught in evil can no longer see it clearly. The wise are those who learn the lessons of memory.

THE JUDGMENT OF THE ADULTERESS

Ezekiel 16:35–43*a*

[35]"Wherefore, O harlot, hear the word of the Lord: [36]Thus says the Lord God, Because your shame was laid bare and your nakedness uncovered in your harlotries with your lovers, and because of all your idols, and because of the blood of your children that you gave to them, [37]therefore, behold, I will gather all your lovers, with whom you took pleasure, all those you loved and all those you loathed; I will gather them against you from every side, and will uncover your nakedness to them, that they may see all your nakedness. [38]And I will judge you as women who break wedlock and shed blood are judged, and bring upon you the blood of wrath and jealousy. [39]And I will give you into the hand of your lovers, and they shall throw down your vaulted chamber and break down your lofty places; they shall strip you of your clothes and take your fair jewels, and leave you naked and bare. [40]They shall bring up a host against you, and they shall stone you and cut you to pieces with their swords. [41]And they shall burn your houses

and execute judgments upon you in the sight of many women; I will make you stop playing the harlot, and you shall also give hire no more. ⁴²So will I satisfy my fury on you, and my jealousy shall depart from you; I will be calm, and will no more be angry. ⁴³Because you have not remembered the days of your youth, but have enraged me with all these things; therefore, behold, I will requite your deeds upon your head, says the Lord God."

After the description of the depths to which the woman in the parable sank, there follows now the first declaration of judgment. In the preceding passage, the parable and its interpretation were closely interwoven; now, though the language still refers to a fallen woman, it is the city of Jerusalem that is coming more prominently into view.

The judgment is declared in a traditional legal manner. In verse 36, the reasons for the judgment are introduced by the word *because*; then, in verse 37, the nature of the judgment is described, introduced by the word *therefore*, which directly relates the penalty to the crime. The scene that follows has the atmosphere of a court. The woman stands there, condemned of various crimes. God is both prosecutor and, in a sense, the offended party. And then all the former lovers are called; they stand around her on every side, seeing her now as she really is, publicly exposed for her licentious ways. To each, words of love had been whispered, but the hollowness of those words echoes from the multitude of so-called lovers assembled in the court. And the lovers perceive that each had been played off against the other by this faithless partner, and all had indulged in their evil activities to the affront of the true husband. The evidence of the court is so overwhelming that "Guilty" can be the only verdict, and in accord with ancient Hebrew law, the woman is condemned to death by stoning (verse 40). Her possessions are to be removed and her properties destroyed. And her dead body, after stoning, would be cut up, a gruesome reminder to others of the consequences of such action.

Though it is the woman of the parable who is addressed, it is the city of Jerusalem that is firmly in the prophet's view. And the lovers on every side are the nations with whom she flirted and to

whom she granted her easy favours. Her possessions and properties represent the falsely gained wealth and the crude fertility
sanctuaries of neighbouring religions. And the execution of judgment on the woman is an anticipation of the coming judgment on
Jerusalem, if it is correct to perceive this parable and its interpretation as having been declared prior to the fall of Jerusalem in 587 B.C. Thus, once again, the prophet returns to his
melancholy theme of judgment; though cut off from his city of
Jerusalem, he returns to it constantly in his ministry, as though
obsessed with its evil and coming downfall, and yet still desperately hoping that the end might be averted.

The passage is one of judgment and thus repeats the already
familiar themes of the preceding chapters; but the new perspective provided by the parabolic approach sheds further light on
both the judged and the judge.

(i) The woman, during the course of the trial, is stripped of
clothing and jewelry by the assembled witnesses and left "naked
and bare" (verse 39). She is reduced, in other words, to the same
sorry state as that in which she was found at birth by a passing
stranger. When first she was found naked, someone had loved
her, cared for her, and provided her with clothing; she had
discovered that it is in the nature of true love to give, But, not
having learned how to love, she had returned to her original
estate. There was a circularity in judgment, from first condition to
last. At every moment of her existence between those points,
there had been the opportunity to break out of the circle into the
freedom of love, but it had not been grasped. Yet the circularity
of it all indicates the character of judgment; though declared by
the judge in the assembled court, there was a sense in which she
had created her own judgment. The human hells that exist in this
world are not always the creation of some external or demonic
force, but are often of our own making. And in the story, the
prophet reminds us again that the source of the woman's terrible
end was that she did not remember the days of her youth (verse
43); having failed to remember them, she created her own kind of
hell in the years of her adult life.

(ii) The character of the Judge is also illuminated in this account of the judgment of the adulteress. At first sight, it is the harshness of character that is evident, yet that is a misleading impression. For what dominates the account is the fact that he loved deeply and was profoundly distraught by the proceedings of the court. When the woman was faithless in love, he could not simply shrug and walk out of the relationship; if he could have done so, he would not have loved deeply in the first place. The rage that characterises this passage is rooted in love; it is not so much anger because the love is not returned, but horror because of the consequences that the loved one had brought upon herself as a result of her actions.

We can only understand the judgmental themes of the prophets when we begin to grasp the profundity of the divine love that always precedes those themes. To read these pronouncements as harsh and uncaring is to misunderstand the prophetic preaching in a fundamental way. It is only those who have loved deeply that truly know the meaning of grief. And it is only those whose commitment is total that grasp the character of righteous anger. The prophetic declarations of God's judgment are thus not only a note of warning, but a constant reminder of the depths of the divine emotion of love.

A SINNER WORSE THAN SISTER SODOM

Ezekiel 16:43b–52

"Have you not committed lewdness in addition to all your abominations? 44Behold, every one who uses proverbs will use this proverb about you, 'Like mother, like daughter.' 45You are the daughter of your mother, who loathed her husband and her children; and you are the sister of your sisters, who loathed their husbands and their children. Your mother was a Hittite and your father an Amorite. 46And your elder sister is Samaria, who lived with her daugthers to the north of you; and your younger sister, who lived to the south of you, is Sodom with her daughters. 47Yet you were not content to walk in their ways, or do according to their abominations; within a very little time you were more corrupt than they in all your ways. 48As I live, says the

Lord God, your sister Sodom and her daughters have not done as you and your daughters have done. [49]Behold, this was the guilt of your sister Sodom: she and her daughters had pride, surfeit of food, and prosperous ease, but did not aid the poor and needy. [50]They were haughty, and did abominable things before me; therefore I removed them, when I saw it. [51]Samaria has not committed half your sins; you have committed more abominations than they, and have made your sisters appear righteous by all the abominations which you have committed. [52]Bear your disgrace, you also, for you have made judgment favourable to your sisters; because of your sins in which you acted more abominably than they, they are more in the right than you. So be ashamed, you also, and bear your disgrace, for you have made your sisters appear righteous."

Now a further elaboration of the parable and the theme of judgment is given. The original story, in this addition, has been so modified and changed that there can be little certainty as to whether this part of the prophetic message was delivered at the same time as the preceding portion of Chapter 16. Nor is there certainty as to whether the passage comes directly from Ezekiel himself, or from one of his disciples. But though the parable is modified, the theme of judgment continues in harmony with the preceding verses and elaborates still further on the folly of the holy city.

The modification of the parable goes back to its beginning. The mother and father are reintroduced, and two sisters are introduced for the first time. The sisters' names, Samaria and Sodom, are the names of cities, and so it is clear that again the parable and its interpretation are closely interwoven—the sins of Jerusalem are to be compared with those of Samaria and Sodom. The evils of the daughter are to be compared with both mother (Jerusalem in her pre-Israelite days) and sisters. The evils of the mother are portrayed as continuing in the life of the daughter, summarised in an ancient proverb: "Like mother, like daughter" (verse 44). And the comparison with the sisters is instructive. Both Samaria (capital of the old northern kingdom) and Sodom had developed international reputations for their evil, but the sins of both paled before the sins of Jerusalem.

Yet of the two sisters, it is Sodom that is emphasised in this dramatic comparison with the so-called holy city. Sodom, since ancient times, had been known for the profligacy of its ways (Genesis 19); its story had been told as a moral tale to the young children of Jerusalem, as the archetype of evil and the symbol of all that was to be avoided. Situated at the south-eastern end of the Dead Sea, even the location had somehow symbolised the character of Sodom. Sir George Adam Smith, one of the greatest Scottish Old Testament scholars of the late nineteenth and early twentieth centuries, wrote this of the region of Sodom in his book, *The Historical Geography of the Holy Land* (1894):

> In this awful hollow, this bit of the infernal regions come to the surface, this hell with the sun shining into it, primitive man laid the scene of the most terrible judgment on human sin. The glare of Sodom and Gomorrah is flung down the whole length of Scripture history. It is the popular and standard judgment of sin.

But in this prophetic declaration of Ezekiel, "the popular and standard judgment of sin" is excelled and surpassed by the sins of Jerusalem. So great were the evils of Jerusalem that the sisters Samaria and Sodom appeared righteous by contrast.

The intent of this prophetic declaration is to achieve its purpose by "shock treatment". The people of Jerusalem, whether at home or in exile, were so deeply imbued with the notion of their city as being the "holy city", that they were blinded to its true character. Yet they all knew, with that marvellous moral insight that detects so clearly the evil in others, how sinful Sodom and Samaria were! The prophetic comparison would at first have elicited outrage from the audience at so horrifying a comparison with God's chosen city. Even to say the word *Jerusalem* in the same breath as the names of those other cities was insulting. Yet the tragedy of the message is that, while the technique may have been to elicit shock followed by sober reflection, the substance of the comparison was essentially true. The few who reflected on the prophetic message would eventually have perceived its truth.

The prophetic comparison points to a familiar human weakness. We are all more acute at perceiving the moral failings of others than we are in perceiving them in ourselves. Moral vision and insight have sometimes a curious bifurcation: they are totally blind to the weakness in oneself that is seen with such penetrating clarity in another. And ironically, this partial blindness is most common in those who have the least excuse, those to whom the greatest opportunity for moral wisdom has been granted. It is more often the religious people of this world than the pagans who perceive and denounce the weakness in others, blithely unaware of its presence in themselves. To the chosen people of the holy city it was a powerful message, but it continues to apply to the people of God from one generation to another.

THE COVENANT RELATIONSHIP RESTORED

Ezekiel 16:53–63

53"I will restore their fortunes, both the fortunes of Sodom and her daughters, and the fortunes of Samaria and her daughters, and I will restore your own fortunes in the midst of them, 54that you may bear your disgrace and be ashamed of all that you have done, becoming a consolation to them. 55As for your sisters, Sodom and her daughters shall return to their former estate, and Samaria and her daughters shall return to their former estate; and you and your daughters shall return to your former estate. 56Was not your sister Sodom a byword in your mouth in the day of your pride, 57before your wickedness was uncovered? Now you have become like her an object of reproach for the daughters of Edom and all her neighbours, and for the daughters of the Philistines, those round about who despise you. 58You bear the penalty of your lewdness and your abominations, says the Lord.

59"Yea, thus says the Lord God: I will deal with you as you have done, who have despised the oath in breaking the covenant, 60yet I will remember my covenant with you in the days of your youth, and I will establish with you an everlasting covenant. 61Then you will remember your ways, and be ashamed when I take your sisters, both your elder and your younger, and give them to you as daughters, but not on account of the covenant with you. 62I will establish my covenant with you, and you shall know that I am the Lord, 63that you may remember and be confounded, and never open your mouth again because of your shame, when I forgive you all that you have done, says the Lord God."

In this concluding portion of Chapter 16, the parable has now almost receded from view, and it is the cities that are in the forefront, though to some extent the language of the parable is retained. The tone of this section is entirely different from that of the preceding verses; the terrible language of judgment gives way to the language of hope and the divine promise of the re-establishment of the covenant (verse 62). The prophetic oracle is located in this context to round out the parable as a whole in its literary form; almost certainly, however, this prophecy would not have been delivered by the prophet to his audience in exile at the same point in time as the immediately preceding prophecies. The purpose of the parable of perverted love is to be found in the message warning of coming judgment; it was that theme that was pertinent both to the citizens of Jerusalem and to those in exile prior to the city's collapse in 587 B.C. But years later, perhaps in the prophet's old age (if he was indeed the prophet through whom this oracle was delivered), this new message of hope was declared; its prospect of a new covenant was all the more powerful because, by that time, Jerusalem had long since fallen and been destroyed.

The message of hope begins gradually with the prospect of restoration (verse 53) and eventually reaches it climax in the announcement that the covenant would be established again (verses 62–63). The restoration would include not only Jerusalem but also its sister cities, Samaria and Sodom, and their "daughters" (viz. satellite cities, or town and suburbs).

The prophetic message is a combination of judgment and grace. On the one hand, God declares: "I will deal with you as you have done" (verse 59). On the other hand, he says: "yet will I remember my covenant with you" (verse 60). Evil behaviour, in the terms of the covenant, required judgment. Yet the covenant had been formed in the first place because of God's love, and ultimately love triumphed over the legal requirements of the covenant relationship. The triumph of love over law can only be achieved after the act of divine forgiveness (verse 63), which (though it creates in the forgiven a sense of shame for that which required forgiveness) culminates in the restoration of the relationship with God.

Thus, in this complex and difficult passage, we are provided with an insight into one of the key aspects of Old Testament theology, the relationship between love and law. From one perspective, the essence of covenant was law. Two parties (God and Israel) entered into a covenant, or contractual relationship. God committed himself to Israel and made certain promises to his chosen people. Israel, in accepting the divinely offered relationship of covenant, also accepted the terms of that relationship, expressed in the law of God. The partners to the relationship of covenant thus each had certain obligations toward each other, which were legally binding. The history of Israel that culminated in the fall of Jerusalem was a history of broken covenant obligations. The sins of the people and of the city of Jerusalem, by virtue of being contraventions of the ancient covenant established at Sinai and renewed by King David in Jerusalem, invited both divine judgment and also the termination of the covenant. The covenant relationship, in other words, remained good only insofar as the partners to that relationship performed their obligations. Israel's failure to fulfil those obligations could culminate in the final termination of the covenant; that is the perspective of *law*.

But it is impossible to view the covenant from the perspective of law alone. While the conduct of the covenant relationship was governed by *law*, the very existence of the covenant presupposed God's *love*. The covenant between God and Israel had never been a contract between two equal parties; it was only offered to Israel because of the prior love of God, as exemplified in the selection of Israel. And thus, though the covenant may be terminated under law because of Israel's failure, it may nevertheless be continued by God as an act of love. For though Jerusalem's sin invoked the legal requirement of the ending of the covenant relationship, there had never been a legal requirement that a covenant be established in the first place. Thus, just as by an act of love, God first established a covenant with Israel, so by a further act of love, he promises to re-establish another covenant. And what is overwhelmingly clear in this prophetic declaration is that neither the original covenant, nor that promised for the future, was based on the merits of the people; both were rooted and grounded in divine love.

Hence, both law and love have a place in the scheme of things, but in the history of covenant, love is both *alpha* and *omega*. And the same is true of the new covenant, which is the central theme of the New Testament. The gospel does not introduce the primacy of *love* for the first time, in contrast to the *law* of the Old Testament, as is sometimes falsely supposed. Love has priority over law in both Testaments and throughout the biblical story of covenant. What we perceive in the New Testament is a new manifestation of love, in the person of Jesus, in his death and resurrection. It was the love of God, as reflected in Jesus, that preceded the establishment of the new covenant of the Christian faith, and the new law of Christian living.

A POLITICAL PARABLE AND PUZZLE

Ezekiel 17:1–10

[1]The word of the Lord came to me: [2]"Son of man, propound a riddle, and speak an allegory to the house of Israel; [3]say, Thus says the Lord God: A great eagle with great wings and long pinions, rich in plumage of many colours, came to Lebanon and took the top of the cedar; [4]he broke off the topmost of its young twigs and carried it to a land of trade, and set it in a city of merchants. [5]Then he took of the seed of the land and planted it in fertile soil; he placed it beside abundant waters. He set it like a willow twig, [6]and it sprouted and became a low spreading vine, and its branches turned toward him, and its roots remained where it stood. So it became a vine, and brought forth branches and put forth foliage.

[7]"But there was another great eagle with great wings and much plumage; and behold, this vine bent its roots toward him, and shot forth its branches toward him that he might water it. From the bed

where it was planted ⁸he transplanted it to good soil by abundant

where it was planted ⁸he transplanted it to good soil by abundant
waters, that it might bring forth branches, and bear fruit, and become a
noble vine. ⁹Say, Thus says the Lord God: Will it thrive? Will he not
pull up its roots and cut off its branches, so that all its fresh sprouting
leaves wither? It will not take a strong arm or many people to pull it
from its roots. ¹⁰Behold, when it is transplanted, will it thrive? Will it
not utterly wither when the east wind strikes it—wither away on the
bed where it grew?"

Now Ezekiel tells his companions in exile another story. It is a
parable, but something of a puzzle too; they must work out for
themselves the identities of the characters in the story. The principal characters are not hard to identify, but the prophet adds an
interpretation in any case (in verses 11–21, the following section),
giving himself the opportunity to press home the meaning of his
story. His role now is something like that of a political cartoonist;
he draws a picture in words, in which living things and plants are
personified; the manner of the personification makes clear the
identity and character of the person or nation so personified.
Ezekiel's political cartoon has two sets of drawings, the first
setting the scene (verses 1–6), and the second set modifying and
developing the first scene (verses 7–10).

(i) In the first scene there is an enormous eagle, with a wide
wingspan and colourful plumage. Flying over Lebanon, the eagle
landed in the upper branches of a great cedar tree, broke off the
uppermost branch, and then flew eastwards carrying the branch
in its beak. When it reached the "land of trade", the eagle planted
the branch in the "city of merchants" (Babylon). Then, returning
to the Mediterranean coastland, the same great eagle planted a
vine seed beside an abundant supply of water; the seed took root
and grew into a vine, its branches and fruit turned towards the
eagle that planted it.

The eagle of the first scene represents the imperial power of
Babylon (just as, in a modern political cartoon, an eagle might
represent the United States, or a bulldog represent Britain); the
eagle may represent the empire as a whole, or its king,
Nebuchadrezzar. The branch of the cedar represents King
David's descendant who ruled in Jerusalem, namely Jehoiachin.

The young king, Jehoiachin, had been taken into exile in 597 B.C., just as the branch of the cedar was planted there by the great eagle. The vine seed planted by the eagle in Palestine represents the regent established in Jerusalem by Nebuchadrezzar, namely Zedekiah (see 2 Kings 24:10–17). As the vine's branches were turned towards the eagle, so was Zedekiah turned towards Nebuchadrezzar, to whom he owed his little power and the vassal nature of his regency. In these first scenes, the information conveyed by the prophet's word pictures was all known to those in exile; the scene was a depiction of the current state of affairs, after the first exile of 597 B.C. and before the final fall of Jerusalem in 587 B.C.

(ii) In the second set of word pictures, a further eagle is depicted. It flies to Palestine and alights close to the newly planted vine. The vine, seeing the new eagle there, turns its branches towards the great bird and hopes to receive better sustenance from the newly arrived bird. The second eagle transplants the vine, so that it might have prospect of bringing forth more fruit.

In this scene, the newly arrived eagle represents the king of Egypt, the great empire lying to the south of Judah. And the turning of the vine's branches towards the second eagle represents the political move of Zedekiah, the regent appointed by Babylon. Though early in his regency Zedekiah was entirely dependent on Nebuchadrezzar, later he seems to have turned for help to the Egyptian Pharaoh, hoping to gain benefit for his nation by setting the two "super eagles" in opposition to each other (2 Kings does not mention this move, but see Jer. 37:5).

To many people, both in exile and in Jerusalem, Zedekiah's Egyptian policy must have been a source of some hope. Perhaps, they may have thought to themselves, if the Pharaoh will only cooperate, we will be liberated from this power of Babylon and set free again. Such were the political events of the time and for many people, they were events containing the seed of hope.

But Ezekiel's parable, as is true of most political cartoons, was not designed to convey hope. For those who reflected on the puzzling parable and sought to understand it, it was clear that there was no hope for the chosen people in either Babylon or

Egypt. For what was the essence of the parable? Two eagles, two birds of prey that is, both having their territorial imperatives that overlapped in the promised land. Each eagle was more concerned about the other eagle and the limits of its power, than about the fate of a transplanted vine in Palestine. So for those in exile, who thought they could discern a glimmer of hope in the news they heard of Zedekiah's pro-Egyptian policy, Ezekiel draws a picture: the homeland they loved so dearly was little more than a scrap of carrion plucked and pulled at between two scrapping eagles. There was no easy hope in Babylon, but it would be folly to seek salvation in a pro-Egyptian policy.

The prophet Ezekiel was thus engaging in a part of his task that was necessary, albeit unpleasant. He was destroying the hope of his companions in exile, not because hope was a bad thing, but because their hope was entirely misplaced. So many in exile perceived their fate to be merely the consequence of the international and political turmoil of their times; if international politics had got them into such a mess, perhaps a shift in the international political situation could get them out of the mess. But their false hopes embodied all the blindness against which the prophet so consistently struggled. Israel's disaster was a consequence of moral and spiritual decline. God had not only permitted it, but directed it. And to seek help in Egypt, while remaining blind to the ultimate cause of the disaster of the moment, was the ultimate folly.

Yet the hopes and aspirations of Israel and its exiles at that point in time typified those of so many men and women at all times. Disaster comes and a solution is sought. But no solution will be successful if the cause of the disaster is not first identified. But most people would prefer to place their hopes in false saviours, rather than going through the agonising examination which identifies the cause of evil, so that then a true saviour could be found. False salvation is the easier hope, though ultimately it has no reality. Seeking true salvation and deliverance is a more painful process, but at least there is substance at the end of the search.

THE PUZZLE EXPLAINED

Ezekiel 17:11–21

11Then the word of the Lord came to me: 12"Say now to the rebellious house, Do you not know what these things mean? Tell them, Behold, the king of Babylon came to Jerusalem, and took her king and her princes and brought them to him to Babylon. 13And he took one of the seed royal and made a covenant with him, putting him under oath. (The chief men of the land he had taken away, 14that the kingdom might be humble and not lift itself up, and that by keeping his covenant it might stand.) 15But he rebelled against him by sending ambassadors to Egypt, that they might give him horses and a large army. Will he succeed? Can a man escape who does such things? Can he break the covenant and yet escape? 16As I live, says the Lord God, surely in the place where the king dwells who made him king, whose oath he despised, and whose covenant with him he broke, in Babylon he shall die. 17Pharaoh with his mighty army and great company will not help him in war, when mounds are cast up and siege walls built to cut off many lives. 18Because he despised the oath and broke the covenant, because he gave his hand and yet did all these things, he shall not escape. 19Therefore thus says the Lord God: As I live, surely my oath which he despised, and my covenant which he broke, I will requite upon his head. 20I will spread my net over him, and he shall be taken in my snare, and I will bring him to Babylon and enter into judgment with him there for the treason he has committed against me. 21And all the pick of his troops shall fall by the sword, and the survivors shall be scattered to every wind; and you shall know that I, the Lord, have spoken."

Having first conveyed his message in the picture language of a puzzle, Ezekiel now extends his purpose further by hammering home his point in a kind of editorial, explaining his political cartoon. The word picture should have been sufficient, but the prophet had learned that his people could be particularly obtuse ("Do you not know what these things mean?", verse 12), and so he leaves nothing to chance. He explains the pictorial parable in terms of the political events of his time, but he selects one or two points for particular emphasis, points that would not have been clear in the word picture alone.

(i) Zedekiah's pro-Egyptian policy was contrary to the *covenant with God*. When he sent ambassadors to Egypt, seeking horses and a large army, he was acting in direct contravention of the ancient Sinai Covenant that had been renewed on the plains of Moab before Moses' death. The ancient law of the king explicitly prohibited a return to Egypt for the purpose of acquiring horses (Deut. 17:16). Thus, whatever political wisdom the policy might have had, it was doomed to failure; the blessings of the covenant could not be acquired by a policy which contravened the covenant.

The moral is clear: the end does not justify the means. The goal of liberation was a noble one in Zedekiah's policy, but its means were entirely wrong. And no goal, no matter how worthy, justifies the breaking of the covenant stipulations. So too, in pursuit of the goals of the New Covenant, the means may not be inconsistent with the end. The goal of liberation, for others or for oneself, is a worthy one, but it must not be sought at the expense of the Covenant itself.

(ii) Zedekiah's pro-Egyptian policy was contrary to his *covenant with the Babylonian king*. It is true that he had little choice in making that covenant, and would rather not have entered such a commitment. It is also true that he could appear to break such a covenant, with his country's best interests at heart. But it was also the case in the ancient world that, when a conquered king entered a covenant with a sovereign king, the vassal king swore his fealty to his new master in the name of his own god. Thus, when Zedekiah broke his oath of fealty to the Babylonian king, he was also breaking an oath taken in the name of his own God. In a way, the behaviour is consistent; he believed the end justified the means. But at a deeper level, the action was typical, not only of Zedekiah, but also of his fellow citizens. They had not taken God seriously in the past, and it was their light and shallow religion that had created the disastrous circumstances in which they found themselves. And still they did not take God seriously. Of course, the young king would swear an oath of loyalty in the name of his God, if that was what circumstances called for! But he would not feel bound by it; if, in his human wisdom, he saw a way out of the dilemma, the oath in God's name could conveniently be forgotten, and the new path pursued with vigour.

In the regent's path towards folly, we see again a mirror, reflecting the folly of so many persons, ourselves included. Our faith is just one part of the baggage of life; we take it seriously when it offers some advantage, but ditch it just as quickly if it looks like becoming a burden. And such action is a blend of folly and hypocrisy, of deceitfulness and false faith. If we do not take God seriously, we have no faith. To treat God as if he were a credit card for times of financial crisis, or a phone number for use in emergency only, is the utmost form of arrogance and conceit. And yet that was the nature of Zedekiah's behaviour, and the tendency that lies constantly latent within us.

The end of Zedekiah's policy would be disaster, not at the hands of a Babylonian king whom he feared, nor even at the hands of an Egyptian Pharaoh in whom he placed such hope; the disaster would come from the hands of God, whose patience would finally be exhausted by the procrastinations of his people in the pursuit of evil. There was a lesson in that for Ezekiel's companions in exile, as there is for all who reflect upon the prophet's words.

GOD, THE PLANTER

Ezekiel 17:22–24

> [22]Thus says the Lord God: "I myself will take a sprig from the lofty top of the cedar, and will set it out; I will break off from the topmost of its young twigs a tender one, and I myself will plant it upon a high and lofty mountain; [23]on the mountain height of Israel will I plant it, that it may bring forth boughs and bear fruit, and become a noble cedar; and under it will dwell all kinds of beasts; in the shade of its branches birds of every sort will nest. [24]And all the trees of the field shall know that I the Lord bring low the high tree, and make high the low tree, dry up the green tree, and make the dry tree flourish. I the Lord have spoken, and I will do it."

One of the difficulties in reading a book like that of Ezekiel is that not all its substance is arranged according to chronological order. If all his prophetic oracles were recorded in strictly the sequence in which they were delivered, then we modern readers might think that his book would be easier to understand. But such is not necessarily the case; there is an inner logic joining together some of the prophet's preaching, even though the sermons themselves may have been delivered at widely separated points in time.

In Ezekiel's earlier preaching, before the city of Jerusalem had been defeated, his principal theme was the warning of coming judgment. There was still time for the people to repent and avert the coming disaster. But in the later years of the prophet's exile, when Jerusalem had long since become a ruined and devastated city, Ezekiel turned his attention more and more to the future and expressed his hope for a new work of God that would be undertaken in that future. Such is the case in Chapter 17; the parable and interpretation that occupy the first twenty-one verses of the chapter precede Jerusalem's downfall, but this short concluding passage reflects a much later date. Jerusalem has collapsed and pro-Egyptian politics have long since been forgotten; now the prophet looks to a more distant future and anticipates a new work of God. But there is a link between these verses and the rest of the chapter; it is to be found in the language of the cedar that the prophet employs.

In this new declaration, God is the principal actor; Ezekiel declares that God will take the topmost branch of a cedar tree. (In the preceding parable, it was the Babylonian eagle that took the cedar's highest branch.) He will plant the branch on "a high and lofty mountain" (Mt. Zion), which is a more natural setting for a cedar than the "city of merchants", in which the eagle had planted the branch in the preceding section of the chapter. On this mountain top, the cedar would flourish; birds of all kinds would seek its shelter and would nest in its branches. And all the other trees of the forest would recognise God's mastery over nature and his ability to make the trees flourish.

The interpretation of the statement is clear. It refers to the re-establishment of Israel in its land at a future date. More specifically, the branch of the cedar refers to a future king of the line of David, whose throne would be established by God at a future date. And in the re-establishment of a royal throne in Jerusalem, all other nations ("trees") would recognise the Lordship of Israel's God, not over nature, but over the course of human history.

Thus, the prophecy is one of hope, contrasting sharply with the judgmental themes of the earlier portion of the chapter. But not only is the substance different; the situation of those who heard the message was also radically different. For the earlier message of judgment, those who heard it still had the opportunity to repent. Now the time of repentance has passed, in a sense; for the chosen people, there was no more future, unless God should act again in mercy. And this statement concerning God taking a branch and planting it on Mt. Zion is a statement of total grace. It is declared to exiles who have no hope, for whom there is no future. Its substance remains a mystery, in detail, but gives new grounds to look towards the future.

The chapter as a whole provides further insight into the two sides of the divine nature, which are in reality but one. God is judge, seeking human repentance that judgment may be turned aside. But God is also gracious, offering a hope that lies beyond the judgment. And the essence of the gospel, in both Testaments, is that beyond judgment there remains yet salvation.

THE ESSENCE OF INDIVIDUAL RESPONSIBILITY

Ezekiel 18:1–20

[1]The word of the Lord came to me again: [2]"What do you mean by repeating this proverb concerning the land of Israel, 'The fathers have eaten sour grapes, and the children's teeth are set on edge'? [3]As I live, says the Lord God, this proverb shall no more be used by you in Israel. [4]Behold, all souls are mine; the soul of the father as well as the soul of the son is mine: the soul that sins shall die.

[5]"If a man is righteous and does what is lawful and right—[6]if he does not eat upon the mountains or lift up his eyes to the idols of the house

of Israel, does not defile his neighbour's wife or approach a woman in her time of impurity, ⁷does not oppress any one, but restores to the debtor his pledge, commits no robbery, gives his bread to the hungry and covers the naked with a garment, ⁸does not lend at interest or take any increase, withholds his hand from iniquity, executes true justice between man and man, ⁹walks in my statutes, and is careful to observe my ordinances—he is righteous, he shall surely live, says the Lord God.

¹⁰"If he begets a son who is a robber, a shedder of blood, ¹¹who does none of these duties, but eats upon the mountains, defiles his neighbour's wife, ¹²oppresses the poor and needy, commits robbery, does not restore the pledge, lifts up his eyes to the idols, commits abomination, ¹³lends at interest, and takes increase; shall he then live? He shall not live. He has done all these abominable things; he shall surely die; his blood shall be upon himself.

¹⁴"But if this man begets a son who sees all the sins which his father has done, and fears, and does not do likewise, ¹⁵who does not eat upon the mountains or lift up his eyes to the idols of the house of Israel, does not defile his neighbour's wife, ¹⁶does not wrong any one, exacts no pledge, commits no robbery, but gives his bread to the hungry and covers the naked with a garment, ¹⁷withholds his hand from iniquity, takes no interest or increase, observes my ordinances, and walks in my statutes; he shall not die for his father's iniquity; he shall surely live. ¹⁸As for his father, because he practised extortion, robbed his brother, and did what is not good among his people, behold, he shall die for his iniquity.

¹⁹"Yet you say, 'Why should not the son suffer for the iniquity of the father?' When the son has done what is lawful and right, and has been careful to observe all my statutes, he shall surely live. ²⁰The soul that sins shall die. The son shall not suffer for the iniquity of the father, nor the father suffer for the iniquity of the son; the righteousness of the righteous shall be upon himself, and the wickedness of the wicked shall be upon himself."

Ezekiel in this chapter turns his teaching toward the nature of responsibility and the justice of God to whom all men and women are responsible. He starts with a popular proverb, one frequently employed no doubt by those who sought to explain their ill-fortune: "The fathers have eaten sour grapes, and the children's teeth are set on edge." It is a subtle and seductive proverb: what the ancestors have done affects their posterity. It not only involves the shifting of responsibility for current disaster, but also produces a kind of pessimism that prohibits preventive measures. And so Ezekiel launches into an analysis that shows to his audience precisely where individual responsibility lies. God holds persons responsible for their own actions, not for those of others. And to make his message plain, the prophet elaborates on it from a number of different angles, as if he were a lawyer providing an exposition of the law to a dull client, making absolutely sure that its thrust is not missed.

(i) If a man is righteous and behaves accordingly, he shall live (verses 5-9). (ii) If he has a son who is a villain and does nothing right, the son will die. His father's righteousness will not save him; the son remains responsible for his own actions (verses 10-13). (iii) But if an evil father has an honest son, the son shall live because of his integrity. The father, nevertheless, will be called to account for his evil actions (verses 14-18). There are to be no exceptions. The good person is responsible for his actions and may reap his own benefits; the evil person is equally responsible for the consequences of his sin.

To an innocent people, Ezekiel's words should have brought good cheer. Yet he declared a disturbing message. His audience, cut off from home and condemned to exile in a foreign land, had clearly found some solace in the thought that their sorry condition was not of their own making. Their lives were hemmed in by the consequences of the evil of former generations, they thought. And, like most profound deceits and delusions, there was an element of truth in their thoughts. Previous generations had indeed been evil, their actions inviting divine judgment. But for each generation, there had been the opportunity to avert the evil of earlier times. Judgment was not a steamroller with no one at the wheel; the brake could always be pulled, if persons exercised their responsibility, turning from evil back to God and to a life of righteousness.

As with so much of the prophet's moral teaching, it seeks to restore a balance in the minds of those who have taken a simple truth and warped it beyond recognition. It was certainly true that the evil actions of a father could have sorry consequences for his children. But it was not true that God held people *responsible* for the actions of others. Each must answer for his or her own life. Those in exile could not blame their entire fate on their predecessors; they needed to recognise their own role and responsibility in creating their prison so far from home. Unless they recognised their own responsibility, they could not turn from their evil; unless they turned from their evil, there could be no hope for a restoration of liberty and the fulness of life.

Just as those prisoners in exile needed to perceive the nature of responsibility before they could find freedom again, so too do we. "Liberty means responsibility," wrote George Bernard Shaw, in his *Maxims for Revolutionists*. "That is why most men dread it." We may perceive the prison we are in and long for liberty, but deep down it is easier for us to remain there, cherishing the illusion that we are prisoners through no fault of our own. To recognise responsibility may necessitate the recognition of fault, and that in turn may require courage followed by repentance. Yet we can never be fully free unless we are willing to shoulder the responsibility for our actions. And in growing into an acceptance of responsibility, we may know that the One to whom we are responsible acts fully in accord with justice. Yet still, responsibility for all our actions may become too heavy a burden to bear; it remains possible throughout life only with a knowledge of the divine forgiveness which lies at the heart of the gospel.

RESPONSIBILITY AND REPENTANCE

Ezekiel 18:21–32

[21]"But if a wicked man turns away from all his sins which he has committed and keeps all my statutes and does what is lawful and right, he shall surely live; he shall not die. [22]None of the transgressions which he has committed shall be remembered against him; for the righteousness which he has done he shall live. [23]Have I any pleasure in the death of the wicked, says the Lord God, and not rather that he should turn from his way and live? [24]But when a righteous man turns away from his

righteousness and commits iniquity and does the same abominable things that the wicked man does, shall he live? None of the righteous deeds which he has done shall be remembered; for the treachery of which he is guilty and the sin he has committed, he shall die.

25"Yet you say, 'The way of the Lord is not just.' Hear now, O house of Israel: Is my way not just? Is it not your ways that are not just? 26When a righteous man turns away from his righteousness and commits iniquity, he shall die for it; for the iniquity which he has committed he shall die. 27Again, when a wicked man turns away from the wickedness he has committed and does what is lawful and right, he shall save his life. 28Because he considered and turned away from all the transgressions which he had committed, he shall surely live, he shall not die. 29Yet the house of Israel says, 'The way of the Lord is not just.' O house of Israel, are my ways not just? Is it not your ways that are not just?

30"Therefore I will judge you, O house of Israel, every one according to his ways, says the Lord God. Repent and turn from all your transgressions, lest iniquity be your ruin. 31Cast away from you all the transgressions which you have committed against me, and get yourselves a new heart and a new spirit! Why will you die, O house of Israel? 32For I have no pleasure in the death of any one, says the Lord God; so turn, and live."

The prophet continues the divine oracle, now focusing on the relationship between responsibility and repentance. In the first part of his teaching, he had supposed lives that were lived, as it were, in a straight line. The person that lived a good life found God's pleasure; the person that lived an evil life must accept responsibility for it, and its end was death. Yet the reality of human living is rarely a straight line from beginning to end. There are good persons, whose lives suddenly switch tracks—they take up the pursuit of evil. Equally, there are evil persons who suddenly perceive the error of their ways and recognise their responsibility for the evil that they do; they turn over a new leaf and recognise their responsibility to do good.

These transitions in life are recognised immediately by God. The man who has been evil, but turned to good, is forgiven and accepted by God, who has no desire that any should die. But the one who for years has done good, but suddenly switches to evil, immediately forfeits the blessing of God. "But surely that is unjust!" some of the people complained. Indeed, it is precisely at this point that the barrack-room lawyers and weekend theologians begin to apply their minds to a knotty problem. "Consider," they argue, "the case of John Doe. For sixty-five years, he has led a totally blameless life. But suddenly, for whatever reason, he turns bad. And for his last few years on this earth, he abdicates responsibility and pursues evil. Surely you are not stating that sixty-five years of good and honest living are wiped out by a little weakness at the end?" But that seems to be precisely what Ezekiel is saying.

So the barrack-room lawyers reverse their case. "Consider the life of John Snoop," they argue. "For sixty-five years, he has been a villain of the darkest dye. He has ignored God. He has exploited his fellow human beings. He has become rich at the expense of the poor and needy. Are you claiming that if, on his death bed, he turns from evil and repents, all will be forgiven? Surely that would be unjust! Yet you claim that God is just!" Yet, for all their complaints, that seems to be precisely what Ezekiel is saying in the divine oracle he declares.

What is wrong with the arguments of the barrack-room lawyers and the half-baked theologians? They do seem to have a point, don't they? Yes—but only because they have misunderstood some of the fundamentals. First, they make the mistake of thinking that God's justice is a simple tally sheet: sixty-five years of good deeds outweigh a few years of bad deeds, so John Doe should be OK. But sixty-five years of villainy totally outbalance a few final moments of repentance, so John Snoop is done for! Yet justice is not a simple weighing of deeds; the knowledge of divine justice must be balanced with a knowledge of divine forgiveness. And the crux of the whole matter is not deeds, but the relationship of a person to God. That is primary. The good person who ackowledges God accepts responsibility for actions and pursues the good, albeit imperfectly. The evil person who turns from God, shuns (or at least tries to shun) responsibility, and lives in evil. The good person may turn from the good and the evil person may turn from the evil. But at the end of the day, all must

know God if they are to know life. And to know God, one must
pursue good, but most of all, one must seek forgiveness. For
whatever the past life has been, there will be need of forgiveness,
and repentance is the spring that releases the flood of divine
forgiveness. Saint Paul takes it further and shows the need of all
mankind, for all have sinned, in the last analysis, and so all need
the forgiveness of God that is in Jesus Christ (Rom. 3:23–24). But
if we have truly recognised the boon that is forgiveness, we will
also shoulder the burden that is responsibility. For failure in
responsibility, we may be forgiven, but we are not absolved from
remaining responsible.

A LAMENT FOR YOUNG LIONS

Ezekiel 19:1–9

[1]And you, take up a lamentation for the princes of Israel, [2]and say:
    What a lioness was your mother
      among lions!
    She couched in the midst of young lions,
      rearing her whelps.
  [3]And she brought up one of her whelps;
      he became a young lion,
    and he learned to catch prey;
      he devoured men.
  [4]The nations sounded an alarm against him;
      he was taken in their pit;
    and they brought him with hooks
      to the land of Egypt.
  [5]When she saw that she was baffled,
      that her hope was lost,
    she took another of her whelps
      and made him a young lion.
  [6]He prowled among the lions;
      he became a young lion,
    and he learned to catch prey;
      he devoured men.
  [7]And he ravaged their strongholds,
      and laid waste their cities;

and the land was appalled and all who were in it
　　at the sound of his roaring.
8Then the nations set against him
　　snares on every side;
　they spread their net over him;
　　he was taken in their pit.
9With hooks they put him in a cage,
　　and brought him to the king of Babylon;
　　they brought him into custody,
　that his voice should no more be heard
　　upon the mountains of Israel.

The prophet's declarations now assume the distinctive form of poetry. To the modern eye, the poetry in this chapter may appear to be typical of other biblical poetry, but it is not. Ezekiel is using a particular poetic form, that of the lament, and his audience, on hearing the words, would immediately have recognised the form. The lament was a kind of dirge, employed in a funeral, bewailing the fate of one who had died. Thus, upon hearing the words, the prophet's people must have wondered immediately whose death the prophet was declaring and lamenting. And yet, as they reflected the words encased in the funereal form, they would have recognised that this was no typical lament. For the substance of the words was that of an allegory concerning a mother lion and her two cubs.

The mother lion was rearing young whelps. One of them grew to be a young lion, with all the force and ferocity that makes such beasts so fearsome. Then the allegory breaks down somewhat and merges into history. The nations round about sent out the alarm concerning this ferocious young lion; he was caught in their pit and transported to Egypt, like a creature of the wild being transferred to a zoo. In desperation, the mother lion reared another lion cub to full strength, and it too developed a reputation throughout the land for its ferocity. Again, the surrounding nations set their traps, and this lion too was caught in a pit. Locked in a cage, it was transported from its mountain home to the king of Babylon, its freedom lost and its lionhood lamented.

As the people heard the prophet's allegory, they would immediately have sought to "translate" it and identify the persons to whom it referred. The first young king must certainly be Jehoahaz, one of Josiah's sons, who had reigned briefly for three months after his father's death. But his kingship was short-lived and soon he was transferred as a prisoner to Egypt; the Pharaoh Neco required a more reliable ally to rule in the province of Judah (see 2 Kings 23:30ff.). The identification of the second young lion is more difficult, not only for the modern reader, but probably also for Ezekiel's original audience. As is often the case with parables and allegories, there is an evident surface meaning (which does not convey the truth), and a deeper meaning, conveying the truth, for those who take time to reflect on it. At first sight, the second young lion might seem to be Jehoiachin, a young prince who ruled briefly in Jerusalem, before being taken into captivity in Babylon. That event had already taken place when Ezekiel declared these words, and his audience might naturally have come to such an interpretation (see 2 Kings 24:8ff.).

But the allegory suggests something deeper. The two young lions had the same mother; they should therefore be brothers. Hence, the second lion is probably not Jehoiachin (a nephew of Jehoahaz), but rather Zedekiah, Jerusalem's puppet king from 597–587 B.C. Zedekiah *was* a brother of Jehoahaz (the first young lion) and their mother was Queen Hamutal (2 Kings 24:18). When the audience recognised the correct identity of the second young lion, then immediately Ezekiel's words took on a different perspective. His lament was not for the fate of two young princes that had already become a part of history. He lamented for Jehoahaz, who some years earlier had been taken to Egypt as a captive, but also he lamented for Zedekiah, who still at that time reigned in Jerusalem. Ezekiel perceived quite clearly, in other words, that though Zedekiah still retained his throne, his days as a young lion were numbered; soon, he too would be brought as a prisoner to Babylon. The prophet lamented not only past tragedies, but also future tragedies that were so soon to come to pass.

When we perceive this deeper thrust of the prophet's message, we see once again how ruthlessly Ezekiel cut and hacked at the false hopes that buoyed up his companions in exile. They still hoped that Zedekiah might change things, that the weight of history might be averted and their redemption secured by a young lion still in Judah. But there was no hope in that direction. And the persistence with which the prophet attacked false hopes, while at first appearance cruel, was in fact an act of kindness. For there could be no true hope for his people until first false hope had been completely eliminated.

There is an old hymn whose words capture the Christian message that runs through the more ancient words of the prophet:

> The Lion of Judah shall break every chain
> and give us the victory again and again.

The young lions of Judah in Ezekiel's time could bring no freedom to Israel in the last days of its collapse. But to all those who in any age are in exile, cut off from the liberty that may be found in God, there is a Liberator. His name is Jesus and he came to bring hope to all human beings in their places of exile.

A PARABLE OF THE VINE AND ITS BRANCH

Ezekiel 19:10–14

10 Your mother was like a vine in a vineyard
  transplanted by the water,
 fruitful and full of branches
  by reason of abundant water.
11 Its strongest stem became
  a ruler's sceptre;
 it towered aloft
  among the thick boughs;
 it was seen in its height
  with the mass of its branches.
12 But the vine was plucked up in fury,
  cast down to the ground;
 the east wind dried it up;
  its fruit was stripped off,

its strong stem was withered;
    the fire consumed it.
[13] Now it is transplanted in the wilderness,
    in a dry and thirsty land.
[14] And fire has gone out from its stem,
    has consumed its branches and fruit,
so that there remains in it no strong stem,
    no sceptre for a ruler.

This is a lamentation, and has become a lamentation.

These verses continue the lament which was introduced with the parable of the lioness and her cubs. But now the imagery changes completely to that of a vine and its branches, though here the theme is developed differently from the allegory of Chapter 17 and the transplanted vine. The vine here represents the queen mother, thus linking the parable to the preceding verses in which the queen mother was portrayed as a lioness. The basic parable is contained in verses 10–12; verses 13–14 probably are a later addition to the parable, reflecting the subsequent purpose of Ezekiel, or his editor, in adapting the significance of the parable to the changing circumstances of history.

The essential parable is this. The mother of the last kings of Israel, Hamutal, was like a vine; transplanted to a well-watered spot, the vine grew prolifically, shooting out numerous tendrils and bearing fruit. One branch on the vine grew larger than all the others; in the parable, this branch represents Zedekiah. Then the vine was pulled up and left lying on the ground, its roots exposed; dried by the east wind from the desert, the vine and its strongest branch withered. Then it was burned.

But the parable has an appendix, introduced by the word *now* (verse 13). The appendix, as both biblical commentators and horticulturalists have observed, is impossible; a vine that has withered and been burned cannot be transplanted in the wilderness. But to say that further transplanting of the vine is impossible is to miss the point. Let us concede that the impossible might be possible, that the burned vine might nevertheless be replanted. The parable still affirms that there is no hope. As if by spontaneous combustion, fire breaks out again, consuming the branches and the fruit. The impossible might be possible, but there is no hope for this vine and its once mighty stem.

The parable prolongs the prophet's message of judgment; it is as if he were pounding in another nail, to make sure the coffin's lid would not come off. The message of the parable to Ezekiel's companions in exile was clear. The royal family in Judah, both the queen mother and her son, King Zedekiah, would fail in their appointed tasks. And even if the royal line survived beyond the promised land in the wilderness, it had no future hope, for there seemed to be deeply rooted within that family a drive to self-destruction. And so the parable, delivered first in anticipation of disaster, becomes eventually a lament for the disasters when they have happened; the closing words of verse 14 toll as a bell for a funeral.

False hopes spring up like weeds in a garden, but the prophet will allow his people no such false consolation. And his apparently ruthless attack on all false forms of hope, here the false hope in God's appointed royal family, is an act of charity in disguise. But we, like Ezekiel's people, would prefer the comfort of a false hope that does not require us to face reality, rather than the horrifying truth beyond which true hope may lie. For in times of calamity, it is easier to think that the source of our calamities lies outside ourselves, rather than within. And it is comforting to think that our salvation comes from without, as some part of the grand purpose of God, rather than recognising the necessity of a change within us before that salvation can be found. If only, we think—if only the impossible would happen, then everything would be all right. And with God, all things are possible! But such thinking is a delusion. When the fault lies within us, nothing but an inner change will make it right. And to think that somehow everything will be solved externally, even to the extent of hoping for a miracle, is a terrible form of blindness and conceit. For often, it is not a miracle that is required, but a simple act of repentance.

REWRITING HISTORY

Ezekiel 20:1–8*a*

> [1]In the seventh year, in the fifth month, on the tenth day of the month, certain of the elders of Israel came to inquire of the Lord, and sat before me. [2]And the word of the Lord came to me: [3]"Son of man, speak to the elders of Israel, and say to them, Thus says the Lord God, Is it to inquire of me that you come? As I live, says the Lord God, I will not be inquired of by you. [4]Will you judge them, son of man, will you judge them? Then let them know the abominations of their fathers, [5]and say to them, Thus says the Lord God: On the day when I chose Israel, I swore to the seed of the house of Jacob, making myself known to them in the land of Egypt, I swore to them, saying, I am the Lord your God. [6]On that day I swore to them that I would bring them out of the land of Egypt into a land that I had searched out for them, a land flowing with milk and honey, the most glorious of all lands. [7]And I said to them, Cast away the detestable things your eyes feast on, every one of you, and do not defile yourselves with the idols of Egypt; I am the Lord your God. [8]But they rebelled against me and would not listen to me; they did not every man cast away the detestable things their eyes feasted on, nor did they forsake the idols of Egypt."

The date is specified once again at the beginning of Chapter 20; approximately a year has passed since the last date specified in the text of Ezekiel (8:1) and the time is now the summer of 591 B.C. Once again, some of the elders of the exiled community have come to the prophet with a question for him to address to God. We are not told the nature of their inquiry, but the prophet makes it very clear that God would not provide an answer in any case (verses 3, 31). The elders receive instead something they had not expected; rather than having their query answered, they are treated to a long discourse on Israel's history.

As Ezekiel begins to deliver the divine oracle on past history, it quickly becomes clear to the audience that this not the same history with which they had become so familiar through constant repetition. The "facts" were the same; the perspective, though, was quite different. The story (in which the extensive narrative of the Pentateuch has been radically condensed) begins in Egypt.

There God chose, or elected, Israel and made himself known to them by name. He promised to liberate his people from their servitude in Egypt and to bring them into a land of plenty, "a land flowing with milk and honey." There was a single condition attached to the promise, namely that the people, in accepting the Lord as their God, would totally dissociate themselves from the idolatrous religion of Egypt.

In broad outline, the story up to this point is a familiar one, but in verse 8 it takes on a new twist. The Israelites in Egypt, despite the gracious invitation of God, would not give up their false religion. The idyllic story of the Exodus from Egypt has already taken on a sour note—and the Israelites are not yet out of Egypt! Thus, what the prophet intends to do is to jar the sensibilities of the elders by radically reshaping and retelling the story that they loved so dearly. The rewriting of ancient history, which is in reality a stripping from the past of the romantic accretions of many centuries, continues in the following verses. But before observing how this new history unfolds, it is worth reflecting on the effect of this oracle on its audience.

A sense of history has always been an essential part of the religion of the Hebrews. The story of the Exodus has been told and retold through centuries long passed, down into the present century. But in any historical recollection, whether it be of a nation's history or a personal biography, there is a natural human tendency to embroider and adapt. The failures are forgotten, the triumphs treated at great length, until eventually the story has little relation to the original events. In Israel's case, there was a double history, for it was a history of covenant relationship. There was the history of God's goodness to his people, and the history of Israel's response to God. The first history was one of continual grace, the second one of constant failure. But in Israel's retelling of its story, there was always an inclination to recall the one side and forget the other. It was comforting to recall the good things, uncomfortable to recall the bad. But it was also dangerous to forget the history of human failure, for forgetfulness could create that malaise which would eventually terminate the history of God's goodness.

And so it is as if the prophet Ezekiel were performing radical surgery on the memory. For the exiles to while away their time remembering the glorious past was dangerous indeed; that would never bring them to a recognition of why they were in exile. Only when they saw clearly the darker chapters of their history would shame drive them to that act of repentance by which the history of God's goodness might be prolonged.

And what was true for the exiles continues to be true for the Christian Church and Christian people. It is right to remember the triumphs, beginning with the first Easter and extending throughout the centuries. But we shall have little future unless we also recall the history of the Church's failure. Like those in exile, we shall sit complacently in our pews, recalling the wonders of the past, but perpetuating the past's failures through future years.

But it is the individual, as much the community, that must recall the past with clarity, stripped of its romantic vision. I met recently a man I had served with, more than twenty-five years ago, in the armed forces. We talked cheerfully of what wonderful times those had been, but we were only deceiving ourselves; they were miserable times. And we all may have the same propensity in the life of faith; forgetting past failures, we do not learn from them and invade the future fully equipped to perpetuate them again.

A HISTORY OF FAILURE AND FORGIVENESS

Ezekiel 20:8b–21a

"Then I thought I would pour out my wrath upon them and spend my anger against them in the midst of the land of Egypt. 9But I acted for the sake of my name, that it should not be profaned in the sight of the nations among whom they dwelt, in whose sight I made myself known to them in bringing them out of the land of Egypt. 10So I led them out of the land of Egypt and brought them into the wilderness. 11I gave them my statutes and showed them my ordinances, by whose observance man shall live. 12Moreover I gave them my sabbaths, as a sign between me and them, that they might know that I the Lord sanctify them. ¹³But the house of Israel rebelled against me in the wilderness; they did not walk in my statutes but rejected my ordinances, by whose observance man shall live; and my sabbaths they greatly profaned.

"Then I thought I would pour out my wrath upon them in the wilderness, to make a full end of them. ¹⁴But I acted for the sake of my name, that it should not be profaned in the sight of the nations, in whose sight I had brought them out. ¹⁵Moreover I swore to them in the wilderness that I would not bring them into the land which I had given them, a land flowing with milk and honey, the most glorious of all lands, ¹⁶because they rejected my ordinances and did not walk in my statutes, and profaned my sabbaths; for their heart went after their idols. ¹⁷Nevertheless my eye spared them, and I did not destroy them or make a full end of them in the wilderness.

¹⁸"And I said to their children in the wilderness, Do not walk in the statutes of your fathers, nor observe their ordinances, nor defile yourselves with their idols. ¹⁹I the Lord am your God; walk in my statutes, and be careful to observe my ordinances, ²⁰and hallow my sabbaths that they may be a sign between me and you, that you may know that I the Lord am your God. ²¹But the children rebelled against me; they did not walk in my statutes, and were not careful to observe my ordinances, by whose observance man shall live; they profaned my sabbaths."

Ezekiel's oracle concerning the retold history of Israel continues relentlessly. The Israelites deserved to remain in Egypt, but God delivered them in any case for the sake of his own name and reputation. He gave them laws by which to live and a sabbath on which to rest, but they rejected the laws and profaned the sabbath. Again, God contemplated leaving this group of thankless refugees to waste in the wilderness, but again he relented. He warned a new generation of the failure of their fathers and made crystal clear the conditions for the future of the covenant. But the new generation was no better than the last, rejecting the commandments and profaning the sabbath; indeed, they were worse than their predecessors, for they compounded their evil in failing to have learned from history.

The message to the exiled elders was becoming more and more forceful. Slaves in Egypt did not obey God. Refugees in the wilderness did not keep his law. A new generation in the wilderness, to whom the ancient promise had been renewed, failed God. One cannot but hear this history without reacting to it. The first reaction, pervaded by the brilliance of hindsight, is to think: What an extraordinarily perverse people! Did they never learn? But the second reaction, for those who were not too blind and arrogant to achieve it, was to ask: Am I any different? Is my generation, also in exile and cut off from the promised land, any different from the perverse generations of the past?

Ezekiel's purpose in retelling ancient history was not academic, but spiritual. There was a repetitive character to human history, a certain circularity to it all. It was not merely the working out of fate, nor was it circular in the sense of the cycles of nature. History was repetitive because it was the story of human behaviour, and human beings persist with remarkable steadfastness in continuing to manifest the same moral and spiritual failings from one century to another. It was those same failures of the distant past, the substance of Ezekiel's story, that had created the situation in which both Ezekiel and the elders found themselves, namely exile. And yet, as would become more clear as the history progressed, the present could never be simply blamed on the family wheel of history, set in motion by the failure of forefathers. That wheel kept turning precisely because each new generation added individually to its momentum. History is often less valuable in explaining the past than it is in indicating a direction for the future. It is one thing to know why we are where we are; it is another thing to know what we must do to move in a new direction, to create a new kind of history. And if Ezekiel appears sometimes to go on at tedious length in hammering home the lessons of history, it is only because they are so hard to learn. They can be grasped with the mind, but are altogether more difficult to convert into a force shaping the future.

A HISTORY OF HORROR

Ezekiel 20:21*b*–31

"Then I thought I would pour out my wrath upon them and spend my anger against them in the wilderness. [22]But I withheld my hand, and acted for the sake of my name, that it should not be profaned in the sight of the nations, in whose sight I had brought them out. [23]Moreover I swore to them in the wilderness that I would scatter them among the nations and disperse them through the countries, [24]because they had not executed my ordinances, but had rejected my statutes and profaned my sabbaths, and their eyes were set on their fathers' idols. [25]Moreover I gave them statutes that were not good and ordinances by which they could not have life; [26]and I defiled them through their very gifts in making them offer by fire all their first-born, that I might horrify them; I did it that they might know that I am the Lord.

[27]"Therefore, son of man, speak to the house of Israel and say to them, Thus says the Lord God: In this again your fathers blasphemed me, by dealing treacherously with me. [28]For when I had brought them into the land which I swore to give them, then wherever they saw any high hill or any leafy tree, there they offered their sacrifices, and presented the provocation of their offering; there they sent up their soothing odours, and there they poured out their drink offerings. [29](I said to them, What is the high place to which you go? So its name is called Bamah to this day.) [30]Wherefore say to the house of Israel, Thus says the Lord God: Will you defile yourselves after the manner of your fathers and go astray after their detestable things? [31]When you offer your gifts and sacrifice your sons by fire, you defile yourselves with all your idols to this day. And shall I be inquired of by you, O house of Israel? As I live, says the Lord God, I will not be inquired of by you."

The morbid history continues; despite the warnings given to a new generation, things get worse rather than better. The perverse wilderness generation are brought into the promised land, but while they are still in the wilderness, they are warned that such evil behaviour will result in their being exiled from the land which they have not yet reached! The only reason for the chosen people being brought into the promised land, Ezekiel states, was for the sake of God's name and reputation; it was never deserved, never a reward, not even at the beginning.

Then there follows an extraordinary passage in which the prophet, speaking on God's behalf, states that God gave to his people evil commandments that could not lead to life. The commandment was to sacrifice children (verses 25–26); it was a practice employed occasionally by the Canaanites (e.g. 2 Kings 3:27) and, indeed, some examples are known in Israel's history: 2 Kings 16:3; 21:6; 23:10. What is so striking in Ezekiel's retelling of history is his direct identification of this evil practice with the commandment of God.

In part, Ezekiel's perspective on this commandment is to be interpreted within the context of divine providence; there is nothing that is done that does not somehow, albeit mysteriously, come under the divine providence. But there is more than the mystery of providence in this passage. Ezekiel implies that one of the commandments of God was interpreted by Israel to establish the practice of child sacrifice. He is almost certainly referring to Exod. 22:29: "You shall give the firstborn of your sons to me". Taken in context, of course, the verse does not command child sacrifice; animals were sacrificed in place of children. But to twisted minds, already warped by the powerful influences of the pagan religion which they so frequently espoused, the command could take on a completely different light. And so the horrifying picture emerges of worshippers devoutly sacrificing children, deceiving themselves in the belief that they were fulfilling the intent of the divine law.

As if child sacrifice were not bad enough, the immigrants developed further foul customs as they settled down in the land of milk and honey. Whenever they saw a hill or a luxuriant and leafy tree, they did not comment on the pleasant countryside of their new home; they decided to make it into a shrine, in which to perpetuate further their false faith. There they offered sacrifices and "soothing odours" (verse 28), but their practices were only further provocation to the God who had brought them into this pleasant land from the harsh and hopeless wilderness.

As the history further unfolds, some penetrating spiritual insights are conveyed to the assembly of exiled elders.

(i) Israel's history is a history of wilfulness; it is, in a sense, a story of a battle of wills. God willed good for his people; they wanted good, but thought they saw a better way to achieve it, contrary to the divine will. So they willed to work out their own salvation; they created a kind of hell, and those in exile knew how different it was from the land of milk and honey. The will of God is always for the human good, but finding that good depends upon the proper exercise of our own wills. To have a will and to exercise it is to be human; to identify that will with the will of God is to discover the meaning of human life. And Ezekiel's tortured history offers sufficient testimony that human beings do not readily identify their wills with that of God.

(ii) A further insight pertains to the sheer perversity of the human mind. The Israelites, in the course of their wilful walk through life, could not only descend to the practice of child sacrifice, but could even identify their practice with the divine law. The mind can become so twisted that it loses the capacity to perceive truth and meaning; it can wrench words out of their context and mould them to an opposite intent. And in this, the Israelites were not unique. A Christian chronicler of the first Crusade described the slaughter of Muslims in the holy city with apparent relish: corpses were piled high in holy places and blood ran freely in the gutters. And, concluded the Christian chronicler, it was a wondrous day in the history of Christianity; he quoted the Bible to prove his point. The murder of Muslims was "justified" by the word of God, but somehow the love of God was forgotten and the heart of the faith was cut out on that terrible day.

Yet child sacrifice in Old Israel, and massacre in Jerusalem, are but two examples of a tendency that always lies within us. We can blind ourselves so totally that we can attempt to justify almost anything we do by quoting Scripture. But it does not lead to life. Ezekiel turns back to his audience and speaks to them again. To paraphrase verse 31: "So, shall I accept any inquiries from you?" God says to the elders. "No. I cannot listen to a word that you say!" That is the point at which the history of human wilfulness and perversity culminates.

MUTINY OR BOUNTY?

Ezekiel 20:32–44

[32]"What is in your mind shall never happen—the thought, 'Let us be

like the nations, like the tribes of the countries, and worship wood and stone.'

³³"As I live, says the Lord God, surely with a mighty hand and an outstretched arm, and with wrath poured out, I will be king over you. ³⁴I will bring you out from the peoples and gather you out of the countries where you are scattered, with a mighty hand and an outstretched arm, and with wrath poured out; ³⁵and I will bring you into the wilderness of the peoples, and there I will enter into judgment with you face to face. ³⁶As I entered into judgment with your fathers in the wilderness of the land of Egypt, so I will enter into judgment with you, says the Lord God. ³⁷I will make you pass under the rod, and I will let you go in by number. ³⁸I will purge out the rebels from among you, and those who transgress against me; I will bring them out of the land where they sojourn, but they shall not enter the land of Israel. Then you will know that I am the Lord.

³⁹"As for you, O house of Israel, thus says the Lord God: Go serve every one of you his idols, now and hereafter, if you will not listen to me; but my holy name you shall no more profane with your gifts and your idols.

⁴⁰"For on my holy mountain, the mountain height of Israel, says the Lord God, there all the house of Israel, all of them, shall serve me in the land; there I will accept them, and there I will require your contributions and the choicest of your gifts, with all your sacred offerings. ⁴¹As a pleasant odour I will accept you, when I bring you out from the peoples, and gather you out of the countries where you have been scattered; and I will manifest my holiness among you in the sight of the nations. ⁴²And you shall know that I am the Lord, when I bring you into the land of Israel, the country which I swore to give to your fathers. ⁴³And there you shall remember your ways and all the doings with which you have polluted yourselves; and you shall loathe yourselves for all the evils that you have committed. ⁴⁴And you shall know that I am the Lord, when I deal with you for my name's sake, not according to your evil ways, nor according to your corrupt doings, O house of Israel, says the Lord God."

The retelling of history has now been completed, but the prophet has not yet completed his declaration of the divine oracle to the elders of Israel. He reverts back to the initial approach of the elders and the question they had intended to put to God; he does not refer to the question explicitly, but he does indicate clearly enough the deeper, unspoken thought that had been in the elders' minds. What they really wanted was to be like everybody else in the world and have their own proper place for worship (verse 32); they could not worship in a temple hundreds of miles away in Jerusalem, and so they needed their own in exile. To have such a formal place of worship would be contrary to the divine law, but that law could hardly be expected to have anticipated the exile! So here were the exiled elders, cut off from home and temple, and their sense of separation was still further aggravated by their inability to worship "properly".

The prophet's response is in two parts. The first anticipates a period of judgment that would be, nevertheless, purging and preparatory (verses 33–39). The second part anticipates a return of the chosen people to the promised land and a restoration of them to relationship with God (verses 40–44). The latter passage is often interpreted as being from a later date in the exile, after Jerusalem's destruction in 587 B.C., but this cannot be certain. The prophet was already so convinced that disaster was coming that his mind was penetrating beyond, to the more distant future.

The experience in the wilderness anticipated by the prophet would not, as such, be a happy experience; it would be a time in which the wrath and judgment of God would be known. But though the experience would not be positive, the purpose would be positive; it would be an interim stage, in a kind of spiritual no-man's land, preparatory to an eventual restoration in the promised land itself. There in the promised land, the proper worship of God would be practised again by a purified people. The faith would flower once again; God's mercy and long-suffering would finally have achieved their goal. And as Ezekiel's vision of the distant future gives the elders a glimpse of what would yet happen in far-off days, concurrently he is answering their unspoken question. There can be no establishment of shrine or temple on the foreign soil of Babylon; one day in the future, the proper worship would again be conducted in the proper place.

Thus, Ezekiel communicates two principles of considerable importance to the elders, who (whatever their faults) had to deal with genuine problems in the community of exiles.

(i) There is grave danger in compromise. One can understand why they might have thought a temple in Tel-Abib would have been good for morale. But in the long run, it would have been disastrous. For compromise does not bolster hope; eventually, it destroys it. If things became too familiar in Babylon, the sense of exile would diminish; they would no longer be exiles in a foreign land, but immigrants in a new land.

And for all who feel cut off from God, the solution to the problem of isolation is not to adapt to the circumstances of separation, though that may indeed remove the separation. The sense of distance, for all its discomfort, must be retained, for only then will a solution be found by which a full restoration of relationship to God may be achieved.

(ii) There must be some element of hope. Ezekiel had little that was cheerful to say to his companions, and his retelling of their history would not evoke much hope. But without hope, a people must eventually die. And so he has a hope to give them; its realisation lies far in the future, beyond the lifespans of those whom he addresses. Yet even that distant ray of hope could provide a perspective of purpose to life. It was not much, and it was very guarded, yet it granted the insight that God's wrath was temporary. Despite their history of mutiny, the bounty of God would eventually be made known to the people. And for every experience of exile and judgment, a strengthening hope is to be found in that God's last word is always one of grace.

THE SWORD IN THE SOUTH

Ezekiel 20:45–21:7

45 And the word of the Lord came to me: 46 "Son of man, set your face toward the south, preach against the south, and prophesy against the forest land in the Negeb; 47 say to the forest of the Negeb, Hear the word of the Lord: Thus says the Lord God, Behold, I will kindle a fire in you, and it shall devour every green tree in you and every dry tree; the blazing flame shall not be quenched, and all faces from south to north shall be scorched by it. 48 All flesh shall see that I the Lord have

kindled it; it shall not be quenched." ⁴⁹Then I said, "Ah Lord God! they are saying of me, 'Is he not a maker of allegories?'"

¹The word of the Lord came to me: ²"Son of man, set your face toward Jerusalem and preach against the sanctuaries; prophesy against the land of Israel ³and say to the land of Israel, Thus says the Lord: Behold, I am against you, and will draw forth my sword out of its sheath, and will cut off from you both righteous and wicked. ⁴Because I will cut off from you both righteous and wicked, therefore my sword shall go out of its sheath against all flesh from south to north; ⁵and all flesh shall know that I the Lord have drawn my sword out of its sheath; it shall not be sheathed again. ⁶Sigh therefore, son of man; sigh with breaking heart and bitter grief before their eyes. ⁷And when they say to you, 'Why do you sigh?' you shall say, 'Because of the tidings. When it comes, every heart will melt and all hands will be feeble, every spirit will faint and all knees will be weak as water. Behold, it comes and it will be fulfilled,'" says the Lord God.

Ezekiel turns once again to allegory to convey the divine message of coming judgment to his people. He declares a prophecy of judgment against the south, specifically the "forest land in the Negeb". A forest fire would be kindled, its flames devouring the trees standing in its path. All the trees would burn, both the green trees and the dry and ageing trees! Nothing would be able to quench the thirsty forest fire in the south, and even the horrified onlookers would be scorched by its heat. To all who saw the devastating fire, its source would be evident; it was God who had kindled the fire!

But as Ezekiel declared his allegory, it quickly became clear to him that his audience did not understand its meaning. They complained that the prophet was a "maker of allegories" and, though they were not a particularly perceptive audience, the allegory nevertheless was not without mystery. To talk of a forest fire in the Negeb was crazy; everybody knew that the Negeb was a great and treeless tract of land in the south of Judah. A forest fire in the Negeb was as improbable as a sandstorm in the Black Forest. And so, with God's permission, Ezekiel explains his allegory.

It is Jerusalem of which the allegory speaks; the word *Negeb* simply designates the south (and the road from Babylon to Judah approached Jerusalem from the north, leading south). And the forest fire is the avenging sword of the Lord, drawn in judgment against the city in the south. As in the forest fire, both green and dry trees would burn, so in the judgment of Jerusalem, both righteous and wicked would perish. The evil of the city had made it like the thirsty summer forest, in which a single spark may release the terrible havoc of destruction.

This allegory and its interpretation illuminate still further the sensitive nature of the prophet and his profound involvement with his prophetic mission.

(i) Ezekiel was deeply concerned that his people understand God's message. He was given an allegory to declare and so he did it, but he could tell quickly enough that his people did not understand. And so he asked permission, and was granted it, to declare also the meaning of the allegory. In a sense he had completed his duty in telling the allegory, but his deeper mission was to make his people understand. And so he went further; he travelled the second mile.

The commission of God involves the fulfilment of duty. But the person who has grasped its deeper involvement will not be satisfied with duty. No effort is too much, if it will help the people to understand the divine word.

(ii) The prophet's ministry not only required of him that he go the second mile, but also exacted an exhausting emotional toll. Ezekiel's task was heartbreaking; he had no cheerful words and his faithful work brought only grief and sighing. In part, the public grief of Ezekiel was a visual part of his message; but it was not merely theatrical drama, enacted without inner grief. He knew that the message he declared would be fulfilled in destruction, and was already grief-stricken as if he had viewed it with his own eyes. And Ezekiel's experience was that of many of the servants of God. For no form of ministry can be a cold and dispassionate task. It brings its own grief and draws forth that sighing of one who sees the world's need, but despairs many a time of the possibility of setting it right.

THE SHARPENED SWORD

Ezekiel 21:8–17

[8]And the word of the Lord came to me: [9]"Son of man, prophesy and say, Thus says the Lord, Say:
  A sword, a sword is sharpened
    and also polished,
[10]sharpened for slaughter,
    polished to flash like lightning!
Or do we make mirth? You have despised the rod, my son, with everything of wood. [11]So the sword is given to be polished, that it may be handled; it is sharpened and polished to be given into the hand of the slayer. [12]Cry and wail, son of man, for it is against my people; it is against all the princes of Israel; they are delivered over to the sword with my people. Smite therefore upon your thigh. [13]For it will not be a testing—what could it do if you despise the rod?" says the Lord God.

[14]"Prophesy therefore, son of man; clap your hands and let the sword come down twice, yea thrice, the sword for those to be slain; it is the sword for the great slaughter, which encompasses them, [15]that their hearts may melt, and many fall at all their gates. I have given the glittering sword; ah! it is made like lightning, it is polished for slaughter. [16]Cut sharply to right and left where your edge is directed. [17]I also will clap my hands, and I will satisfy my fury; I the Lord have spoken."

The *sword* is the central theme of Chapter 21; indeed, it is possible that the various prophecies collected in this chapter were given at different times, but were brought together because of the common theme, *sword*. In the preceding verses, the prophet has spoken of the coming sword of judgment against the people of the holy city. In the verses that follow, he speaks of the sword of the king of Babylon (verse 18) and the sword drawn against the Ammonites (verse 28). But in this short passage, the artistic work of the editor may be seen; it forms a focal point for the chapter as a whole. Its emphasis is not on the judgment that the sword will undertake, nor on the person grasping it in his hand; here it is as though the sword takes on life and force of its own. The effect is to draw the attention to the *instrument* of judgment, rather than the judgment itself, and thus to lend coherence to the whole chapter.

The details of this short passage are difficult to interpret with certainty; it is possible that the text has not survived in its complete form. But there are both words and actions related to the sword, and it is probable that an enacted prophecy should be understood in these verses. There is, first, the "Song of the Sword" (verses 9–10, and possibly portions of other verses). Second, there were to be a number of actions: the actual sharpening and polishing of the sword (verse 11), wailing (verse 12), hand clapping (verse 14), and various dramatic motions with the sword (verses 12, 14, 16).

Ezekiel has already demonstrated to his people his ability to act out, with extraordinary dramatic power, the substance of his prophetic message, but now he goes further. He uses a "sword dance" (whether Hebrew or Babylonian cannot be known with certainty), with its chanted words and the sweeping motions of a flashing sword, to illustrate the destructive power of the sword, which is the instrument of God's judgment. The image is powerful, grasping both sight and hearing. Initially, it conjures up one of the most ancient beliefs about God in Israel, that of the Lord as *Warrior* (see Exod. 15:3; Ps. 24:8); but whereas in the ancient language of worship, the Lord was a warrior *for* Israel, here his sword is drawn in judgment *against* Israel.

Though the message of this chapter is the now familiar theme of coming judgment, there are two aspects to the substance of this particular presentation of the message that give it striking force.

(i) Simply reading the words can hardly convey adequately the force of the sight and sounds that grasped the audience of exiles. They saw no solemn, prophetic preacher: Ezekiel was dancing before them like a demented dervish, chanting war-like words, sword slashing to left and right in the ritual drama of the sword dance. One must imagine, perhaps, a Scottish minister grasping the two swords of the Highland Dance and swirling them round his head, to appreciate the impact of the performance. Or a minister in the old American West, twirling six-guns on his fingers, declaring the word of God. The performance must have been sensational, yet the prophet was not by nature a sensationalist; by any means at his disposal, he sought to attract his people's attention. His message must be heard; the future depended on it. And if his antics in conveying the message made him the object of mirth, he knew that its essence was conveyed.

(ii) The second dramatic dimension of Ezekiel's sword dance was his reversal of familiar Hebrew imagery to force home his point. All his people knew that the Lord was a Warrior, but that language had always meant that he would fight for his chosen people against Israel's enemies. Now they perceived that the wrath of the warrior was turned against themselves. And knowing from past experience the warrior's invincibility, they had reason to fear.

But we must all be careful of the ancient images that give us comfort, for by our evil actions and rejection of God, we can convert the images of comfort into spectres of terror. We may sing from time to time the old "Battle Hymn of the Republic", thinking (as indeed it says in the Hymnbook) that it is a song of Christian hope:

> Mine eyes have seen the glory of the coming of the Lord,
>> He is trampling out of the vintage where the grapes of wrath are
>> stored;
> He has loosed the fateful lightning of his terrible swift sword;
>> His truth is marching on.

If we have listened carefully to Ezekiel, we will have learned that God's "terrible swift sword" is not always a basis for hope. Ezekiel would have us look within, and then turn back to God in repentance and in search of forgiveness.

THE SWORD OF THE KING OF BABYLON

Ezekiel 21:18–27

[18]The word of the Lord came to me again: [19]"Son of man, mark two ways for the sword of the king of Babylon to come; both of them shall come forth from the same land. And make a signpost, make it at the head of the way to a city; [20]mark a way for the sword to come to

Rabbah of the Ammonites and to Judah and to Jerusalem the fortified. [21]For the king of Babylon stands at the parting of the way, at the head of the two ways, to use divination; he shakes the arrows, he consults the teraphim, he looks at the liver. [22]Into his right hand comes the lot for Jerusalem, to open the mouth with a cry, to lift up the voice with shouting, to set battering rams against the gates, to cast up mounds, to build siege towers. [23]But to them it will seem like a false divination; they have sworn solemn oaths; but he brings their guilt to remembrance, that they may be captured.

[24]"Therefore thus says the Lord God: Because you have made your guilt to be remembered, in that your transgressions are uncovered, so that in all your doings your sins appear—because you have come to remembrance, you shall be taken in them. [25]And you, O unhallowed wicked one, prince of Israel, whose day has come, the time of your final punishment, [26]thus says the Lord God: Remove the turban, and take off the crown; things shall not remain as they are; exalt that which is low, and abase that which is high. [27]A ruin, ruin, ruin I will make it; there shall not be even a trace of it until he comes whose right it is; and to him I will give it."

This third prophecy concerning the *sword* is also difficult to interpret in its details; it is almost certainly concerned with contemporary political and military events. In the year 589 B.C. the small states of Judah and Ammon signed a treaty of alliance; they hoped that, by standing together, they might offer some resistance to the threatening power of the Babylonian Empire. And to those in exile, news of this new alliance must have come, creating a sense of hope in those who could not see clearly the political and military realities of their time. Ezekiel's prophetic word is addressed to those who had heard the news and who once again were cultivating delusive hope.

The difficulty in interpreting the passage lies in the fact that again prophetic action and prophetic word are combined; yet the account of the enacted prophecy is so concise that it is not easy to reconstruct all the actions to which the words of interpretation are so closely related.

The prophet is told to "mark two ways" (verse 19); he could have done this by making a drawing on a tile (as he had done before; see 4:1), or else by drawing in the dust of the ground. In effect, he was to draw a road map, with a single road leading on out of Babylon; the single road split, in a Y-junction, with one road leading to the city of Rabbah in Ammon (the modern city of Amman, Jordan), and the other to Jerusalem, the capital city of Judah. Standing at the junction of the two ways was the king of Babylon, with sword drawn, attempting to determine which road to take. The destinations of the two roads were written on a signpost, represented in Ezekiel's drawing. Up to this point, the prophetic action and oracle were probably an approximate description of the state of current events. And the citizens of Jerusalem, no less than their compatriots in exile, were desperately hoping that the Babylonian king would choose the road to Ammon!

Whether the next part of the prophecy was developed by further drawing, or simply in words, is uncertain. In either case, Ezekiel depicts the elaborate lengths to which the Babylonian king goes in order to determine which is the right road to take. He makes use of all the methods of divination available to him, which (in the ancient Near East) were a crucial part of military intelligence. Marked arrows were mingled in a quiver and one drawn out (as in the drawing of lots), to provide some indication of the appropriate choice. The lines marking the livers of slaughtered sheep were examined carefully to see what they indicated (an ancient "science" not unlike palm-reading). By these and other means, the Babylonian king took the most scrupulous care to determine what was, as he understood it, the will of the gods.

The signs were clear: it was the road to Jerusalem that the king must take. The citizens of that unholy city would claim, in their desperation, that the Babylonian foe had been led by a false divination. But complaints would be to no avail; true or false in divinatory acumen, the king of Babylon would set forth for Jerusalem. In his hand he carried a sword, and though to those in Jerusalem, it was the sword of an enemy, Ezekiel saw clearly enough that it was also the sword of the Lord. And so Jerusalem and its "prince" (verse 25; King Zedekiah) could await with fear the coming ruin of destruction; it would come not as a misfortune of history, but as the judgment of God in recompense for a history of evil.

In this difficult passage, the prophet provides his people with a striking contrast between the "piety" of the pagan king and the blindness of the elect in exile.

(i) The pagan king of Babylon is not in any strict sense praised for true piety, though in his actions he was to be an instrument of God's judgment. But in a certain sense, his "piety" shows; he may have been a pagan, but, according to the lights of his own religion, he was scrupulous in determining what was the divine will for him to perform. His careful acts of divination, albeit prohibited in the religion of Israel, were the acts of a faithful man. Thus, Ezekiel's prophecy draws out not only contrast, but irony! If only the chosen people had been half as scrupulous in their faith as was the enemy king, they would not have found themselves in such a terrible plight. And in this, they are not so different from modern generations, who heartily harangue "godless communists" and the like, but cannot perceive the fault within themselves. Those to whom light had been revealed had not walked in the light even as faithfully as those that were blind, and therein in part lay the source of their judgment.

(ii) But Ezekiel was also concerned with crushing false hope, both in the breasts of his companions and in the citizens of Jerusalem. It was not unkindness that drove him to the task, but the perception that his people were truly blind. There is an epitaph in Elgin Cathedral which reads:

> Here lie I, Martin Elginbrodde:
> Hae mercy o' my soul, Lord God,
> As I would do were I Lord God,
> And ye were Martin Elginbrodde.

I do not know whether this ancient Scot was a godly man, but there is a certain presumption in his words! If he were God, he would know exactly what to do. Likewise, if the exiles were in God's place, they would know exactly how to guide the Babylonian king, as he stood at the junction pondering the path to pursue. They would send him to Ammon, a natural human reaction. But it would be a blind action, nevertheless. They could not understand that a pagan king could be an instrument of judgment, precisely because they still did not perceive the nature of their own evil, and the way in which it cried out for judgment.

Thus the prophet's goal for his people was one which is perpetually pertinent. He sought to remove their blindness, whether by pointing to a faithful pagan or crushing their false hope bolstered by a moral blindness. For there is little hope of any person choosing the road to righteousness, if his blindness is such that he cannot read the words on the signpost. Ezekiel, in declaring God's words, was as a signpost to his people.

THE SWORD AGAINST THE AMMONITES

Ezekiel 21:28-32

> 28"And you, son of man, prophesy, and say, Thus says the Lord God concerning the Ammonites, and concerning their reproach; say, A sword, a sword is drawn for the slaughter, it is polished to glitter and to flash like lightning—29while they see for you false visions, while they divine lies for you—to be laid on the necks of the unhallowed wicked, whose day has come, the time of their final punishment. 30Return it to its sheath. In the place where you were created, in the land of your origin, I will judge you. 31And I will pour out my indignation upon you; I will blow upon you with the fire of my wrath; and I will deliver you into the hands of brutal men, skilful to destroy. 32You shall be fuel for the fire; your blood shall be in the midst of the land; you shall be no more remembered; for I the Lord have spoken."

These few verses bring to an end the series of oracles concerning the *sword*. For a number of reasons they are difficult to interpret; although the reference to *Ammon* links the verses with the passage immediately preceding, its reference in time seems to be quite different. In the preceding section, the disaster threatening Ammon was averted and fell upon Jerusalem instead; now, however, it is the judgment of Ammon that is foretold, or described. For this reason, it is possible that the passage was given by Ezekiel at a later date, or else that it was added by a disciple, to convey a message to later readers of the text.

The prophet is instructed to prophesy, but this time his words refer not to the chosen people, but to their neighbours and allies, the Ammonites. He sees that a sword of judgment has been drawn for their slaughter. Their evil had been no less than that of Judah, and so their time of reckoning would inevitably come. There is also a suggestion in verse 29 that a part of the evil of Ammon lay in their misleading the gullible Israelites with lies and false visions intimating a rosy future. From the later perspective of a reader of this chapter on the sword, it becomes clear that although Judah was the first to be judged by the Babylonian king, her evil ally Ammon would not escape; punishment was merely postponed. The final verses (verses 30–32) are extremely difficult to understand. In all probability, they bring the prophecy of judgment to a full and complete conclusion by describing the punishment of the sword itself, namely the Babylonian king and his armies. The sword, God's instrument of destruction, would also be destroyed when its task was done.

Though Ezekiel (or his disciple) conveys little by way of good cheer in this oracle of judgment, its substance is nevertheless something which, in another time and another place, was a source of joy. Above all, the passage declares God's sovereignty in the world of individuals and nations. His sovereignty was exercised, not according to favouritism, but according to principles of justice. If God's people were evil, he would bring judgment upon them, even employing a pagan people to that end. But the executioner would also be summoned for execution for crimes committed.

Centuries in the past, when the Hebrews were oppressed slaves in Egypt, God's sovereignty and capacity to judge were a source of joy; because of that power, he had given them freedom in exodus. But in their history of ingratitude, the chosen people had forgotten that they too must live by righteousness, or bear the consequences of their actions. In all this, it was not God who had changed; the smile of love had not been changed for the frown of hatred. It was the same God, long-suffering and merciful, but the people had changed: they had abandoned that for which they were redeemed, and then they had joined the ranks of their former persecutors.

God's favour is never a perpetual guarantee of sunny days and trouble-free decades. The favour of God was experienced by his people only insofar as they maintained their relationship with him. And so it is with all who encounter the judgmental power of God's sovereignty. In another time and another place, that sovereignty might be a source of hope, but when the relationship with God has lapsed, that same sovereignty offers no more bright horizons than do the dreary prophecies of doom declared by an exiled prophet in Babylon.

A CATALOGUE OF CRIME

Ezekiel 22:1-16

[1]Moreover the word of the Lord came to me, saying, [2]"And you, son of man, will you judge, will you judge the bloody city? Then declare to her all her abominable deeds. [3]You shall say, Thus says the Lord God: A city that sheds blood in the midst of her, that her time may come, and that makes idols to defile herself! [4]You have become guilty by the blood which you have shed and defiled by the idols which you have made; and you have brought your day near, the appointed time of your years has come. Therefore I have made you a reproach to the nations, and a mocking to all the countries. [5]Those who are near and those who are far from you will mock you, you infamous one, full of tumult.

[6]"Behold, the princes of Israel in you, every one according to his power, have been bent on shedding blood. [7]Father and mother are treated with contempt in you; the sojourner suffers extortion in your midst; the fatherless and the widow are wronged in you. [8]You have despised my holy things, and profaned my sabbaths. [9]There are men in you who slander to shed blood, and men in you who eat upon the mountains; men commit lewdness in your midst. [10]In you men uncover their fathers' nakedness; in you they humble women who are unclean in their impurity. [11]One commits abomination with his neighbour's wife; another lewdly defiles his daughter-in-law; another in you defiles his sister, his father's daughter. [12]In you men take bribes to shed blood; you take interest and increase and make gain of your neighbours by extortion; and you have forgotten me, says the Lord God.

[13]"Behold, therefore, I strike my hands together at the dishonest gain which you have made, and at the blood which has been in the

midst of you. ¹⁴Can your courage endure, or can your hands be strong, in the days that I shall deal with you? I the Lord have spoken, and I will do it. ¹⁵I will scatter you among the nations and disperse you through the countries, and I will consume your filthiness out of you. ¹⁶And I shall be profaned through you in the sight of the nations; and you shall know that I am the Lord.''

The prophet's attention now returns to the city of Jerusalem. The city was still standing, but it is clear from Ezekiel's words that its days were numbered. The city that is still thought of today as the "Holy City" is here described as the "bloody city" (verse 2); the bloodthirsty deeds of its citizens had transformed the character of the city. The prophecy is declared in a manner reminiscent of the law courts: Ezekiel, on behalf of God, is to declare to the city the catalogue of its crimes and the condemnation that must come. But though the words are formally addressed to Jerusalem, in reality they are declared in the hearing of the Hebrews in exile. And as Ezekiel's companions heard the words of this prophecy, their few remaining hopes of rescue coming from Jerusalem would have been shattered. The crimes of their capital city demanded punishment.

The condemnation of Jerusalem moves from the general to the specific, and from the sacred to the secular. Jerusalem had been guilty of idolatry and bloodshed, and so had hastened the day of its judgment (verses 4–5). The city had lost its true faith, in its acts of idolatry (verse 3); but in addition, its citizens had committed a multitude of social crimes, making it the "sin city" of the ancient world. The social crimes included acts of violence, sexual violations, bribery, extortion, and the exploitation of the poor and needy.

What is clear in the prophet's declaration is the close interrelationship between the faith of the city and the moral behaviour of its citizens. When the faith of a nation or individual is healthy, moral behaviour towards human beings will flow from that faith. When the faith collapses, it undermines the foundation of the moral life, so that crime and immorality flourish. Thus the root of Jerusalem's evil, in this depressing catalogue of crime, is idolatry; the worship of false gods, or of the true God in the form of an idol, was an indication that the true knowledge of the God of Israel had been lost. From that fundamental flaw, the multitude of evils grew and prospered. Thus, in a way, the more immediately horrifying part of this catalogue of crime (murder, adultery, exploitation) is secondary; the root of the problem is the loss of faith, as exemplified in idolatry.

The close relationship between the life of faith and that of morality is illustrated over and over again in the Old Testament; it is a lesson that needs to be learned if any human life is to be successful. The Ten Commandments deal first with the life of faith (the prohibition of gods other than the Lord, the prohibition of idolatry, etc.), before moving on to the social and moral areas of human behaviour (theft, adultery, murder, and the like). Likewise, ancient Israel's educational system, as developed in the Book of Proverbs, started with the foundation of faith and then developed the nature of moral behaviour. "The beginning of wisdom is the reverence (or "fear") of the Lord" (Prov. 1:7); when that foundation has been established, it is possible to learn the way of morality.

The lesson is true with respect to both individuals and nations. In our individual lives, moral behaviour flows from a healthy faith. In a sense, faith and morality are part of a circle, but when the circle is broken in a collapse or perversion of the faith, the drive and capacity for moral behaviour are weakened. And the same is true in the life of a nation or city: the loss of faith is accompanied by a decline in morality. There is no longer a commonly shared vision as to what constitutes the good, and so evil may flourish unnoticed.

The tragedy in this process of decline is the transformation of character that is an integral part of the process. The "holy city" becomes the "bloody city"; the good person becomes the evil person. And both invite the judgment of a God who is both good and holy.

SCRAP CITY

Ezekiel 22:17–22

¹⁷And the word of the Lord came to me: ¹⁸"Son of man, the house of Israel has become dross to me; all of them, silver and bronze and tin and iron and lead in the furnace, have become dross. ¹⁹Therefore thus says the Lord God: Because you have all become dross, therefore, behold, I will gather you into the midst of Jerusalem. ²⁰As men gather silver and bronze and iron and lead and tin into a furnace, to blow the fire upon it in order to melt it; so I will gather you in my anger and in my wrath, and I will put you in and melt you. ²¹I will gather you and blow upon you with the fire of my wrath, and you shall be melted in the midst of it. ²²As silver is melted in a furnace, so you shall be melted in the midst of it; and you shall know that I the Lord have poured out my wrath upon you."

In the city where I live, there is a scrap metal merchant whose business establishment is proudly labelled "Scrap City." His yard is piled high with the rusting hulks of ancient automobiles and various other tangled remains of machinery made of metal. It is the ancient equivalent of this image which Ezekiel employs now of the city of Jerusalem: the city is a scrap metal yard and Israel as a whole is dross. More precisely, the image is that of a smelter. Various types of metal ores (bronze, tin, iron and lead, verse 18) are dumped into a furnace. The purpose is to reduce the ores to their various base metals, namely the dross, and to remove any silver that might be present. But, in this case, there is no silver present.

The text is slightly difficult to read in the original language; the word *silver* is probably not original in verse 18. But the sense is this: when the smelter puts various scraps of metal ores into the furnace (verse 20), his purpose is to find silver, and to throw away the useless dross. In the same way, God acts as a smelter. Jerusalem is a furnace, or smelter's crucible; the people are cast into the furnace and melted down, a metaphorical way of describing the coming judgment of Jerusalem and the people of Israel. But although in theory the purpose of the undertaking is to find silver, there is none to be found; Israel as a whole has become dross, scrap metal of no value (verse 18).

Here, the prophet takes one of the familiar metaphors of the Old Testament and converts it from one with an element of hope to one of total hopelessness. The prophet Isaiah describes God as a smelter, but his message has an element of hope: the judgment of God would remove the dross, but it would also be a process of refinement and restoration (Isa. 1:21–27). But Ezekiel sees no such prospect of refinement; beyond the smelting, there remains only dross. Israel's evil has been taken so far that the prophet, at this point in his ministry, cannot see any prospect beyond judgment.

The prophecy is one concerning waste. In every life, there is the potential both for dross and for silver; that is true both of individuals and of nations. Life's purpose, from one perspective, is to remove the dross and refine the silver; the goal may be achieved in maintaining a relationship with the living God. But when that relationship is lost, and dross dominates where silver might have been, life has lost its purpose. And so Ezekiel's epitaph for Jerusalem, as a city with no remaining silver, is not simply a saying of judgment; it is also a declaration of tragedy. To have lived without knowing the purpose of human existence is surely the greatest of human tragedies and waste. And perhaps it is for this reason that Ezekiel, though later he recaptures a vision of hope, here can see nothing more than the end of the sacred city and the chosen people.

PRINCES, PRIESTS, PROPHETS AND PEOPLE CONDEMNED

Ezekiel 22:23–31

23And the word of the Lord came to me: 24"Son of man, say to her, You are a land that is not cleansed, or rained upon in the day of indignation. 25Her princes in the midst of her are like a roaring lion tearing the prey; they have devoured human lives; they have taken treasure and precious things; they have made many widows in the midst of her. 26Her priests have done violence to my law and have profaned my holy things; they have made no distinction between the holy and the common, neither have they taught the difference between the unclean and the clean, and they have disregarded my sabbaths, so that I am profaned among them. [27]Her princes in the midst of her are like wolves tearing the prey, shedding blood, destroying lives to get dishonest gain. [28]And her prophets have daubed for them with white-wash, seeing false visions and divining lies for them, saying, 'Thus says the Lord God,' when the Lord has not spoken. [29]The people of the land have practised extortion and committed robbery; they have oppressed the poor and needy, and have extorted from the sojourner without redress. [30]And I sought for a man among them who should build up the wall and stand in the breach before me for the land, that I should not destroy it; but I found none. [31]Therefore I have poured out my indignation upon them; I have consumed them with the fire of my wrath; their way have I requited upon their heads, says the Lord God."

Now Ezekiel's condemnation of Israel becomes quite specific in terms of the various segments of society that made up the population as a whole. The picture is that of an enormous court; before the court, the people are lined up in various ranks, according to the part of the society to which they belonged. First, there were the *princes* (verse 25), who were responsible for the government and administration of the nation. Second, there were the *priests* (verse 26), to whom were entrusted the worship and spiritual welfare of the nation. The *prophets* were third (verse 28); they were responsible for declaring God's word to his people. And fourth, there was the great mass of the citizenry as a whole. Each of these groups is summoned in the court and condemned for its evil.

(i) The princes had power; it should have been exercised in the course of their leadership for the good of the nation, but instead it was abused. They no longer saw their people as sheep entrusted to their care, but rather behaved like hungry lions, pouncing on their own people as if they were prey. They destroyed people's lives and seized their wealth, forgetting their responsibilities as protectors.

(ii) The priests were responsible for maintaining the divine law and guarding the sanctity of worship, but in this they had failed miserably. They had neither fulfilled their own responsibilities with respect to worship and the sabbath, nor had they taught the people the fundamentals of the faith.

(iii) The prophets had succumbed to the pressure of popular demand. No one wanted to hear bad news, and so they had declared none. They had whitewashed the dark truth of Israel's terrible estate and declared instead the cheerful things the people wanted to hear. They claimed the authority of God for all their hollow pronouncements, but God had not spoken.

(iv) The people as a whole were just as guilty. They committed every kind of crime, exploited the poor, and exercised no concern for the rights of immigrants and other marginal members of their society.

In this prophetic condemnation by rank and file, a number of things become clear about God's judgment of the chosen people.

(a) The judgment was to be all-inclusive, as the preceding prophecy made clear (verses 17–22), and no single class of people could claim innocence or exclusion from the judgment. All had been involved; all had sinned. Indeed, if there had been a single person to "stand in the breach" (verse 30), judgment could have been turned aside, but none was found. Thus the overwhelming and total character of the judgment Ezekiel describes was not only justified, but also demanded by the national collapse of faith and morality amongst the people as a whole.

(b) The prophet's declaration removes a natural human tendency, in time of trouble, to blame someone else. When a nation has gone wrong, we blame the government. When the economy is in a state of crisis, we blame the "workers" (ourselves excluded). When the Church is in decline, we blame the clergy. And so it goes on; the fault must always be laid at somebody else's doorstep. Yet the fault, albeit rampant elsewhere, lies also within. And Ezekiel, in this condemnation by rank, seeks to bring home to the people not only the pervasiveness of evil, but also the responsibility of individuals for evil, regardless of rank or vocation.

(c) The condemnation also brings home the important responsibility of each group and profession that makes up a society. If only the princes had retained their integrity, a judgment such as this would not have come. If only the priests, or prophets, had retained a faithfulness in their calling, the national crisis might have been averted. If only the people had kept the faith, even a few of them, there would still have been hope. But there was no honest person left, and so there was no hope.

Thus, the declaration of judgment also contains for us a challenge to accept responsibility. In times of crisis, when governments and church leadership fail, it is no reason for despair. God always seeks one person to "stand in the breach". And though we may not be able to see the influence and impact of one such person, we are required to stand, not despair and conform to the tenor of our times. Ezekiel, though addressing a nation, has much to say on individual responsibility, both here and elsewhere in his book. If we truly grasp his message, we will learn the responsibility of faithfulness, even in a time of faithlessness.

A TALE OF TWO CITIES

Ezekiel 23:1–21

¹The word of the Lord came to me: ²"Son of man, there were two women, the daughters of one mother; ³they played the harlot in Egypt; they played the harlot in their youth; there their breasts were pressed and their virgin bosoms handled. ⁴Oholah was the name of the elder and Oholibah the name of her sister. They became mine, and they bore sons and daughters. As for their names, Oholah is Samaria, and Oholibah is Jerusalem.

⁵"Oholah played the harlot while she was mine; and she doted on her lovers the Assyrians, ⁶warriors clothed in purple, governors and commanders, all of them desirable young men, horsemen riding on horses. ⁷She bestowed her harlotries upon them, the choicest men of Assyria all of them; and she defiled herself with all the idols of every one on whom she doted. ⁸She did not give up her harlotry which she had practised since her days in Egypt; for in her youth men had lain with her and handled her virgin bosom and poured out their lust upon her. ⁹Therefore I delivered her into the hands of her lovers, into the hands of the Assyrians, upon whom she doted. ¹⁰These uncovered her nakedness; they seized her sons and her daughters; and her they slew

with the sword; and she became a byword among women, when judgment had been executed upon her.

¹¹"Her sister Oholibah saw this, yet she was more corrupt than she in her doting and in her harlotry, which was worse than that of her sister. ¹²She doted upon the Assyrians, governors and commanders, warriors clothed in full armour, horsemen riding on horses, all of them desirable young men. ¹³And I saw that she was defiled; they both took the same way. ¹⁴But she carried her harlotry further; she saw men portrayed upon the wall, the images of the Chaldeans portrayed in vermilion, ¹⁵girded with belts on their loins, with flowing turbans on their heads, all of them looking like officers, a picture of Babylonians whose native land was Chaldea. ¹⁶When she saw them she doted upon them, and sent messengers to them in Chaldea. ¹⁷And the Babylonians came to her into the bed of love, and they defiled her with their lust; and after she was polluted by them, she turned from them in disgust. ¹⁸When she carried on her harlotry so openly and flaunted her nakedness, I turned in disgust from her, as I had turned from her sister. ¹⁹Yet she increased her harlotry, remembering the days of her youth, when she played the harlot in the land of Egypt ²⁰and doted upon her paramours there, whose members were like those of asses, and whose issue was like that of horses. ²¹Thus you longed for the lewdness of your youth, when the Egyptians handled your bosom and pressed your young breasts."

The whole of Chapter 23 is taken up with the story of Oholah and Oholibah, together with its various levels of interpretation. On the surface, it is a story of two sisters, whose lives are characterised by blatant immorality and eventual failure. But the story serves as an allegory: it is really a tale of two cities and their fate in the history of the world nations. One sister is called Oholah and represents Samaria, the capital city of the northern state of Israel. The other sister is Oholibah, representing the capital of the kingdom of Judah, namely Jerusalem.

The story concerning the cities is one of horror and unfaithfulness in terms of international relationships. But to many people, international relationships are such weighty matters, and seem so distant from daily life, that the horror cannot be seen. And so the story is told as an allegory; it is expressed as a horrifying tale of moral turpitude, easily understood and easily abhorred by any listener.

Because the purpose of the story is entirely negative, namely the declaration of judgment on the cities, it is told flatly, with little charm or attractiveness. This tale has none of the beauty, or even sadness, of the parable in Chapter 16. The story-teller's purpose is simply to convey the facts of his condemnation as directly and forcibly as possible. By using terrible and blunt allegory, the force of the story is conveyed more directly and compellingly than if allegory had not been employed.

The story contains virtually no bright asides to lighten its gloomy progression. It begins with two sisters living in Egypt; there, as young women, they had already adopted the casual ways and easy favours of the life of a prostitute. But despite their unworthy condition, God took them (in the language of the allegory) to be his wives: "they became mine" (verse 4). The family moved to another land, away from the sinful associations of youth. But the behaviour of the sisters had been set in youth; in their new homes, they continued to act with the same abandonment as they had done in youth. Oholah (Samaria) continued to take lovers and be unfaithful to her husband. She fancied the young warriors of the Assyrians and devoted her fickle attentions to them, until at last her husband despaired and handed her over to the Assyrians. Only then did she discover the true violence of her so-called lovers; they slew her, and in death she became a "byword among women", one whose immoral life was told to the young to warn them of the final end of the profligate. (Samaria fell to the Assyrians in 722 b.c.)

The sister Oholibah was worse, not better; knowing full well the fate of Oholah, she continued to behave in the same fashion. Sometimes it was the Assyrians that caught her fancy, and sometimes her fickle feelings turned to the Babylonians, until she too had gone so far beyond the limits, that her husband turned from her in disgust (verse 18). Even that did not halt her, and she continued the lewd lifestyle that had been her only companion since youth.

The story is not yet complete, but already its themes are emerging.

(a) Judah's history is horrible and totally offensive to God. No doubt the exiles, and their relatives in Jerusalem, had convinced themselves that their history was not too bad; there had been failures, certainly, but still there was hope for change. Yet the words of the allegory draw a broader perspective. Oholibah had been delinquent from the time of adolescence down through the years of maturity; it was too late now to look for change. And so too had Jerusalem been perpetually delinquent, so that the ways of her evil had become a fundamental and permanent part of her character. The perpetual and disciplined practice of evil makes it eventually a part of the essential personality; such was the case with Jerusalem.

(b) The story's sense of hopelessness emerges from the fact that it describes *two* sisters, both similarly reprobate, but one of them (at the time of telling) was long dead. For most of the Israelites in Ezekiel's time, Samaria was only a memory; it used to be the capital city of a nation that used to exist. But the story links Samaria with sister Jerusalem, so that the fate of the one, long since accomplished, must inevitably become eventually the fate of the other. The effect of the story would have been telling on the proud citizens of Jerusalem, at home and in exile, who had nothing but scorn for the city that once had lain to the north. Gradually they would perceive that the same fate would be coming to them, that the scorners would also be scorned.

(c) The method of the story is to cause comprehension by shock. It is a lewd tale, told in a vulgar fashion. It would have raised eyebrows and offended sensibilities when first it was told, as it continues to do today. Yet the complacency of many people is so firmly set, that only a shocking approach can break the shell of hardness. "If you think this story is crude," the prophet is saying, "what do you think God's reaction must be to the story of your life?"

And for the modern reader of the ancient tale, it is most important that we let its thrust penetrate our complacency. For if, in a genteel fashion, we pass on too quickly to the next chapter, we have not seen that this lurid anecdote, for all its tastelessness, is in part a mirror of each of our lives.

THE LOT OF THE LEWD

Ezekiel 23:22–35

²²Therefore, O Oholibah, thus says the Lord God: "Behold, I will rouse against you your lovers from whom you turned in disgust, and I will bring them against you from every side: ²³the Babylonians and all the Chaldeans, Pekod and Shoa and Koa, and all the Assyrians with them, desirable young men, governors and commanders all of them, officers and warriors, all of them riding on horses. ²⁴And they shall come against you from the north with chariots and wagons and a host of peoples; they shall set themselves against you on every side with buckler, shield, and helmet, and I will commit the judgment to them, and they shall judge you according to their judgments. ²⁵And I will direct my indignation against you, that they may deal with you in fury. They shall cut off your nose and your ears, and your survivors shall fall by the sword. They shall seize your sons and your daughters, and your survivors shall be devoured by fire. ²⁶They shall also strip you of your clothes and take away your fine jewels. ²⁷Thus I will put an end to your lewdness and your harlotry brought from the land of Egypt; so that you shall not lift up your eyes to the Egyptians or remember them any more. ²⁸For thus says the Lord God: Behold, I will deliver you into the hands of those whom you hate, into the hands of those from whom you turned in disgust; ²⁹and they shall deal with you in hatred, and take away all the fruit of your labour, and leave you naked and bare, and the nakedness of your harlotry shall be uncovered. Your lewdness and your harlotry ³⁰have brought this upon you, because you played the harlot with the nations, and polluted yourself with their idols. ³¹You have gone the way of your sister; therefore I will give her cup into your hand. ³²Thus says the Lord God:

"You shall drink your sister's cup
   which is deep and large;
you shall be laughed at and held in derision,
   for it contains much;
³³you will be filled with drunkenness and sorrow.
   A cup of horror and desolation,
      is the cup of your sister Samaria;
³⁴you shall drink it and drain it out,
      and pluck out your hair,
      and tear your breasts;

for I have spoken, says the Lord God. [35]Therefore thus says the Lord
God: Because you have forgotten me and cast me behind your back,
therefore bear the consequences of your lewdness and harlotry."

In the first part of the story, the fate of one sister was described
(verse 10), but that of the second was not. In this passage, the
second sister's fate is described, and as the story continues, the
veil of the allegory is gradually drawn back; it is increasingly the
city, not the sister, that forms the substance of the narrative. The
fate of Oholibah/Jerusalem is declared in four divine sayings,
each introduced by the words: "thus says the Lord God" (verses
22, 28, 32, 35). The general substance of the four sayings does not
differ greatly; their effect is to compound the finality of the divine
sentence, in part through repetition and in part through saying
the same thing in a different and more forceful manner.

The essence of Oholibah's judgment was that the lovers, from
whom she had eventually turned in disgust, would return to her.
But now they would not come seeking love; they would desire
only to unleash their violence on a former lover. And Oholibah,
who formerly had been enchanted by the uniforms and accoutre-
ments of war that adorned her eastern lovers, would learn bitterly
that they were indeed soldiers and bearers of the implements of
death. The former night-time lovers would become, in the cruel
light of day, the executioners of her sons and daughters. They
would disfigure her by cutting off her ears and nose (the latter
being a penalty for adultery under Mesopotamian law). Her
clothes and jewelry would be removed and her life of lewdness at
last laid to rest.

The condemnation of the sister is given further striking expression in the song contained in verses 32–34. It is written in the form
of a lament; it is possible that the prophet adapted to his purpose
a popular song of his day to give more power to his expression of
judgment. Oholibah would drink of the same cup that her sister
had drunk; it was a cup of "horror and desolation" (verse 33), a
symbolic foretaste of the terrible end that now was near.

Underlying the allegory, which is now but a thin veneer on the
surface of the narrative, Jerusalem's political history is clear.

(Jerusalem here represents Judah and the chosen people as a whole.) The covenant with God demanded total allegiance from the people; they could not be faithful in that covenant and concurrently enter into covenants (or treaties) with foreign and pagan nations. Just as, in the story, the sister had been perpetually unfaithful in terms of her covenant of marriage, so too Judah had been unfaithful with respect to its national covenant. And just as the sister would be devastated by former lovers, so too would Judah be judged by former allies, those to whom the people had turned in their history of unfaithfulness to God. The force of the allegory lies in the fact that the Hebrew word, commonly translated *covenant*, can be used to describe: (a) marriage; (b) political alliances; and (c) the covenant relationship between God and Israel. In any such covenant, the essence (in Hebrew law) was to be found in faithfulness. The tragedy of the prophet's narrative is that it describes in virtually every verse one act of unfaithfulness after another.

For all the bleakness of this continuing tale of two sisters, two positive messages emerge.

(i) The source of all the sins (both of the city and the sister) was *unfaithfulness*. Covenants of every kind required faithfulness between the partners. The first of the Ten Commandments specified the primary requirement of Israel, namely that it be faithful to the one, true God. Failure in the first requirement of the relationship with God naturally leads to collapse elsewhere. And so we learn the hard way, from this tragic tale, that to fail in faithfulness is to fail in life. That is true of marriage, of covenants with other people, and ultimately of the covenant that may exist between each person and God.

(ii) Yet there is a deeper diagnosis of Israel's failure in this sordid narrative. Acts of unfaithfulness culminated in disaster, but behind the unfaithfulness lay *forgetfulness*: "you have forgotten me" (verse 35). A healthy memory was an essential part of a healthy covenant relationship (Deut. 8:11–20). By forgetting God's past mercies, Israel had no brake in its headlong rush towards disaster.

These two characteristics, absent in Israel, are essential in any person's walk through life. Faithfulness is required, but forgetfulness will contribute to its decline. A healthy memory and a healthy faith each support the other and may lead to a life very different from that portrayed in the tale of the two sisters.

THE TWO SISTERS: A RECAPITULATION

Ezekiel 23:36–49

36The Lord said to me: "Son of man, will you judge Oholah and Oholibah? Then declare to them their abominable deeds. 37For they have committed adultery, and blood is upon their hands; with their idols they have committed adultery; and they have even offered up to them for food the sons whom they had borne to me. 38Moreover this they have done to me: they have defiled my sanctuary on the same day and profaned my sabbaths. 39For when they had slaughtered their children in sacrifice to their idols, on the same day they came into my sanctuary to profane it. And lo, this is what they did in my house. 40They even sent for men to come from far, to whom a messenger was sent, and lo, they came. For them you bathed yourself, painted your eyes, and decked yourself with ornaments; 41you sat upon a stately couch, with a table spread before it on which you had placed my incense and my oil. 42The sound of a carefree multitude was with her; and with men of the common sort drunkards were brought from the wilderness; and they put bracelets upon the hands of the women, and beautiful crowns upon their heads.

43"Then I said, Do not men now commit adultery when they practise harlotry with her? 44For they have gone in to her, as men go in to a harlot. Thus they went in to Oholah and to Oholibah to commit lewdness. 45But righteous men shall pass judgment on them with the sentence of adulteresses, and with the sentence of women that shed blood; because they are adulteresses, and blood is upon their hands."

46For thus says the Lord God: "Bring up a host against them, and make them an object of terror and a spoil. 47And the host shall stone them and despatch them with their swords; they shall slay their sons and their daughters, and burn up their houses. 48Thus will I put an end to lewdness in the land, that all women may take warning and not commit lewdness as you have done. 49And your lewdness shall be requited upon you, and you shall bear the penalty for your sinful idolatry; and you shall know that I am the Lord God."

The allegory draws to a close in this passage, in which some elements of the preceding story are recapitulated and a number of minor new elements are introduced. The sins of the sisters are summarised. They had committed adultery, they had engaged in idolatry, they had sacrificed their children, they had defiled God's sanctuary and profaned his sabbaths, and they had engaged in drunken orgies that were offensive to God. In the language of these verses, the appropriateness of the allegory becomes still more clear. At a superficial level, the loose sexual behaviour of the sisters is an allegory of the loose political behaviour of the cities. But it gradually becomes clear that the reality of the decline in the two cities involved, in actuality, loose sexual behaviour, in part a consequence of the influence of the foreign and pagan religions. The reality of sexual laxity in the societies of those two cities illustrates forcefully the apposite nature of the allegory.

The behaviour, of cities and sisters, invited judgment, and so God summoned judgment (verse 46). An enemy host would come and destroy them, thus ending at last their lewd lives and behaviour. They would be stoned, like adulteresses, their children executed, and their houses burned. All remnant of them would be destroyed in the final purging of evil.

In this conclusion of Ezekiel's allegory, only one small positive note emerges: "all women may take warning and not commit lewdness as you have done" (verse 48). Translated from the allegory, all nations could observe the terrible consequences that came to the two cities, and their nations, as a consequence of their histories of perpetual unfaithfulness. There was little consolation in that thought for the exiled citizens of Jerusalem. And yet, if they or their children were fortunate enough to survive exile and return again to city life in Jerusalem, it was a lesson they should take with them. The only future was for the faithful. If, in exile, they were to hope once again for a future for their native city and land, first they would have to relearn the daily practice of faithfulness to God.

THE ALLEGORY OF THE RUSTY POT

Ezekiel 24:1–14

[1]In the ninth year, in the tenth month, on the tenth day of the month, the word of the Lord came to me: [2]"Son of man, write down the name of this day, this very day. The king of Babylon has laid siege to Jerusalem this very day. [3]And utter an allegory to the rebellious house and say to them, Thus says the Lord God:

> Set on the pot, set it on,
>> pour in water also;
> [4]put in it the pieces of flesh,
>> all the good pieces, the thigh and the shoulder;
>> fill it with choice bones.
> [5]Take the choicest one of the flock,
>> pile the logs under it;
> boil its pieces,
>> seethe also its bones in it.

[6]"Therefore thus says the Lord God: Woe to the bloody city, to the pot whose rust is in it, and whose rust has not gone out of it! Take out of it piece after piece, without making any choice. [7]For the blood she has shed is still in the midst of her; she put it on the bare rock, she did not pour it upon the ground to cover it with dust. [8]To rouse my wrath, to take vengeance, I have set on the bare rock the blood she has shed, that it may not be covered. [9]Therefore thus says the Lord God: Woe to the bloody city! I also will make the pile great. [10]Heap on the logs, kindle the fire, boil well the flesh, and empty out the broth, and let the bones be burned up. [11]Then set it empty upon the coals, that it may become hot, and its copper may burn, that its filthiness may be melted in it, its rust consumed. [12]In vain I have wearied myself; its thick rust does not go out of it by fire. [13]Its rust is your filthy lewdness. Because I would have cleansed you and you were not cleansed from your filthiness, you shall not be cleansed any more till I have satisfied my fury upon you. [14]I the Lord have spoken; it shall come to pass, I will do it; I will not go back, I will not spare, I will not repent; according to your ways and your doings I will judge you, says the Lord God."

Once again, Ezekiel specifies a date for the saying he is about to declare. The last date referred to was the summer of 591 B.C. (20:1); now, some two and a half years later, he specifies a winter date, probably in January, 588 B.C. But on this occasion, the date is presented in a distinctive fashion. The prophet is instructed to write down the date, thereby clearly specifying to his companions in exile the day on which the prophecy that follows was declared. The date was important, for it was the day on which Ezekiel was instructed to announce that the Babylonian king had begun the siege of the city of Jerusalem. Although no doubt the siege was expected (those in exile would doubtless have heard of the departure of the Babylonian armies on a campaign to Palestine), its date could not have been known by normal means. Indeed, many interpreters take this passage to imply that Ezekiel must have been writing in Jerusalem! But such an interpretation is hardly necessary, unless one excludes *a priori* not only the possibility that God could reveal this knowledge to his servant, but also such phenomena as clairvoyance, extra-sensory perception, and even what used to be called the "second sight". Indeed, the whole point of Ezekiel writing down the date is the fact that he could not have known it by normal means, an exercise that would have been futile in Jerusalem! And later, as the truth of his announcement was established, the writing down of the date would be pertinent to his continuing authority as a prophet. Thus, though the event is quite beyond verification, it seems best to accept it and interpret it at face value.

Then the prophet is instructed to declare an allegory. It begins with a song, probably a popular work song in use by members of the exiled community. The song as such is not particularly allegorical; it introduces the theme of the detailed allegory that is to follow. The song, indeed, simply typifies a daily incident in domestic life: a pot is set on the fire, and raw meat and bones are added to the water in the pot to make a tasty stew. The domesticity of the scene is to be sharply transformed in the allegorical development that follows the song.

The pot, it seems, has not been properly cared for; it is corroded with rust and cannot do its job properly. The rust mixes into the stew, making the meat inedible so that it must be removed. The cook, perceiving the pot to be useless, pours out the gravy and puts the pot back onto the blazing logs of the cooking fire. On the fire, the dry flesh and bones burn, and eventually the pot itself melts down to a chunk of useless metal. The initial scene of domesticity is converted to one of destruction: permeated by rust, the pot is no good for the task for which it was created and so must be destroyed.

Interpreting the allegory, the pot is the city of Jerusalem; the flesh and bones within it are its citizens. The fire beneath the pot represents the Babylonian enemy. A sturdy pot, rust-free and in good condition, uses fire to its own end; the water boils the meat, making it edible and providing gravy. But a rusty pot contaminates the meat and poisons the gravy. When the tainted gravy is poured out, the heat eventually scorches the contents and melts the pot itself. Likewise, a healthy city can utilise external "heat" to its own ends, strengthening those within it in times of adversity. But when there is corruption within the city, external adversity first destroys the inhabitants; eventually the city itself will be destroyed.

This is the message that Ezekiel conveys to his companions, marking its contemporaneity by writing down the date. And it may be that the prophet declared his allegory more forcibly by illustrating it visually with a rusty pot melting on a fierce fire; but of this we cannot be sure. The message to those in exile was clear and horrifying. The beginning of the end was starting. In most such conflicts, the observers can at least observe the siege and hope for a successful outcome. But such was not possible for those in exile. The siege had begun, and on its first day their prophet declared to them what the outcome would be: disaster. The siege was to be a long one, but when Ezekiel's companions received confirmation of the date on which it began, they would also be convinced of the inevitability of its conclusion. Thus, in this allegory of the rusty pot, many of Ezekiel's earlier prophecies are moving towards a hopeless climax; he had spoken of the coming destruction of their native city, but many no doubt consoled themselves with the thought that the prophet's sayings were merely the ravings of a religious fanatic. Now, the time of truth was near; Ezekiel claimed the siege had started. If he were to be wrong, all the exiles could relax; if he were right, then there was no future. Only when his companions perceived that there was no future, would Ezekiel turn his attention to the future again and convey a message that contained a distant hope.

The nature of the allegory introduces the theme of uselessness. A normal pot need fear no fire; it was designed to sit on fire. So too a nation need not fear adversity; it exists not only to cope with adversity, but to flourish under stress. But Jerusalem had forgotten the reason for its existence, and so had become useless to its Founder. The rust that corroded the nation's soul had been allowed to spread, so that it had no strength in adversity. Those who would seek to retain the usefulness for which they were created must constantly scour out the rust. If it is allowed to spread, usefulness diminishes and there remains no capacity for converting adversity into strength. What is useless is eventually destroyed.

THE DEATH OF EZEKIEL'S WIFE

Ezekiel 24:15–27

¹⁵ Also the word of the Lord came to me: ¹⁶ "Son of man, behold, I am about to take the delight of your eyes away from you at a stroke; yet you shall not mourn or weep nor shall your tears run down. ¹⁷ Sigh, but not aloud; make no mourning for the dead. Bind on your turban, and put your shoes on your feet; do not cover your lips, nor eat the bread of mourners." ¹⁸ So I spoke to the people in the morning, and at evening my wife died. And on the next morning I did as I was commanded.

¹⁹ And the people said to me, "Will you not tell us what these things mean for us, that you are acting thus?" ²⁰ Then I said to them, "The word of the Lord came to me: ²¹ 'Say to the house of Israel, Thus says the Lord God: Behold, I will profane my sanctuary, the pride of your power, the delight of your eyes, and the desire of your soul; and your sons and your daughters whom you left behind shall fall by the sword. ²² And you shall do as I have done; you shall not cover your lips, nor eat the bread of mourners. ²³ Your turbans shall be on your heads and your shoes on your feet; you shall not mourn or weep, but you shall pine away in your iniquities and groan to one another. ²⁴ Thus shall Ezekiel be to you a sign; according to all that he has done you shall do. When this comes, then you will know that I am the Lord God.'

²⁵"And you, son of man, on the day when I take from them their stronghold, their joy and glory, the delight of their eyes and their heart's desire, and also their sons and daughters, ²⁶on that day a fugitive will come to you to report to you the news. ²⁷On that day your mouth will be opened to the fugitive, and you shall speak and be no longer dumb. So you will be a sign to them; and they will know that I am the Lord."

The event described here probably took place after the preceding dated allegory (24:1–14), although it cannot be determined how long afterwards; it may have been as long as eighteen months, in the fateful summer of 587 B.C., when Jerusalem finally fell.

God's word to Ezekiel on this occasion must have caused him instant shock: the Lord declares that the prophet's wife is about to die. In the book as a whole, she is an anonymous person, and little is known of her relationship to the prophet. But here she is described as the "delight of [Ezekiel's] eyes" (verse 16), indicating something of the intimacy of the relationship between them. The shock is compounded by the further instruction delivered to Ezekiel: when his wife is dead, he is not to mourn her in the conventional manner, but to hold his grief to himself. And furthermore, he is instructed to announce this coming event to the people; he did that on the same morning that he received the revelation.

In the evening, Ezekiel's wife died; the following morning he exhibited none of the customary signs of mourning, as required by convention and compelled by grief. We do not know exactly how Ezekiel's wife died, beyond the fact that she died "at a stroke" (verse 16), indicating the suddenness of the event. Nor do we know whether she was sick, and vulnerable to death, so that the prophet simply saw that her end was at last near. All that is known for certain is that the death was announced, and later on the same day the woman died.

Ezekiel's companions were naturally curious about the sequence of events and questioned him as to the absence of formal mourning on the following day. Usually on such an occasion, the bereaved would have been weeping loudly; his priestly turban would have been removed, his sandals left off, and sackcloth and ashes would have been the fitting garb. The people asked for an explanation of the death and the prophet's reaction; instead, they received a prophetic declaration about their native land. As the prophet's wife had been the "delight of his eyes", so, in a different sense, was the temple in Jerusalem the "delight of the eyes" of the exiles (verse 21). That striking temple, beautiful in architectural form and profound in its symbolism of God's presence, would "die" as the prophet's wife had died. The pride of Jerusalem would be profaned. And as he had kept control of his grief at his wife's demise, so too would the people control their grief at the temple's destruction. For both parties, the tragedies would be too great for resort to formal grief. As one part of the prophet's life and hope died with his wife, so too hope would die for those in exile when the temple was destroyed. The destruction of the temple in Jerusalem would seem to mark, in an external sense, the end of the religion of Israel. God's presence would no longer be among them. Thus Ezekiel's loss and his response to it were to function as a sign: as he did, so too would his people do in the loss of the central symbol of their faith.

The last verses in the chapter (verses 25–27) present a number of difficulties of interpretation. In general terms, the sense seems to be this: that from the time of his wife's death until news was received by those in exile of the temple's destruction, Ezekiel would be totally speechless. Only when he received news of the temple, brought by a fugitive fleeing from the city, would he be able to speak again. Then, when his speech returned, his people would be speechless with horror, for they too would have heard the tidings from Jerusalem. The difficulties arise from the details. Verses 25–26 seem to imply that a fugitive would arrive in Tel Abib with the bad news on the same day that the terrible event took place. Clearly, it would take some time for the news to travel back from Jerusalem. Though there is debate as to the appropriate method of resolving the difficulty, probably the verses should be interpreted as written in a conflated style, collapsing the difference in time between the event as such and the report of it reaching those in exile.

While the symbolism of this passage is clear, it brings home forcefully once again the trials of the life of the prophet and his family. Death occurs in all families from time to time; it is never easy to cope with and mourning offers some solace. But for Ezekiel to have been asked to "use" his wife's death as a part of his prophetic ministry must have been terribly difficult for him. Was it not enough that she had died? Did her death also have to be bandied about as a part of his prophetic ministry? Must he be denied even the decency of proper mourning?

There is no easy answer to such questions. We know only that Ezekiel was obedient and faithfully fulfilled his instructions. We completely misread the man if we think that his obedience came easily. He was a man who loved deeply, and true grief is born of true love. Yet even the prophet's grief was to be used in the service of God; no part of his human existence was excluded from the totality of his vocation. And if we imagine the scene, we can perceive something of the power of its message. Here was a man, grasped by human and personal grief, who nevertheless saw beyond the immediacy of the moment to a greater grief that lay in store for all his people in the future. And the reality of the prophet's immediate loss declared more powerfully than any sermon could just how real was the coming loss for Israel.

We begin to perceive how the real tribulations of mortal existence may be more direct messengers than the words of sermons and speeches. A colleague of mine taught, for many years, a course entitled "death and dying". It is always a difficult subject, but lacks a certain reality when taught by a healthy middle-aged man to younger and healthier students. But one year there was a visiting lecturer in the course, a professor of chemistry who knew nothing in theory about "death and dying." But he *was* dying; he was in the terminal weeks of cancer, and knew it, when he taught in that course. His words and presence were more effective than any textbook or pastoral theories of coping with dying. He spoke simply from the painful knowledge of dying, just as Ezekiel spoke from the painful experience of grief. And both illustrate how the agonising experiences of human living and dying, the very experiences which we would prefer to be secret, may be used to a greater purpose. Whatever the experience to which we are called in life, we need to remember that it may speak to others more coherently than any speech or sermon.

ORACLES AGAINST THE NATIONS

Ezekiel 25:1–7

¹The word of the Lord came to me: ²"Son of man, set your face toward the Ammonites, and prophesy against them. ³Say to the Ammonites, Hear the word of the Lord God: Thus says the Lord God, Because you said, 'Aha!' over my sanctuary when it was profaned, and over the land of Israel when it was made desolate, and over the house of Judah when it went into exile; ⁴therefore I am handing you over to the people of the East for a possession, and they shall set their encampments among you and make their dwellings in your midst; they shall eat your fruit, and they shall drink your milk. ⁵I will make Rabbah a pasture for camels and the cities of the Ammonites a fold for flocks. Then you will know that I am the Lord. ⁶For thus says the Lord God: Because you have clapped your hands and stamped your feet and rejoiced with all the malice within you against the land of Israel, ⁷therefore, behold, I have stretched out my hand against you, and will hand you over as spoil to the nations; and I will cut you off from the peoples and will make you perish out of the countries; I will destroy you. Then you will know that I am the Lord."

At the end of the account of the death of Ezekiel's wife, it is indicated that the prophet began a period of silence, until the news was brought concerning the destruction of Jerusalem's temple. The theme that is left off at the end of Chapter 24 is not resumed until Chapter 33; breaking the continuity of the narrative is a large section of the book (Chapters 25–32) containing oracles against various foreign nations. It is possible that this narrative is inserted at this point in the text to create, in a literary sense, an awareness of the time of silence separating Chapters 24 and 33.

Chapters 25–32 form a self-contained unit, almost a separate little book, with the declaration of God's word against foreign nations as their unifying theme. Despite the difference in objective, these oracles are also from the prophet Ezekiel, though in a number of places his disciples may have made editorial additions to the original words of the prophet. The oracles shed new light on the thought and perspective of Ezekiel; whereas, in the preceding chapters, his primary focus had been on the chosen people, now the perspective is international. We begin to perceive that the prophet was by no means a narrow-minded man; he had a quite remarkable insight into the international affairs of his time. And another of the prophet's gifts also becomes more evident in these chapters. Many of his oracles against foreign nations are poetic in form, and the poetry illustrates clearly Ezekiel's gift of language.

The first oracle is directed against Ammon, one of Judah's neighbours in Palestine. The Ammonites lived to the north-east of Judah in territory that is now a part of the modern kingdom of Jordan; their capital city was Rabbah. In political terms, the Ammonites had sometimes been Judah's enemy, and sometimes an ally, though alliance was only for selfish ends; there was little love between the two nations.

The crime of the Ammonites that elicited Ezekiel's oracle of judgment was their malicious delight over the fate of Judah. The destruction of Jerusalem's temple, the defeat of the land, and the exile of its inhabitants caused no grief to the Ammonites; they clapped their hands and rejoiced at the downfall of their neighbours. As a consequence, Ezekiel declared that their own land would be made desolate and taken over by foreign invaders. Their capital city would be converted to a pasture for the camels of invading Bedouin, and the neighbouring towns, in their desolation, would be as folds for the invader's flocks. The Ammonites would perish, destroyed by the outstretched hand of the sovereign God.

The crime of Ammon was the absence of compassion, exemplified in a surfeit of malicious glee. They did not even have the wisdom to guard themselves against the sorry end of their neighbours. They learned nothing from the crises taking place around them, complacently pursuing their path through history, unaware that their own doom was drawing nigh. They were not only heartless, but also blind.

The message in this oracle, as in the other oracles against foreign nations, is that God is sovereign over all nations, not only his chosen people. To take delight in the downfall of another at the hands of God, is to fail to recognise that God's sovereignty extends not only over others, but also over oneself. If we are to avoid the error of Ammon, we will learn not to take delight in the disaster that befalls our neighbour, but to feel compassion and grief. And if we are wise, we will seek to understand the cause of another's fall, and avoid it in our own practice of living.

ORACLES AGAINST MOAB, EDOM, AND PHILISTIA

Ezekiel 25:8–17

[8]"Thus says the Lord God: Because Moab said, Behold, the house of Judah is like all the other nations, [9]therefore I will lay open the flank of Moab from the cities on its frontier, the glory of the country, Beth-jeshimoth, Baal-meon, and Kiriathaim. [10]I will give it along with the Ammonites to the people of the East as a possession, that it may be remembered no more among the nations, [11]and I will execute judgments upon Moab. Then they will know that I am the Lord.

[12]"Thus says the Lord God: Because Edom acted revengefully against the house of Judah and has grievously offended in taking vengeance upon them, [13]therefore thus says the Lord God, I will stretch out my hand against Edom, and cut off from it man and beast; and I will make it desolate; from Teman even to Dedan they shall fall by the sword. [14]And I will lay my vengeance upon Edom by the hand of my people Israel; and they shall do in Edom according to my anger and according to my wrath; and they shall know my vengeance, says the Lord God.

[15]"Thus says the Lord God: Because the Philistines acted revengefully and took vengeance with malice of heart to destroy in never-ending enmity; [16]therefore thus says the Lord God, Behold, I will stretch out my hand against the Philistines, and I will cut off the Cherethites, and destroy the rest of the seacoast. [17]I will execute great vengeance upon them with wrathful chastisements. Then they will know that I am the Lord, when I lay my vengeance upon them."

The oracle against Ammon (verses 1–7) is followed by oracles against three other small nations that were Judah's geographical neighbours. Moab lay to the east of the Jordan, immediately south of Ammon. Edom lay still further south, on the eastern flank of the Arabah. Philistia was Judah's neighbour in the southwest, occupying a strip of land alongside the Mediterranean, in the vicinity of Gaza. The oracles addressed to these three nations are introduced by an abbreviated form of the prophetic formula ("Thus says the Lord God": verses 8, 12, 15) and are ascribed, by many scholars, to a disciple of Ezekiel. In each case, a crime is briefly stated, followed by an indication of the divine judgment that would come.

(i) Moab's sin was its conviction that Judah was "like all other nations". The statement had religious implications. Judah's God was no more powerful than any other god, in the view of the Moabites, and so the state had been defeated in war like any other state. They did not perceive that Judah's defeat was an act of judgment by a universal God, and so they could not perceive that the same God could judge them for the same kinds of sins. Hence, their fate would be like that of Ammon: they would be invaded from the east, and all their proud cities would collapse.

(ii) Edom's sin was that of acts of vengeance against the nation of Judah (presumably in the aftermath of the Babylonian invasion), and so its territories would be laid waste from north to south ("from Teman to Dedan", verse 13). As Edom had acted in vengeance towards Judah, so God would act against Edom.

(iii) Philistia's crime was like that of Edom: in acting vengefully against Judah, it gave vent to malice and perpetual enmity. Hence, their territory by the ocean would be destroyed. The Cherethites, one of the Philistine tribes, were formerly associated with Crete; their name means, in effect, the *Cretans*. This particular name is used because it is, in Hebrew, very similar in sound to the verb "cut off".

These three oracles addressed to Judah's neighbour states illustrate still further the prophetic concept of God's sovereignty in the realm of human history. From one perspective, the primary focus of the prophets was on the chosen people, their history and destiny. Ezekiel was concerned with Judah's history and the manner in which the divine purpose for the world was being worked out through God's chosen ones. Yet the narrowness of historical and theological interest did not produce a corresponding narrowness in theological vision. God was a universal God; his power, in an historical sense, was international, not merely national. All the world was God's realm, and thus all nations, in some sense, were God's people. Israel and Judah could be judged in the light of the special revelation they had received, yet all nations were responsible before God with respect to a universal code of morality and national behaviour.

To grasp the universal sovereignty of God is always a difficult task, for our minds are constrained by that which we can more easily know and understand. Yet if we are to penetrate, even in a small way, the mystery of the affairs of all men and nations, we must perceive that ultimately all such matters are within the divine sovereignty. Nations act with freedom, as do individuals, but like individuals, they are also held responsible for their actions. And the rise and fall of human nations, though rarely comprehensible in the short term, are not unrelated to the behaviour of those nations in the eyes of God.

(*Note*: the small states neighbouring Judah seem to have been relatively untouched in the invasion of 587 B.C., but we have evidence from extra-biblical sources that Ammon and Moab were devastated by Nebuchadrezzar in 582 B.C.; it is highly likely that Philistia and Edom were subjugated during the same expedition, which was directed against Egypt.)

A TIRADE AGAINST TYRE

Ezekiel 26:1–14

[1]In the eleventh year, on the first day of the month, the word of the Lord came to me: [2]"Son of man, because Tyre said concerning Jerusalem, 'Aha, the gate of the peoples is broken, it has swung open to me; I shall be replenished, now that she is laid waste,' [3]therefore thus says the Lord God: Behold, I am against you, O Tyre, and will

bring up many nations against you, as the sea brings up its waves. ⁴They shall destroy the walls of Tyre, and break down her towers; and I will scrape her soil from her, and make her a bare rock. ⁵She shall be in the midst of the sea a place for the spreading of nets; for I have spoken, says the Lord God; and she shall become a spoil to the nations; ⁶and her daughters on the mainland shall be slain by the sword. Then they will know that I am the Lord.

⁷"For thus says the Lord God: Behold, I will bring upon Tyre from the north Nebuchadrezzar king of Babylon, king of kings, with horses and chariots, and with horsemen and a host of many soldiers. ⁸He will slay with the sword your daughters on the mainland; he will set up a siege wall against you, and throw up a mound against you, and raise a roof of shields against you. ⁹He will direct the shock of his battering rams against your walls, and with his axes he will break down your towers. ¹⁰His horses will be so many that their dust will cover you; your walls will shake at the noise of the horsemen and wagons and chariots, when he enters your gates as one enters a city which has been breached. ¹¹With the hoofs of his horses he will trample all your streets; he will slay your people with the sword; and your mighty pillars will fall to the ground. ¹²They will make a spoil of your riches and a prey of your merchandise; they will break down your walls and destroy your pleasant houses; your stones and timber and soil they will cast into the midst of the waters. ¹³And I will stop the music of your songs, and the sound of your lyres shall be heard no more. ¹⁴I will make you a bare rock; you shall be a place for the spreading of nets; you shall never be rebuilt; for I the Lord have spoken, says the Lord God."

The city state of Tyre was situated on the Mediterranean coast, about 100 miles north-west of Jerusalem. Although in geographical terms it was a relatively small state, it was immensely rich and exerted considerable influence by virtue of its involvement in international trade. It was, at that time, the wealthiest of the Phoenician city-states, and it saw Jerusalem as a competitor in terms of trade and political influence in Syria and Palestine. Tyre was also something of a political agitator in that part of the world at the beginning of the 6th century B.C. It had been involved briefly in a revolt against Babylon in 594 B.C.; and by virtue of encouraging Jerusalem's rebellion, it precipitated the speedy end of the holy city. To an extent, Tyre's self-confidence was based upon the defensive capacities of its geographical location. The city was in two parts; one part lay on the mainland, the other on a small rocky island just off-shore. Each part of the city had a port and, for much of its history, the two parts of the city were joined by a causeway. Thus, it was both a gateway to maritime trade, and concurrently a gateway to the overland trading routes. And, from a military perspective, it had an immense advantage: the island was difficult to capture from the sea, but if a land-based military force threatened the city its inhabitants could retreat in safety to the city's insular port.

The prophecy against Tyre is dated; though there are some problems with the Hebrew text, it is generally agreed that the date of this prophecy was early in 586 B.C., probably the month of February. Set in a larger context, the prophecy was delivered after the downfall of Jerusalem, and after the news of that tragic event had reached Ezekiel in exile.

The sin for which Tyre is condemned is its selfish delight at the fall of Jerusalem. Instead of grief for a city that had once been an ally, the Tyrians saw only the selfish advantage that they could reap from its devastation. They hoped to be "replenished" (verse 2); that is, they hoped that they would be able to capture a greater share of the revenues from international trade, now that Jerusalem, and Judah, no longer survived as an independent power. But their selfish ambition evoked the divine opposition: "Behold, I am against you, O Tyre" (verse 3).

The divine judgment is expressed in terms of the enmity of foreign nations that would eventually bring Tyre to its knees in defeat. The island part of the city would eventually become no more than an area of dry rocks, used by the fishermen along the coast for spreading out their nets to dry in the sun. The mainland part of the city would be attacked by powerful armies and destroyed. The latter part of the prophecy was speedily fulfilled. In 586 B.C. the Babylonian Empire undertook a 13-year siege of the city, destroying its mainland territories. But it was not until the 4th century B.C., in the time of Alexander the Great, that the island part of the city fell. Today, the island is little more than a tourist attraction.

Apart from Tyre's political intrigues, it is primarily the city's commercial avarice that is the focus of the divine condemnation. Greed is a destructive force; as wealth is accumulated, it creates an arrogant power, accompanied eventually by a sense of invincibility. Over the centuries, a number of ports on the eastern Mediterranean seaboard have risen to power, growing from the commercial wealth that arose from their trading activities. Before Tyre, Ugarit flourished, further to the north. After Tyre, other cities rose and fell. In our own century, Beirut once held the power that Tyre used to control; but Beirut too has tumbled from its former position of pre-eminence. The commercial empires that human beings build are for a time wealthy and powerful; but their cities are not enduring cities. Avarice is a destructive appetite, having the seeds of its own destruction within it.

LAMENT FOR A LOST CITY

Ezekiel 26:15–21

[15]"Thus says the Lord God to Tyre: Will not the coastlands shake at the sound of your fall, when the wounded groan, when slaughter is made in the midst of you? [16]Then all the princes of the sea will step down from their thrones, and remove their robes, and strip off their embroidered garments; they will clothe themselves with trembling; they will sit upon the ground and tremble every moment, and be appalled at you. [17]And they will raise a lamentation over you, and say to you,
'How you have vanished from the seas,
    O city renowned,
that was mighty on the sea,
    you and your inhabitants,
who imposed your terror
    on all the mainland!
[18]Now the isles tremble
    on the day of your fall;
yea, the isles that are in the sea
    are dismayed at your passing.'

¹⁹"For thus says the Lord God. When I make you a city laid waste, like the cities that are not inhabited, when I bring up the deep over you, and the great waters cover you, ²⁰then I will thrust you down with those who descend into the Pit, to the people of old, and I will make you to dwell in the nether world, among primeval ruins, with those who go down to the Pit, so that you will not be inhabited or have a place in the land of the living. ²¹I will bring you to a dreadful end, and you shall be no more; though you be sought for, you will never be found again, says the Lord God."

The long oracle against Tyre (extending from Chapter 26 to Chapter 28) continues now with a lament for the downfall of the island-city. In a manner common to the prophets, a formal lament, such as would be used at a funeral, is employed before the "death" of Tyre has actually happened; the lament reinforces the inevitability of the city's demise.

The prophet paints a poignant picture of the funeral of the island of Tyre. The princes of other island-states have gathered together; they have set aside their royal robes and sit trembling on the ground beside the corpse of their former distinguished neighbour. And then, they begin to wail the words of the lament (verses 17–18). The mighty maritime city has gone; all the ocean's islands tremble with dismay at its passing!

The verses that follow (verses 19–21) pursue still further the ocean imagery. The waters are no longer those of the Mediterranean; Tyre is being covered by the primeval waters of the ancient Flood story, cutting the city off from the immediate world and despatching it to Sheol, the netherworld beneath the primeval ocean. There in Sheol, or the *Pit* (verse 20), Tyre is cut off from the land of the living. The scene is like that of a naval funeral, where the body of the deceased is dropped into the ocean after the funeral words have been spoken. But here, an entire island is dropped into the ocean depths, never again to see the light of this world. Thus, with powerful poetry, the prophet announces the end of the island empire's era.

In a penetrating manner, the prophet brings home to us the temporal nature of mankind's most enduring symbols. Tyre, it seemed, had always been there. Its location made it impregnable.

For generations of sailors along the Mediterranean coastline, Tyre had been a familiar and welcome sight. It was a port of call, a place of refuge, a market for goods, and a *permanent* place. But nothing in this world is permanent, and no city lives for ever. Well may the maritime princes have trembled at the funeral of Tyre, for in that event, they saw the writing on the wall for themselves. For all persons, ancient princes or modern paupers, something more permanent in life must be sought than the strong cities of this world. It was the sovereign God that declared Tyre's fate; the same sovereign God is the only one that offers a permanent and enduring city.

THE GOOD SHIP "TYRE"

Ezekiel 27:1–25*a*

[1]The word of the Lord came to me: [2]"Now you, son of man, raise a lamentation over Tyre, [3]and say to Tyre, who dwells at the entrance to the sea, merchant of the peoples on many coastlands, thus says the Lord God:

"O Tyre, you have said,
    'I am perfect in beauty.'
[4]Your borders are in the heart of the seas;
    your builders made perfect your beauty.
[5]They made all your planks
    of fir trees from Senir;
  they took a cedar from Lebanon
    to make a mast for you.
[6]Of oaks of Bashan
    they made your oars;
  they made your deck of pines
    from the coasts of Cyprus,
    inlaid with ivory.
[7]Of fine embroidered linen from Egypt
    was your sail,
    serving as your ensign;
  blue and purple from the coasts of Elishah
    was your awning.
[8]The inhabitants of Sidon and Arvad
    were your rowers;

skilled men of Zemer were in you,
> they were your pilots.
9The elders of Gebal and her skilled men were in you,
> caulking your seams;
all the ships of the sea with their mariners were in you,
> to barter for your wares.

10"Persia and Lud and Put were in your army as your men of war; they hung the shield and helmet in you; they gave you splendour. 11The men of Arvad and Helech were upon your walls round about, and men of Gamad were in your towers; they hung their shields upon your walls round about; they made perfect your beauty.

12"Tarshish trafficked with you because of your great wealth of every kind; silver, iron, tin, and lead they exchanged for your wares. 13Javan, Tubal, and Meshech traded with you; they exchanged the persons of men and vessels of bronze for your merchandise. 14Beth-togarmah exchanged for your wares horses, war horses, and mules. 15The men of Rhodes traded with you; many coastlands were your own special markets, they brought you in payment ivory tusks and ebony. 16Edom trafficked with you because of your abundant goods; they exchanged for your wares emeralds, purple, embroidered work, fine linen, coral, and agate. 17Judah and the land of Israel traded with you; they exchanged for your merchandise wheat, olives and early figs, honey, oil, and balm. 18Damascus trafficked with you for your abundant goods, because of your great wealth of every kind; wine of Helbon, and white wool, 19and wine from Uzal they exchanged for your wares; wrought iron, cassia, and calamus were bartered for your merchandise. 20Dedan traded with you in saddlecloths for riding. 21Arabia and all the princes of Kedar were your favoured dealers in lambs, rams, and goats; in these they trafficked with you. 22The traders of Sheba and Raamah traded with you; they exchanged for your wares the best of all kinds of spices, and all precious stones, and gold. 23Haran, Canneh, Eden, Asshur, and Chilmad traded with you. 24These traded with you in choice garments, in clothes of blue and embroidered work, and in carpets of coloured stuff, bound with cords and made secure; in these they traded with you. 25The ships of Tarshish travelled for you with your merchandise."

The oracles against the city-state of Tyre continue in this chapter; the precise relation of these verses to the preceding chapter remains uncertain, but it is probable that the two chapters are

closely linked, rather than simply being a record of different
oracles against Tyre from different periods of the prophet's ministry. The preceding chapter closed with an anticipation of Tyre's
demise; the poem which dominates Chapter 27 converts that
threat into the reality of ruin.

The chapter as a whole contains a poetic passage of striking
beauty concerning a ship and its eventual shipwreck. The poetry
is interrupted (verses 10–25a) by a passage in prose, describing
the "ship's" crew and the international dimensions of its trade.
The metaphor recedes in the prose passage, so that the words
appear to describe simply the city itself; the substance and the
form of the prose verses may thus be secondary to the original
poem (verses 3a–9, 25b–36). Nevertheless, the prose section adds
to the literary effect of Chapter 27 as a whole. The first part of the
poem (verses 3a–9) contains only praise of a truly magnificent
ship, whereas the latter part (verses 25b–36) describes the wreck.
The prose insertion, elaborating upon Tyre's fame, heightens the
glory described in the first part of the poem and thus makes more
dramatic the disaster with which the chapter concludes.

The poet's panegyric upon Tyre is not in the least tainted with
criticism. "I am perfect in beauty," Tyre says (verse 3); one
expects such a statement of pride to be followed by rebuke, but
only praise is added to the proud words at this stage in the poem.
On a Cadillac, a small plate announces "Coachwork by Fisher";
this poem is similar, indicating that the material and craftsmen
utilised in the construction of the good ship Tyre were only the
best. No expense was too much: the planks and mast were of the
finest wood, the oars of strong oak and the decks of sturdy pine,
inlaid with fine ivory. The sails and awning were of the finest
material, imported without thought of cost. The crew and pilots
were employed for their excellence and experience; only the best
of merchant seamen should serve on the finest of ships. And, as
the prose passage makes clear, the great trading ship was immensely successful, specialising in the best commodities with
all the significant trading nations of the ancient world.

The absence of criticism in this part of the chapter is entirely
appropriate, for in these verses there is no real ground for the

declaration of judgment. Excellence is something to be sought after; it is no cause for being ashamed. And, from one perspective, Tyre had achieved excellence. The Tyrians had sought to build a strong and beautiful "ship", and in that they had been successful. They were engaged in trade, and they did it well, trading with every nation that had something to offer to international commerce. In many ways Tyre deserved praise: it had set itself the goal of excellence, and in external things, at least, it had attained its goal. It was a valuable gem in the crown of nations.

But the reader of Chapter 27 has already read the preceding chapter and thus is aware of the rot within the good ship Tyre, hidden behind the fine exterior. The consequence of that inner deterioration is developed in the latter part of the chapter, but at this stage we must be careful lest we fail to recognise merit where merit is deserved. Tyre had chalked up extraordinary achievements; for that, the city deserved praise. Excellence is a goal worth striving for; Tyre laboured toward that goal and achieved it in extraordinary measure. And we would miss the point of this chapter if we thought that the wreck, of which the description follows, was a consequence of excellence and massive strength. Greatness does not invite judgment.

But fame and strength, if they can be achieved, bring their own temptations. As goals, they may sometimes bring out the best qualities, those of dedication and hard work. Once achieved, the greatness that was a noble goal may become a debilitating disease, of which the symptoms include pride and arrogance. And thus all those who would honestly seek to achieve excellence in its variety of forms, whether for an individual or a nation, must prepare themselves for the more difficult task of living with the achievement, if it is attained. The temptation to pride is enormous, precisely because of the great work and skill that went into attaining the goal. But, like rot in the hull of a great ship, pride will lead eventually to shipwreck, and it is of this that the prophet speaks in the latter part of his poem.

THE WRECK OF THE "TYRE"

Ezekiel 27:25*b*–36

"So you were filled and heavily laden
    in the heart of the seas.
²⁶Your rowers have brought you out
    into the high seas.
The east wind has wrecked you
    in the heart of the seas.
²⁷Your riches, your wares, your merchandise,
    your mariners and your pilots,
your caulkers, your dealers in merchandise,
    and all your men of war who are in you,
with all your company
    that is in your midst,
sink into the heart of the seas
    on the day of your ruin.
²⁸At the sound of the cry of your pilots
    the countryside shakes,
²⁹and down from their ships
    come all that handle the oar.
The mariners and all the pilots of the sea
    stand on the shore
³⁰and wail aloud over you,
    and cry bitterly.
They cast dust on their heads
    and wallow in ashes;
³¹they make themselves bald for you,
    and gird themselves with sackcloth,
and they weep over you in bitterness of soul,
    with bitter mourning.
³²In their wailing they raise a lamentation for you,
    and lament over you:
'Who was ever destroyed like Tyre
    in the midst of the sea?
³³When your wares came from the seas,
    you satisfied many peoples;
with your abundant wealth and merchandise
    you enriched the kings of the earth.

³⁴Now you are wrecked by the seas,
in the depths of the waters;
your merchandise and all your crew
have sunk with you.
³⁵All the inhabitants of the coastlands
are appalled at you;
and their kings are horribly afraid,
their faces are convulsed.
³⁶The merchants among the peoples hiss at you;
you have come to a dreadful end
and shall be no more for ever.'"

The metaphor of the ship "Tyre", with which the chapter begins,
continues towards its dreadful climax. Heavily laden with the
merchandise that brought it prosperity, the ship is caught in a
storm at sea, as the east wind blows and stirs up a storm of such
violence that the ship is crushed by its power. The "Tyre" sinks in
the midst of the ocean, taking with it beneath the waves its crew
and valuable cargo. And as the news of the wreck spreads along
the coast, mariners from the coastal ports come out to stand on
the shore, where flotsam from the once mighty vessel is washed
up by the ocean waves.

There on the shore, the mariners lament the loss of the mighty
ship, knowing from their own experience the power of a storm at
sea. They raise a lament for the "Tyre"; other ships had been
wrecked in the past, but the loss of one of the finest ships ever to
have braved the waves was a terrible event indeed. Perhaps with
irony, the poet elaborates on the significance of the loss; it is not
the drowned crew that are the focus of the lament, but the loss of
a great ship that provided the people and kings of the earth with
such valuable merchandise (verse 33).

In his metaphorical lament, the prophet draws out a number of
lessons that pertain to all of life's voyages.

(i) The first lesson has already been noted in the preceding
verses; pride leads inevitably to shipwreck (see the commentary
on verses 1–25).

(ii) In every voyage, one remains vulnerable. The "Tyre" was a
ship built of the finest materials, served by the ablest crew, and

directed by those experienced from many years on the ocean. Yet when the east wind blew, the power of the ocean was too great for all the accumulated quality and experience in the ship. For all true "seafarers", quality and experience are essential; it would be foolhardy to venture out into the ocean of life without them. Yet there is also the need for recognising forces greater than those with which human beings can cope alone. The east wind and its power of storm were beyond human control, but within the power of God.

> Thou dost rule the raging of the sea;
> when its waves rise, thou stillest them.
> (Ps. 89:9)

Recognising powers beyond those for which preparation can be made, all voyagers should confess the need for faith as well as competence. The crew of the "Tyre", experienced in the minor storms of the ocean, foolishly thought themselves able for anything the elements could offer. But they had forgotten the One who controlled the raging of the seas and who had the power to still those waves.

(iii) The lament of the mariners on the shore introduces an irony in the wreck of the "Tyre". The city's sin had been its perverse delight over the ruin of Jerusalem (26:2); confident in its own power, it had nothing but delight in the wreck of a neighbour. But those that lamented the "Tyre" perceived what the crew of the ship had not perceived, namely that a wreck should always be lamented. Every loss of a ship at sea was a reminder to the mariners on the shore of their own vulnerability.

And as we perceive the shipwrecks of life, they should never be a source of derision or delight. Nor should they evoke self-confidence and arrogance. For in all life's experiences, there are storms that are greater than our capacity to survive. Recognising and lamenting tragedy should introduce a knowledge of our own vulnerability, and thus draw forth from us that trust in God who alone can still the violent ragings of the sea.

THE PRIDE OF THE PRINCE OF TYRE

Ezekiel 28:1–10

¹The word of the Lord came to me: ²"Son of man, say to the prince of Tyre, Thus says the Lord God:
"Because your heart is proud,
    and you have said, 'I am a god,
I sit in the seat of the gods,
    in the heart of the seas,'
yet you are but a man, and no god,
    though you consider yourself as wise as a god—
³you are indeed wiser than Daniel;
    no secret is hidden from you;
⁴by your wisdom and your understanding
    you have gotten wealth for yourself,
and have gathered gold and silver into
    your treasuries;
⁵by your great wisdom in trade
    you have increased your wealth,
    and your heart has become proud in your wealth—
⁶therefore thus says the Lord God:
"Because you consider yourself
    as wise as a god,
⁷therefore, behold, I will bring strangers upon you,
    the most terrible of the nations;
and they shall draw their swords against the beauty of your wisdom
    and defile your splendour.
⁸They shall thrust you down into the Pit,
    and you shall die the death of the slain
    in the heart of the seas.
⁹Will you still say, 'I am a god,'
    in the presence of those who slay you,
though you are but a man, and no god,
    in the hands of those who wound you?
¹⁰You shall die the death of the uncircumcised
    by the hand of foreigners;
    for I have spoken, says the Lord God."

This further oracle against Tyre is addressed specifically to its prince, or king; in Ezekiel's time, the ruler of Tyre was Ithobaal II. In the oracle, the king is condemned on the basis of his crimes toward God, not specifically toward Israel. That he did not worship the one true God is neither here nor there. His crimes spoke for themselves. He should have known better, and had no excuse.

The principal sin of which the prince was condemned was *hubris*, that overweening form of pride that created the conviction that "I am a god" (verse 2). In the ancient Near East, there were various understandings of the nature of human kingship. In general terms, the view typical of Syria and Mesopotamia was that kings were human beings, but appointed by a god, and thus in some special sense they were the instruments of that god's authority. In Egypt, by way of contrast, the Pharaoh or king was believed to be in some sense divine, a god amongst the larger family of divine beings. In Tyre, the concept of kingship was essentially that typical of Syria or Mesopotamia, though it may well have been influenced by Egyptian concepts, for Tyre had intimate trading links with Egypt.

The essence of the prophet's critique, however, is not against the Tyrian notion of kingship in general, but against the particular puffed-up notion of divine kingship acquired by actual Tyrian kings. The extraordinary achievements of prince and people in Tyre led to such enormous pride that delusion replaced reality; in the immense conceit of the prince, it was but a small step to take from being a human ruler to becoming a divine prince.

In the prophet's oracle, the wisdom and human achievements are acknowledged, albeit with a touch of sarcasm. "You are indeed wiser than Daniel" (verse 3); the figure Daniel (see also 14:14) was a traditional wise man in the ancient world, referred to in the Ugaritic texts, excavated from Ras Shamra, a little further north on the Mediterranean coast than Tyre. The ancient texts recognise Daniel's wisdom, but give no suggestion that he committed the sin of *hubris*; the Tyrian prince, wiser than Daniel in a material sense, was also a fool, for he allowed his real wisdom to blind him to the truth of his mortal estate.

Thus, the prophet moves from an honest acknowledgment of human achievement to an oracle of judgment against the prince of Tyre. The reason for the judgment was not human success, but pride: "Because you consider yourself as wise as a god..." (verse 6). Enemies would come with destructive force, and the prince and his people would die. The prophet, in this oracle, makes powerful use of language the force of which is not easily captured in English translation. The human prince considers himself (as his name suggests) to be a god like Baal, yet he would die "in the heart of the seas". In Hebrew, *sea* is *yam*; in Ugaritic (and presumably, therefore, Tyrian) mythology, *Yam* was a chaotic god who, after conflict, killed *Baal*. In poetic language, the prophet suggests that the human prince, whose power had been established by apparent mastery of the *sea*, would die in the midst of that same *sea*. The one who would be like *Baal*, would be consumed by *Yam*. But lying behind this adaptation of mythological language is the prophet's solid conviction that there is but one God; those who would aspire to the status of divinity were doomed to fall.

Of all the themes running through this prophetic oracle, it is the true character of human *wisdom* that is the most striking. From one perspective there is no doubt that the prince of Tyre possessed wisdom; by the exercise of his wisdom, he gathered for himself and his kingdom extraordinary wealth and power. Wisdom, in a strictly human sense, could be demonstrated in success and achievement. But the prince's perspective on wisdom was different from that of the biblical tradition: "the beginning of wisdom is the fear of the Lord" (Prov. 1:7). Wisdom itself, from a biblical perspective, might lead to achievements like those of the prince of Tyre, but rooted in the fear and reverence of the Lord, it would prohibit the possibility of overweening pride emerging from its accomplishments. One who starts with the "fear of the Lord" cannot go on to say: "I am a god."

All human beings may have and develop the various attributes of wisdom which, in the biblical perspective, embrace both skills and knowledge. And the exercise of wisdom may lead to success; its fruit may be wealth, reputation, power, influence, and various forms of advancement in life. But the possessor of wisdom must know not only how to use it, but also how to live with its results.

Wisdom is God-given, but its development and use are a human responsibility. And because, very often, the success that follows the exercise of human wisdom may have been achieved in part by hard work, it is easy to remember one's own effort and forget the divine gift without which all effort would have been futile. The pride that may emerge from the successes of wisdom is a pride rooted in forgetfulness. The one who masters the truth of human wisdom is the one who remembers its source in God.

EXIT FROM EDEN

Ezekiel 28:11–19

[11]Moreover the word of the Lord came to me: [12]"Son of man, raise a lamentation over the king of Tyre, and say to him, Thus says the Lord God:

"You were the signet of perfection,
  full of wisdom
  and perfect in beauty.
[13]You were in Eden, the garden of God;
  every precious stone was your covering,
carnelian, topaz, and jasper,
  chrysolite, beryl, and onyx,
sapphire, carbuncle, and emerald;
  and wrought in gold were your settings
  and your engravings.
On the day that you were created
  they were prepared.
[14]With an anointed guardian cherub I placed you;
  you were on the holy mountain of God;
  in the midst of the stones of fire you walked.
[15]You were blameless in your ways
  from the day you were created,
  till iniquity was found in you.
[16]In the abundance of your trade
  you were filled with violence, and you sinned;
so I cast you as a profane thing from the mountain of God,
  and the guardian cherub drove you out
  from the midst of the stones of fire.

¹⁷Your heart was proud because of your beauty;
　　you corrupted your wisdom for the sake of your splendour.
　I cast you to the ground;
　　I exposed you before kings,
　　to feast their eyes on you.
¹⁸By the multitude of your iniquities,
　　in the unrighteousness of your trade
　　you profaned your sanctuaries;
　so I brought forth fire from the midst of you;
　　it consumed you,
　and I turned you to ashes upon the earth
　　in the sight of all who saw you.
¹⁹All who know you among the peoples
　　are appalled at you;
　you have come to a dreadful end
　　and shall be no more for ever."

This concluding oracle against Tyre and its ruler is expressed once again (see 26:15–18) in the form of a funeral lament. But in addition to the poetic form of lament, the prophet has made use of ancient religious traditions to give expression to his announcement of the coming death of the Tyrian king. He has taken the ancient stories of primeval paradise, both the biblical story of Eden (verse 13) and Canaanite traditions concerning a holy mountain (verse 14), and adapted the themes to his immediate purpose.

The king of Tyre is presented as the primeval man in the Garden of Eden, "full of wisdom and perfect in beauty" (verse 12). There in the garden, with its holy mountain and guardian cherub, the king's life began in blamelessness. But, as in the original story, innocence was followed by fall. The growth of Tyre's trade led to the abandonment of justice and the growth of violence. Proud of beauty, Tyre's beauty was destroyed; successful and splendid, Tyre's wisdom was corrupted. And so the prince in Eden was cast forth from the garden; his demise outside the garden was a source of horror to all who perceived it.

The prophet has framed his oracle in such a way as to bring out its perpetual relevance.

(i) By adapting the story of Eden, the prophet shows that the tale of the Tyrian prince is really the tale of every man and woman. We do not understand Eden aright if we think of the exit from Eden as merely the consequence of some primeval ancestor's action. Just as the prince embodied Adam's action in his own behaviour, so too may we. The exit from Eden is the consequence ultimately of one's own actions.

(ii) The cause of the fall, in this version of the story, is *trade*. It is not trade as such that is evil, but the possible effect of the activity on the trader. Trade leads to profit, and profit may stoke the fires of greed and desire. Unchecked desire, in turn, may lead to the use of violence in pursuit of greater profits. And the acquisition of profits may corrupt wisdom, and pride in beauty and achievement completes the corruption of the whole person. And when innocence has been lost and corruption embraced, it is impossible to remain in Eden.

The prophet's anatomy of evil, and his tracing of the road out of Eden, are as true today as in his own time. Desire, greed, violence, and pride are the scourges of the human race that have removed all signs of Eden from our world. There can be no return to Eden until the corruption that expels humans from the garden has been dealt with and banished.

(iii) The prophet's oracle captures the dilemma of all human existence. In every person, there is the deep-seated longing to find Eden; but there is also in each of us the corruption that expels from Eden. We are made in such a way that we perpetually desire the divine presence in the garden, but we act in such a way that we cannot achieve it. The predicament of the king of Tyre is our predicament: in the pursuit of a goal that is so deeply set within us, we perversely destroy the possibility of reaching that goal.

The solution to the dilemma is to be found in yet another version of the story of Eden. Adam was a type of all human beings (Rom. 5:14), including the king of Tyre and ourselves. But Jesus Christ, the "new Adam", transforms the ancient story. Whereas the old Adam typified the human pursuit of evil and its culmination in death, the new Adam offers the promise of life (1 Cor. 15:42–50) and the possibility of a return to Eden.

SORROW FOR SIDON AND HOPE FOR ISRAEL

Ezekiel 28:20–26

²⁰The word of the Lord came to me: ²¹"Son of man, set your face toward Sidon, and prophesy against her ²²and say, Thus says the Lord God:

"Behold, I am against you, O Sidon,
    and I will manifest my glory in the midst of you.
And they shall know that I am the Lord
    when I execute judgments in her,
    and manifest my holiness in her;
²³ for I will send pestilence into her,
    and blood into her streets;
and the slain shall fall in the midst of her,
    by the sword that is against her on every side.
Then they will know that I am the Lord.

²⁴"And for the house of Israel there shall be no more a brier to prick or a thorn to hurt them among all their neighbours who have treated them with contempt. Then they will know that I am the Lord God.

²⁵"Thus says the Lord God: When I gather the house of Israel from the peoples among whom they are scattered, and manifest my holiness in them in the sight of the nations, then they shall dwell in their own land which I gave to my servant Jacob. ²⁶And they shall dwell securely in it, and they shall build houses and plant vineyards. They shall dwell securely, when I execute judgments upon all their neighbours who have treated them with contempt. Then they will know that I am the Lord their God."

These concluding verses of Chapter 28 bring to a close the first part of the collection of oracles against foreign nations (Chapters 25–28). The oracle against the city-state of Sidon, some twenty-five miles north of Tyre on the Mediterranean coast, brings to six the total number of nations addressed in this part of the prophet's oracles: Ammon, Moab, Edom, Philistia, Tyre, and Sidon. The foreign-nation oracles that follow (Chapters 29–32) are directed against Egypt, giving a final total of seven nations addressed by the prophet. The first six nations stand together as Israel's most immediate neighbours, in a geographical context, and thus they are followed by some words addressed to Israel (verses 24–26), indicating the eventual consequences for the chosen people of the exercise of God's judgment against foreign nations.

The oracle against Sidon clearly proclaims God's opposition to that city, though no explicit reason for the coming judgment is stated, as is the case for the other nations. Sidon had been a great city in the past, though it did not have the power and pre-eminence of Tyre in Ezekiel's time; later in history, after Tyre's collapse, Sidon was to grow once again in influence. Though it is only speculation, one may assume that Sidon's political alignments had contributed, as had Tyre's, to the eventual collapse of Judah before the Babylonians, and thus the city-state came within the purview of the prophet as a candidate for judgment. The city would be attacked and destroyed in war, its judgment demonstrating the glory of God to all those who observed it.

There follow some words addressed to the chosen people, which emerge as a consequence of the divine judgment that has been declared as about to fall on Israel's neighbouring nations. No longer would the Israelite state of Judah have to suffer the insults and derision of arrogant neighbours; in the sorrow that would befall its neighbours, there lay the seed of new hope for Israel.

It is probable that the words of hope which the prophet expresses in verses 25–26 come from the later period of his ministry and were placed here by him or one of his disciples at a later date. The nation of the chosen people has collapsed; its former citizens have been scattered the world over, as exiles having no longer a permanent home. And it is to these people, who have no longer any human grounds for hope of a return to the precious homeland, that Ezekiel imparts some words of hope. Beyond the insecurity of exile lay a secure dwelling once again in the promised land, together with a renewed knowledge of God's sovereignty over human nations and affairs. But at this point the prospect of restoration is only hinted at. There is some way still to go before it occupies the centre of Ezekiel's preaching.

ORACLES AGAINST EGYPT

Ezekiel 29:1–16

¹In the tenth year, in the tenth month, on the twelfth day of the month, the word of the Lord came to me: ²"Son of man, set your face against Pharaoh king of Egypt, and prophesy against him and against all Egypt; ³speak, and say, Thus says the Lord God:

"Behold, I am against you,
   Pharaoh king of Egypt,
the great dragon that lies in the midst of his streams,
   that says, 'My Nile is my own;
     I made it.'
⁴I will put hooks in your jaws,
   and make the fish of your streams stick to your scales;
and I will draw you up out of the midst of your streams,
   with all the fish of your streams which stick to your scales.
⁵And I will cast you forth into the wilderness,
   you and all the fish of your streams;
you shall fall upon the open field,
   and not be gathered and buried.
To the beasts of the earth and to the birds of the air
   I have given you as food.
⁶"Then all the inhabitants of Egypt shall know that I am the Lord. Because you have been a staff of reed to the house of Israel; ⁷when they grasped you with the hand, you broke, and tore all their shoulders; and when they leaned upon you, you broke, and made all their loins to shake; ⁸therefore thus says the Lord God: Behold, I will bring a sword upon you, and will cut off from you man and beast; ⁹and the land of Egypt shall be a desolation and a waste. Then they will know that I am the Lord.

"Because you said, 'The Nile is mine, and I made it,' ¹⁰therefore, behold, I am against you, and against your streams, and I will make the land of Egypt an utter waste and desolation, from Migdol to Syene, as far as the border of Ethiopia. ¹¹No foot of man shall pass through it, and no foot of beast shall pass through it; it shall be uninhabited forty years. ¹²And I will make the land of Egypt a desolation in the midst of desolated countries; and her cities shall be a desolation forty years among cities that are laid waste. I will scatter the Egyptians among the nations, and disperse them among the countries.

[13] "For thus says the Lord God: At the end of forty years I will gather the Egyptians from the peoples among whom they were scattered; [14] and I will restore the fortunes of Egypt, and bring them back to the land of Pathros, the land of their origin; and there they shall be a lowly kingdom. [15] It shall be the most lowly of the kingdoms, and never again exalt itself above the nations; and I will make them so small that they will never again rule over the nations. [16] And it shall never again be the reliance of the house of Israel, recalling their iniquity, when they turn to them for aid. Then they will know that I am the Lord God."

Chapters 29–32 round out the collection of oracles against foreign nations and are devoted entirely to the proclamation of judgment against Egypt. These four chapters contain, in all, seven prophecies against Egypt; six of them are explicitly identified by date, and it is clear that they were delivered at various different times in the prophet's ministry. In their present literary arrangement, the oracles may seem to the reader somewhat tedious and repetitive; when it is remembered that initially each oracle was delivered on a separate occasion in history, the force of the various oracles may be perceived. It is not always possible, however, to determine what particular event might have given rise to each oracle.

The general background to the oracles is provided by a knowledge of the long history of tense relationships between the chosen people and Egypt. The relationship began in the days of slavery before the Exodus; after the Exodus, when the Israelites formed their own state, Egypt was always too close and too powerful a neighbour to be ignored. And from Egypt's perspective, the territory inhabited by the Israelites was of vital geopolitical significance. The principal threat to Egypt's existence lay always to the north, not in Palestine as such, but in Syria and Mesopotamia. It was from the north that the successive empires of Assyrians and Babylonians threatened Egypt; Israel's land was the buffer zone, part of Egypt's defence against northern aggression. And thus, when Egypt was friendly towards Israel, it was always out of self-interest and towards the goal of self-protection; equally, Egypt's enmity was rooted in the same political purpose, namely that of securing the northern approach to the nation against the encroachments of dangerous foreign powers.

The first oracle is dated in the winter months of 588/587 B.C. (29:1), only a few months before the siege and eventual destruction of Jerusalem. To those in exile who heard the words, the oracle must have destroyed a possible hope for Jerusalem's salvation. There were some in Jerusalem, and no doubt others in exile, who believed that the holy city's rescue from the Babylonians depended on the forging of an alliance with Egypt. But the prophet's opening words remove any such hope: "I am against you, Pharaoh king of Egypt" (verse 3).

Egypt's greatness throughout history was the fruit of the Nile. It was that great river which made habitation in the valley possible. It provided the rich soil in which to plant crops, the water with which to irrigate those crops, a means of transportation, and supply for drinking. Without the river, there could have been no Egypt. And so in this statement of judgment, the Pharaoh is described in metaphorical language as a "great dragon", namely the crocodile that was the master beast of the waters of the Nile. The arrogance of the beast is revealed in its words: "My Nile is my own; I made it" (verse 3). Yet, as is so true of many of the causes of arrogance, the reverse was the truth: Egypt was the *product* of the Nile, not vice versa. As an act of judgment, the great beast would be dragged from the river and left to die on dry land, there to become the food of the birds of the air.

Arrogance was not Egypt's only crime. It had also been, throughout its history, a false friend to Israel, a reed that purported to offer support, but broke under the least pressure. For all its crimes, the land would be laid desolate by God for a period of forty years; after that, the land would be restored as a kingdom, but it would never again return to its powerful position among the world's great nations.

The oracle against Egypt illustrates two flaws in character that are as commonly the characteristics of individual humans as of nations.

(i) The first flaw is *delusion*, an offshoot of pride and arrogance. So self-centred had Egypt become in its power, that it persuaded itself that both the nation and the river on which it was based were its own creations. This delusion of grandeur, spoken of as a form of national omnipotence, was dangerous in the extreme; it could only be shattered by the truly omnipotent God, whose words the prophet declares.

The most dangerous lies that are told are those that delude the liar. Egypt really believed its own lie, that its strength was its own creation. In this self-delusion, it typified not only all great nations that express a similar conviction, but also all individuals who think they are self-made and that their achievements are entirely the consequence of their own abilities and efforts. It is the mighty, more than the weak, that succumb to this tempting delusion. It is incumbent on all those who achieve a degree of pre-eminence in this world to recognise that ultimately such pre-eminence is the gift of God.

(ii) The second flaw is *selfishness*. From time to time Egypt offered friendship to its neighbour, but it was only a tool with which to engineer its own benefit. False friendship, offered for selfish reasons and hastily withdrawn at the least sign of cost, undermined the entire fabric of human and national relationships and invited judgment.

Friendship is fundamental to all human relationships, holding individuals and societies together. It can only be strong if it is engendered in the spirit of self-sacrifice; the friendship that takes, but is not willing to give, is not true friendship at all. There is no greater insight into the nature of true friendship than that contained in the teaching and ministry of Jesus: "Greater love has no man than this, that a man lay down his life for his friends" (John 15:13). True friendship must eliminate the power of selfishness.

THE SECOND ORACLE AGAINST EGYPT

Ezekiel 29:17–21

17In the twenty-seventh year, in the first month, on the first day of the month, the word of the Lord came to me: 18"Son of man, Nebuchadrezzar king of Babylon made his army labour hard against Tyre; every head was made bald and every shoulder was rubbed bare; yet neither he nor his army got anything from Tyre to pay for the labour that he had performed against it. ¹⁹Therefore thus says the Lord God: Behold, I will give the land of Egypt to Nebuchadrezzar king of Babylon; and he shall carry off its wealth and despoil it and plunder it; and it shall be the wages for his army. ²⁰I have given him the land of Egypt as his recompense for which he laboured, because they worked for me, says the Lord God.

²¹"On that day I will cause a horn to spring forth to the house of Israel, and I will open your lips among them. Then they will know that I am the Lord."

This oracle, the second in the series of seven addressed to Egypt, is nevertheless the latest-dated oracle in the book of Ezekiel; the information provided in verse 17 indicates that it was delivered in the spring of the year 571 B.C., some sixteen years later than the preceding oracle. Although reference is made to the Babylonian emperor, the oracle is in fact addressed to Egypt, and in substance it is related intimately to the prophet's earlier oracles addressed to Tyre (Chapters 26–28).

The prophet begins by describing Nebuchadrezzar's long siege of the city of Tyre. His army had become old and weary in the effort, yet the limited success of the enterprise had hardly repaid the expenditure of time and money. The siege of Tyre had extended over thirteen years; although the city became a vassal of the Babylonian Empire and paid tribute to the emperor, the island portion of the city was not fully conquered. Certainly, the Babylonians never captured the treasure of Tyre. Whether it was simply spent in the defence of the city, or whether it was evacuated by ship to Egypt, is not known. For those of his listeners who remembered Ezekiel's earlier prophecies, the siege of Tyre must have been disturbing; they had expected the city's total annihilation (26:14), but after a fashion it seemed to survive. (The island port was eventually captured in 332 B.C. by Alexander the Great.)

As a consequence of the disappointment over Tyre, the prophet declares, the Babylonian emperor would be given the opportunity of plundering Egypt and carrying off its wealth. The spoil of Egypt would serve as compensatory wages for the fruitless work of the Babylonian soldiers in the long siege of Tyre. The event anticipated by the prophet took place a few years later: in

568/567 B.C., an expeditionary force from Babylon invaded Egypt. Though little is known of the event from the historical sources, it is presumed that the Pharaoh, Amasis II, came to terms with the invading army by paying massive tribute.

The oracle concludes with an element of hope: a "horn" (or perhaps "grass shoots") would spring forth in Israel, indicating new life and thus new hope. The words fit into the larger mosaic of the prophet's growing hope for a new future, which characterised the later years of his ministry.

THE THIRD ORACLE AGAINST EGYPT

Ezekiel 30:1–19

¹The word of the Lord came to me: ²"Son of man, prophesy, and say, Thus says the Lord God:

"Wail, 'Alas for the day!'
   ³For the day is near,
      the day of the Lord is near;
   it will be a day of clouds,
      a time of doom for the nations.
⁴A sword shall come upon Egypt,
      and anguish shall be in Ethiopia,
   when the slain fall in Egypt,
      and her wealth is carried away,
      and her foundations are torn down.
⁵Ethiopia, and Put, and Lud, and all Arabia, and Libya, and the people of the land that is in league, shall fall with them by the sword.
⁶"Thus says the Lord:
   Those who support Egypt shall fall,
      and her proud might shall come down;
   from Migdol to Syene
      they shall fall within her by the sword,
   says the Lord God.
⁷And she shall be desolated in the midst of desolated countries
      and her cities shall be in the midst of cities that are laid waste.
⁸Then they will know that I am the Lord,
      when I have set fire to Egypt,
      and all her helpers are broken.

⁹"On that day swift messengers shall go forth from me to terrify the unsuspecting Ethiopians; and anguish shall come upon them on the day of Egypt's doom; for, lo, it comes!

¹⁰"Thus says the Lord God:

I will put an end to the wealth of Egypt,
    by the hand of Nebuchadrezzar king of Babylon.

¹¹He and his people with him, the most terrible of the nations,
    shall be brought in to destroy the land;
and they shall draw their swords against Egypt,
    and fill the land with the slain.

¹²And I will dry up the Nile,
    and will sell the land into the hand of evil men;
I will bring desolation upon the land and everything in it,
    by the hand of foreigners;
I, the Lord, have spoken.

¹³"Thus says the Lord God:

I will destroy the idols,
    and put an end to the images, in Memphis;
there shall no longer be a prince in the land of Egypt;
    so I will put fear in the land of Egypt.

¹⁴I will make Pathros a desolation,
    and will set fire to Zoan,
    and will execute acts of judgment upon Thebes.

¹⁵And I will pour my wrath upon Pelusium,
    the stronghold of Egypt,
    and cut off the multitude of Thebes.

¹⁶And I will set fire to Egypt;
    Pelusium shall be in great agony;
Thebes shall be breached,
    and its walls broken down.

¹⁷The young men of On and of Pibeseth shall fall by the sword;
    and the women shall go into captivity.

¹⁸At Tehaphnehes the day shall be dark,
    when I break there the dominion of Egypt,
and her proud might shall come to an end;
    she shall be covered by a cloud,
    and her daughters shall go into captivity.

¹⁹Thus I will execute acts of judgment upon Egypt.
    Then they will know that I am the Lord."

This third oracle is the only undated one among the collection of seven oracles against Egypt (Ezek. 29–32). The prophet anticipates the coming judgment and defeat of the mighty nation; the forces of history and nature would combine to bring Egypt to ruin.

The prophecy begins with a reference to the coming "day" of the Lord (verses 2–3). Earlier, Ezekiel had anticipated the great day of judgment when the "end" would come for the land of Israel (7:1–13); in this oracle, he makes it clear that God's judgment would be universal and international in character. A sword of judgment would devastate Egypt and its southern neighbour, Ethiopia, just as a sword of devastation had already been declared for the land of the chosen people (Ezek. 21).

Two sources are specified as the instruments of God's coming judgment, one in the sphere of history and the other in the sphere of nature. The Babylonian emperor, Nebuchadrezzar, would invade the land and cover its soil with the corpses of the slain. But God would also dry up the River Nile, upon whose waters the nation was totally dependent (verse 12), and thus would mock the hollow boast that even the Nile was controlled by Egypt (29:9). God's coming judgment would be complete. The catalogue of coming destruction for all the great Egyptian cities (verses 13–19) indicates the comprehensiveness of the prophet's vision. The cities of Lower Egypt and Upper Egypt, from the north-eastern reaches of the Delta area to the southern reaches of the River Nile, all would succumb to the divine devastation. The archaeological remains that may still be seen by the modern traveller indicate just how splendid the ancient cities of Egypt were. They embodied extraordinary human achievement in their fine architecture and massive structures. But the cities, symbols of human strength and progress, would be unable to withstand the onset of judgment. No human structure can withstand the might of God.

In this oracle of judgment, Ezekiel penetrates the facade of strength and continuity upon which so much of the false confidence of the human race is based. The nation of Egypt represented a truly extraordinary civilisation in the 6th century B.C. It had been strong for some two and half millennia, an achievement without parallel in any modern form of civilisation. Its great architectural achievements embodied this same sense of continuity; its pyramids must have seemed to be as ancient as the Nile itself and the surrounding sands of the desert. Yet this ancient and seemingly perpetual civilisation was as vulnerable to the judgment of God as any other nation or people. Its confidence and pride could be shattered when the foundations upon which it was built were summoned to judgment.

The oracle against Egypt stands as a perpetual reminder of the omnipotence of God, over and against the temporary potency of mankind. And what was true of ancient Egypt is equally true of modern nations and empires. The most enduring of mankind's creations are marked indelibly with the sign of temporality. And for all of us who are the citizens of modern nations and civilisations, the temporary nature of Egypt's greatness comes as a solemn reminder. The durability of a nation or civilisation does not depend simply on the singular achievements of its various members; it is subject to the sovereignty of God. And the qualities that permit survival are not greatness and strength. Rather, they are the fruits of humility and morality that emerge from the recognition of the ultimate sovereignty of God in all human affairs.

THE FOURTH ORACLE:
THE FRACTURE OF PHARAOH'S ARMS

Ezekiel 30:20–26

20In the eleventh year, in the first month, on the seventh day of the month, the word of the Lord came to me: 21"Son of man, I have broken the arm of Pharaoh king of Egypt; and lo, it has not been bound up, to heal it by binding it with a bandage, so that it may become strong to wield the sword. 22Therefore thus says the Lord God: Behold, I am against Pharaoh king of Egypt, and will break his arms, both the strong arm and the one that was broken; and I will make the sword fall from his hand. 23I will scatter the Egyptians among the nations, and disperse them throughout the lands. [24] And I will strengthen the arms of the king of Babylon, and put my sword in his hand; but I will break the arms of Pharaoh, and he will groan before him like a man mortally wounded. [25] I will strengthen the arms of the king of Babylon, but the arms of Pharaoh shall fall; and they shall know that I am the Lord. When I put my sword into the hand of the king of Babylon, he shall stretch it out against the land of Egypt; [26] and I will scatter the Egyptians among the nations and disperse them throughout the countries. Then they will know that I am the Lord."

The fourth oracle against Egypt is dated in the spring of 587 B.C., just a few months before the final siege and defeat of the city of Jerusalem. For Ezekiel's companions in exile, it was a time of great anxiety and uncertainty; the news that filtered back to them from the homeland would have been bleak, but still the exiles would have hoped desperately for some support to avert what seemed like inevitable disaster. A few months prior to the delivery of this oracle, the Pharaoh Hophra had sent an army to Jerusalem in response to Zedekiah's urgent plea (see Jer. 37:1–10). The Pharaoh's force had not been successful, but many in exile must still have been hoping for another such intervention by the Pharaoh.

Ezekiel's prophecy declares the folly of hoping for further help from Egypt. In the traditional metaphor of the ancient world, the might of a king and his army was symbolised by the *arm*. A royal arm, successfully wielding a sword, was a symbol of strength. Pharaoh's arm had been fractured once, Ezekiel declared, referring back in time to the fruitless campaign of the Pharaoh Hophra; that arm had never healed, and the other arm would be fractured in the future! In declaring that the Pharaoh's other arm would be broken, the prophet was in effect fracturing the false hopes of those in exile, who still believed that salvation might be found in Egypt. The prophet's message is strengthened further by the announcement that the Babylonian king's arm would be strengthened. The one from whom deliverance was sought was the one who would destroy a false hope of deliverance.

In this short oracle, the prophet illuminates a number of significant themes.

(i) It is folly to seek human deliverance from the instrument of God's judgment. Both those in Jerusalem and those in exile were terrified of the Babylonian army; they thought salvation might be found with the Pharaoh. But both were blind; they could not perceive the truth, namely that God was using the Babylonian king as the executor of his will and judgment. Thus, to seek a human or political solution to a national and spiritual problem was an exercise in folly. It was almost too late to find salvation in the month this oracle was delivered, yet if there was any hope, it would be in national repentance, by citizens and exiles alike. Only a return to God could avert disaster, for it was God who strengthened the Babylonian king's arm, just as surely as he fractured Pharaoh's arm.

In all human crises, we must attempt to see beyond the immediate crisis to that which lies behind. When human actions have precipitated external crisis, it is the internal roots of corruption that must be dealt with more urgently than the external danger.

(ii) This fourth oracle illustrates the deep-seated theological blindness of the chosen people prior to the collapse of Jerusalem. The oracle is addressed to Egypt, yet its impact was felt by those Israelites who looked to Egypt for strength. They hoped that the Babylonian king's arm would be broken and that of the Pharaoh strengthened. The prophet declares that the reverse would be the case. But lying behind false hope and the prophetic declaration was the ancient fundamental of Hebrew theology, that ultimately it was only the arm of God that was strong.

> O sing to the Lord a new song,
>   for he has done marvellous things!
> His right hand and his holy arm
>   have gotten him victory.   (Ps. 98:1)

The chosen people had once been a great nation, but only because of the strength of God's "holy arm". Having forgotten the strength of God's arm, they would fall victim to the arms of human enemies strengthened by God for judgment.

Over and again, the Old Testament writers and prophets warn against the danger of forgetting the original source of human strength. What strength we have is a God-given capacity. Forgetting the source of strength, we automatically undermine it and create weakness.

THE FIFTH ORACLE: THE COSMIC TREE

Ezekiel 31:1–18

[1]In the eleventh year, in the third month, on the first day of the month, the word of the Lord came to me: [2]"Son of man, say to Pharaoh king of Egypt and to his multitude:
    'Whom are you like in your greatness?
 [3]Behold, I will liken you to a cedar in Lebanon,
   with fair branches and forest shade,
      and of great height,
      its top among the clouds.
 [4]The waters nourished it,
      the deep made it grow tall,
   making its rivers flow
      round the place of its planting,
   sending forth its streams
      to all the trees of the forest.
 [5]So it towered high
      above all the trees of the forest;
   its boughs grew large
      and its branches long,
      from abundant water in its shoots.
 [6]All the birds of the air
      made their nests in its boughs;
   under its branches all the beasts of the field
      brought forth their young;
   and under its shadow
      dwelt all great nations.
 [7]It was beautiful in its greatness,
      in the length of its branches;
   for its roots went down
      to abundant waters.
 [8]The cedars in the garden of God could not rival it,
      nor the fir trees equal its boughs;

     the plane trees were as nothing
       compared with its branches;
    no tree in the garden of God
       was like it in beauty.
⁹I made it beautiful
       in the mass of its branches,
    and all the trees of Eden envied it,
       that were in the garden of God.'

¹⁰"Therefore thus says the Lord God: Because it towered high and set its top among the clouds, and its heart was proud of its height, ¹¹I will give it into the hand of a mighty one of the nations; he shall surely deal with it as its wickedness deserves. I have cast it out. ¹²Foreigners, the most terrible of the nations, will cut it down and leave it. On the mountains and in all the valleys its branches will fall, and its boughs will lie broken in all the watercourses of the land; and all the peoples of the earth will go from its shadow and leave it. ¹³Upon its ruin will dwell all the birds of the air, and upon its branches will be all the beasts of the field. ¹⁴All this is in order that no trees by the waters may grow to lofty height or set their tops among the clouds, and that no trees that drink water may reach up to them in height; for they are all given over to death, to the nether world among mortal men, with those who go down to the Pit.

¹⁵"Thus says the Lord God: When it goes down to Sheol I will make the deep mourn for it, and restrain its rivers, and many waters shall be stopped; I will clothe Lebanon in gloom for it, and all the trees of the field shall faint because of it. ¹⁶I will make the nations quake at the sound of its fall, when I cast it down to Sheol with those who go down to the Pit; and all the trees of Eden, the choice and best of Lebanon, all that drink water, will be comforted in the nether world. ¹⁷They also shall go down to Sheol with it, to those who are slain by the sword; yea, those who dwelt under its shadow among the nations shall perish. ¹⁸Whom are you thus like in glory and in greatness among the trees of Eden? You shall be brought down with the trees of Eden to the nether world; you shall lie among the uncircumcised, with those who are slain by the sword.

    "This is Pharaoh and all his multitude, says the Lord God."

The fifth oracle against Egypt is dated in the summer of 587 B.C., some two months after the preceding dated oracle (30:20). In historical context, Jerusalem was in the final weeks of its struggle for survival when this oracle was delivered. Although the prophetic words do not directly address the fate of Jerusalem, they do elaborate upon the international crises amongst which the holy city's fate must be seen. The oracle is addressed specifically to the Egyptian Pharaoh and his retinue (31:2), although the immediate audience for the spoken words would have been, as before, the prophet's companions in exile.

The prophecy is in the form of an allegory, which is introduced by a description of a great tree (verses 3–9). The poetic description of the tree is followed by a prosaic account of the fall of the great tree (verses 10–14) and its consignment to the "Pit" (verses 15–18).

The description of the great tree, on which the allegory is based, is in the form of a poem or song. In all probability this poetic passage had an independent and popular existence beyond the words of the prophet; Ezekiel took the well-known passage and adapted it to his purpose, by indicating at the very beginning that the Pharaoh's greatness was like that of the great tree (verse 2). The poetic passage as such is simply descriptive, implying no criticism of the extraordinary greatness of its subject. Echoing ancient traditions about the garden of Eden and its phenomenal tree of life, the poem portrays a tree that seems to reach from earth to heaven.

It is only in verse 10, when the prophet moves from description to declaration of judgment, that it becomes clear that greatness is also a source of weakness. The very height which was a source of greatness became also the substance of pride (verse 10). And thus inevitably, once pride has been identified, it is intimated that the tree will be cut down (verse 12). The once mighty tree would lie fallen, its boughs broken, a moral tale to other great trees of the danger of pride that could come from achieving great height.

The latter part of the prophecy (verses 15–18) modifies the allegory somewhat: the great tree, now cut down, would be shipped to Sheol, where it would lie horizontally alongside other once great trees. The fall and demise of the great tree would cause deep anxiety among other strong trees with aspirations for altitude. Converting the allegory: if the great tree that was Egypt could be cut down and despatched to the netherworld, what tree was safe?

The allegory of the great tree presents in a new and distinctive fashion several of the prophet's familiar themes.

(i) Pride leads to a fall. Two dimensions of this common theme are given vivid illustration in the allegory. First, in the language of the allegory, there is nothing wrong with a tall and strong tree; it is the attitude to strength and greatness that is crucial. Egypt, the object of the oracle, was genuinely great; it was the self-centred focus on that greatness that led to weakness. Second, pride involves looking down on others, just as in the judgment of the allegory the great tree looked down on the lesser trees of the forest.

True greatness comes to only a few people in this world, though many may be privileged with the minor forms of greatness. Greatness is neither something to be ashamed of, nor something to be proud of. If it leads to pride, both in the form of self-conceit and the despising of others, then greatness cannot be retained. For true greatness, whether in the local or international aspects of human living, can only grow on humility and respect for others.

(ii) The fall of the mighty is a loss to the weak. When the great tree was cut down, all those who had benefited from its strength and shade were among the losers. We cannot limit the effect of the fall of the mighty; it is not only an individual tragedy, but a disaster that impinges upon the lives of others. And not least of the reasons why those privileged with greatness must guard their positions with humility and care, is that the lives of so many others are dependent on them.

(iii) The great tree of the allegory symbolises in many ways mankind's longing for permanence, for a continuity in life not disrupted by death. If one has seen one of the great North American redwood trees that has survived, one may sense the power of the symbol. The "General Sherman Tree", in the Sequoia National Park, is reputed to be some 3,500 years old. It stands more than 270 feet high, with a trunk more than 36 feet in diameter. Such a great tree, growing before the birth of modern civilisation, expresses in a subtle way the human aspiration for perpetuity. Egypt thought it had attained such continuity of life and, on a smaller scale, many humans seek within life the same kind of permanence.

Yet the essence of being human is to be mortal, and that is as true of human beings as it is of human nations. Job perceived clearly enough that, when a tree was cut down, it was possible for fresh sprouts to grow around the stump, but when a man died, there was no more life (Job 14:7–17). The deep-seated desire for perpetuity, represented here by the tree, can only find fulfilment in the One who, in the words of St Paul, "hung upon a tree", thereby removing the curse of mortality and offering the promise of life (Gal. 3:13–14).

THE SIXTH ORACLE: MOURNING THE MONSTER

Ezekiel 32:1–16

¹In the twelfth year, in the twelfth month, on the first day of the month, the word of the Lord came to me: ²"Son of man, raise a lamentation over Pharaoh king of Egypt, and say to him:

"You consider yourself a lion among the nations,
    but you are like a dragon in the seas;
you burst forth in your rivers,
    trouble the waters with your feet,
    and foul their rivers.
³Thus says the Lord God:
    I will throw my net over you
    with a host of many peoples;
    and I will haul you up in my dragnet.
⁴And I will cast you on the ground,
    on the open field I will fling you,
  and will cause all the birds of the air to settle on you,
    and I will gorge the beasts of the whole earth with you.
⁵I will strew your flesh upon the mountains,
    and fill the valleys with your carcass.
⁶I will drench the land even to the mountains
    with your flowing blood;
    and the watercourses will be full of you.
⁷When I blot you out, I will cover the heavens,

and make their stars dark;
I will cover the sun with a cloud,
    and the moon shall not give its light.
8All the bright lights of heaven
    will I make dark over you,
    and put darkness upon your land, says the Lord God.
9"I will trouble the hearts of many peoples, when I carry you captive
among the nations, into the countries which you have not known. 10I
will make many peoples appalled at you, and their kings shall shudder
because of you, when I brandish my sword before them; they shall
tremble every moment, every one for his own life, on the day of your
downfall. 11For thus says the Lord God: The sword of the king of
Babylon shall come upon you. 12I will cause your multitude to fall by
the swords of mighty ones, all of them most terrible among the nations.
    "They shall bring to naught the pride of Egypt,
    and all its multitude shall perish.
13I will destroy all its beasts
    from beside many waters;
and no foot of man shall trouble them any more
    nor shall the hoofs of beasts trouble them.
14Then I will make their waters clear,
    and cause their rivers to run like oil, says the Lord God.
15When I make the land of Egypt desolate
    and when the land is stripped of all that fills it,
when I smite all who dwell in it,
    then they will know that I am the Lord.
16This is a lamentation which shall be chanted; the daughters of the
nations shall chant it; over Egypt, and over all her multitude, shall they
chant it, says the Lord God."

The sixth oracle against Egypt is dated in the early spring of 585
B.C., some months after the time at which those in exile would
have received news of the downfall of their city, Jerusalem.
(Some of the ancient versions give an earlier date, in 586 B.C., so
that the precise date of this oracle is uncertain.) The prophecy is
identified as a *lamentation* (verses 2, 16) but, as is commonly the
case with such prophetic laments, it is in part an anticipation and
warning of a coming disaster which, when it came to pass, would
be followed by lamentation. The passage contains an allegory,
likening Egypt to a marine monster (verses 2–8), followed by an
historical interpretation and application.

The poetry begins with a striking contrast. The Egyptian king thought of himself in terms of the royal metaphor of a bold lion, the king of the beasts. In reality, he was little more than a dragon, fouling the waters as he flopped about in the mud. The prophet declares that the dragon would be caught: God would cast his net in the waters and drag the beast onto the dry land for slaughter. Then, the birds would pick at its flesh and the wild animals gnaw at its meat; the monster's blood would flow in rivers through the land. The day of the marine monster's death would be a day of deep darkness in the land.

The demise of the monstrous dragon that was Egypt would be a source of great concern to other nations. And in the historical interpretation, the king of Babylon is identified as the one whose sword would kill the Egyptian Pharaoh (verse 11), a reiteration of the prophet's familiar theme that God would use the Babylonian king as an instrument of judgment. For all the mourning for the monster, it is a mourning based on anxiety, not a little touched with relief that the monster is no longer around to threaten and do damage.

It is not at first apparent in the English translation of this oracle how the prophet has made use of ancient mythological themes from the land of his captivity to convey his message. The Babylonian creation story, *Enuma Elish*, describes the emergence of an ordered world from primeval chaos in terms of a great battle. The most powerful of the forces of chaos was a great marine monster, the goddess Tiamat. While Tiamat flourished, order and peace could not develop in the world. But a young champion among the gods of order, Marduk of Babylon, challenged the chaotic monster and slew it; from the carcase of Tiamat, in the language of the myth, the ordered and structured world gradually emerged. The adaptation of the language in the prophecy portrays Egypt in the role of the monster Tiamat and the Babylonian king appropriately playing the role of Marduk. Such adaptation of the mythological language of creation must have had a striking effect on the captives who lived in the land of Marduk. Yet the adaptation of language is significant; whereas in the Babylonian myth, Tiamat and Marduk were independent deities, in Ezekiel's oracle, Babylon and Egypt were but pawns in the hands of a universal God.

It is only when the mythological background of this oracle of judgment has been identified that one begins to grasp its deeper theological message. It concerns not merely judgment, but the gradual emergence of the divine order from a world still gripped in primeval chaos. The ancient creation stories were not concerned with the origin of *matter*; rather, they were concerned with the origin of *order* and the subjugation of *chaos*. And the judgment against Egypt, portrayed here as the conquest of chaos, depicts a further stage in the emergence of world order from world chaos.

Seen in this light, and from this larger perspective, all the prophet's oracles of judgment take on a more positive purpose. They reflect not simply acts of divine punishment for particular evils, but are episodes in a cosmic history in which gradually the powers of evil and chaos are being conquered. All judgment is in some sense a part of the battle with chaos, and hence all judgment has ultimately a positive purpose, the creation of a world in which the forces of evil are held back and the powerful structures of the divine order are established. And thus what may seem to be a morbid preoccupation with judgment in the words of the prophet is in reality not morbid at all. All judgment is a part of the subjugation of the chaotic forces of evil. Beyond judgment, there lies a better world, in which it is God's good order that rules supreme.

THE FINAL ORACLE AGAINST EGYPT: THE DENIZENS OF THE NETHERWORLD

Ezekiel 32:17–32

[17]In the twelfth year, in the first month, on the fifteenth day of the month, the word of the Lord came to me: [18]"Son of man, wail over the multitude of Egypt, and send them down, her and the daughters of majestic nations, to the nether world, to those who have gone down to the Pit:

¹⁹'Whom do you surpass in beauty?

Go down, and be laid with the uncircumcised.'

²⁰They shall fall amid those who are slain by the sword, and with her shall lie all her multitudes. ²¹The mighty chiefs shall speak of them, with their helpers, out of the midst of Sheol: 'They have come down, they lie still, the uncircumcised, slain by the sword.'

²²"Assyria is there, and all her company, their graves round about her, all of them slain, fallen by the sword; ²³whose graves are set in the uttermost parts of the Pit, and her company is round about her grave; all of them slain, fallen by the sword, who spread terror in the land of the living.

²⁴"Elam is there, and all her multitude about her grave; all of them slain, fallen by the sword, who went down uncircumcised into the nether world, who spread terror in the land of the living, and they bear their shame with those who go down to the Pit. ²⁵They have made her a bed among the slain with all her multitude, their graves round about her, all of them uncircumcised, slain by the sword; for terror of them was spread in the land of the living, and they bear their shame with those who go down to the Pit; they are placed among the slain.

²⁶"Meshech and Tubal are there, and all their multitude, their graves round about them, all of them uncircumcised, slain by the sword; for they spread terror in the land of the living. ²⁷And they do not lie with the fallen mighty men of old who went down to Sheol with their weapons of war, whose swords were laid under their heads, and whose shields are upon their bones; for the terror of the mighty men was in the land of the living. ²⁸So you shall be broken and lie among the uncircumcised, with those who are slain by the sword.

²⁹"Edom is there, her kings and all her princes, who for all their might are laid with those who are slain by the sword; they lie with the uncircumcised, with those who go down to the Pit.

³⁰"The princes of the north are there, all of them, and all the Sidonians, who have gone down in shame with the slain, for all the terror which they caused by their might; they lie uncircumcised with those who are slain by the sword, and bear their shame with those who go down to the Pit.

³¹"When Pharaoh sees them, he will comfort himself for all his multitude, Pharaoh and all his army, slain by the sword, says the Lord God. ³²For he spread terror in the land of the living; therefore he shall be laid among the uncircumcised, with those who are slain by the sword, Pharaoh and all his multitude, says the Lord God."

The seventh and final oracle against Egypt is dated somewhere in 586/585 B.C. The Hebrew text omits any reference to the month in which the oracle was delivered; the translation above, "in the first month", is taken from the early translation of the text into Greek, but its authenticity remains uncertain. Regardless of the precise date, this prophecy is appropriately placed at the end of the series of oracles addressed to Egypt; for it concerns the final resting place of Egypt in Sheol, or the Pit.

The prophet is instructed to "wail" over the Egyptian multitudes and declare their departure for the netherworld. The picture of Sheol that follows is poetic in character; it captures the essence of the Hebrew notion of existence beyond the grave, but cannot be taken as a literal description of the underworld.

Sheol is a place of shadowy existence, a ghostly world that is the grave of all mankind. Yet even the netherworld had its own fine shades of distinction: there were those who died honestly and retained some honour, and those who died ignominiously and without honour. Greeted at the entrance to Sheol by the honourable chiefs of antiquity, the Egyptians would be sent to a farther corner of the dark world, there to lie among those without honour, "the uncircumcised, slain by the sword" (verse 21).

And thus finally, lying among the deceased, the judged Egyptians would find their rightful place in death. They are given, as it were, a tour of the Pit, to see their companions in the grave. Conquerors and purveyors of terror are there, great and small alike. The great nations of the living are numbered among the dead: Assyria, Elam, Meshech and Tubal. The smaller states are also there: Edom and Sidon. And to this moribund company, the Pharaoh and his people would be despatched in an act of divine judgment.

Ezekiel's final oracle against Egypt contains not only basic Hebrew theology, but also new insights for his time that were not to be given fuller amplification until subsequent centuries.

(i) The basic theology was that death, both of human beings and of nations, was followed by the grave, Sheol. This theology was not unique to the Hebrews but was shared, in a variety of forms, among the various religions of the ancient Near East. It was not a developed form of religious thought, nor was it particularly cheerful, yet it was characterised by hard-nosed realism. And it is not so different from the popular "theology" of the great mass of people in the modern world: aspiring to no hope beyond this world, they acknowledge at least that the grave is the end. But Ezekiel goes a little further and draws out the logical conclusion of this observation. If death is the end, then the grave makes mockery of some of the fierce strivings of human beings and nations. The grave is the great leveller—those who strove for pre-eminence in life lie horizontally together in death. A recognition of this basic truth should shape the conduct of living; if one cannot live beyond the grave, the meaning of human living as such must be explored for its true and lasting meaning.

(ii) But Ezekiel goes a step further, and anticipates later developments in Jewish theology, to find even later fulfilment in Christian theology. Existence in Sheol was not the same for all, as commonly supposed in ancient Hebrew theology. Though the prophet knows no distinction between "heaven" and "hell", he does have a notion of levels of distinction within Sheol. There are places of honour and places of dishonour. The places of dishonour are inhabited by those "who spread terror in the land of the living" and as a consequence had a position of shame in Sheol (verse 24). And Egypt, the prophet indicates, would lie with those whose living culminated in a death of shame.

Thus the prophet's oracles against Egypt conclude with a sombre note. The judgment declared of the living always leaves open the possibility of perceiving evil and turning from it. The judgment declared of the dead allows no such possibility, but rings with the dreadful finality of the terminal epitaph.

THE PARABLE OF THE WATCHMAN I

Ezekiel 33:1–20

[1]The word of the Lord came to me: [2]"Son of man, speak to your people and say to them, If I bring the sword upon a land, and the people of the land take a man from among them, and make him their

watchman; ³and if he sees the sword coming upon the land and blows the trumpet and warns the people; ⁴then if any one who hears the sound of the trumpet does not take warning, and the sword comes and takes him away, his blood shall be upon his own head. ⁵He heard the sound of the trumpet, and did not take warning; his blood shall be upon himself. But if he had taken warning, he would have saved his life. ⁶But if the watchman sees the sword coming and does not blow the trumpet, so that the people are not warned, and the sword comes, and takes any one of them; that man is taken away in his iniquity, but his blood I will require at the watchman's hand.

⁷"So you, son of man, I have made a watchman for the house of Israel; whenever you hear a word from my mouth, you shall give them warning from me. ⁸If I say to the wicked, O wicked man, you shall surely die, and you do not speak to warn the wicked to turn from his way, that wicked man shall die in his iniquity, but his blood I will require at your hand. ⁹But if you warn the wicked to turn from his way, and he does not turn from his way; he shall die in his iniquity, but you will have saved your life.

¹⁰"And you, son of man, say to the house of Israel, Thus have you said: 'Our transgressions and our sins are upon us, and we waste away because of them; how then can we live?' ¹¹Say to them, As I live, says the Lord God, I have no pleasure in the death of the wicked, but that the wicked turn from his way and live; turn back, turn back from your evil ways; for why will you die, O house of Israel? ¹²And you, son of man, say to your people, The righteousness of the righteous shall not deliver him when he transgresses; and as for the wickedness of the wicked, he shall not fall by it when he turns from his wickedness; and the righteous shall not be able to live by his righteousness when he sins. ¹³Though I say to the righteous that he shall surely live, yet if he trusts in his righteousness and commits iniquity, none of his righteous deeds shall be remembered; but in the iniquity that he has committed he shall die. ¹⁴Again, though I say to the wicked, 'You shall surely die,' yet if he turns from his sin and does what is lawful and right, ¹⁵if the wicked restores the pledge, gives back what he has taken by robbery, and walks in the statutes of life, committing no iniquity; he shall surely live, he shall not die. ¹⁶None of the sins that he has committed shall be remembered against him; he has done what is lawful and right, he shall surely live.

¹⁷"Yet your people say, 'The way of the Lord is not just'; when it is their own way that is not just. ¹⁸When the righteous turns from his

righteousness, and commits iniquity, he shall die for it. [19]And when the wicked turns from his wickedness, and does what is lawful and right, he shall live by it. [20]Yet you say, 'The way of the Lord is not just.' O house of Israel, I will judge each of you according to his ways."

Chapter 33 begins not only a new section in the Book of Ezekiel, but also a new period in the prophet's ministry. The preceding chapters (25–32), containing a collection of prophecies against foreign nations, form from a literary perspective a tense hiatus between the death of Ezekiel's wife (24:15–27) and the anticipated news of Jerusalem's collapse. The latter event is described later in Chapter 33, but first we are presented with the parable of the watchman and its interpretation. One might expect this chapter to begin with the event described in verses 21–22, namely the arrival of a fugitive from Jerusalem bearing news of the fall of the city; it was only then that Ezekiel recovered the power of speech lost at the time of his wife's death. Yet it is appropriate for this new section of the book to begin with the parable, although he must have told it after the sad news came; it marks a renewal of Ezekiel's vocation, and hence a new direction in his ministry.

The notion of the watchman is already familiar; in shorter form, it was a part of the description of Ezekiel's initial vocation, as described in 3:16–21. Its elaboration here, with the development of the earlier metaphor into a full parable, marks the renewal of the prophet's vocation for a new type of ministry; whereas his former ministry had been focused on the past and current history of the chosen people, the collapse of Jerusalem marks the beginning of a new future emphasis in the prophet's words. But there is a further difference between the parable presented here and the earlier reference to the prophet as watchman. In 3:16–21 Ezekiel was told that he had been appointed a watchman, but that office was not made public. In the passage now under discussion, the parable of the watchman and its interpretation are specifically to be addressed by the prophet to his people (verse 1). The prophet's role as watchman, and the people's responsibility to respond to the watchman's warning, are both made explicit.

The parable drew upon knowledge familiar to the people and was thoroughly contemporary in terms of current events, specifically the fall of the holy city in battle. One must envisage a city-state; the city itself was a military stronghold offering protection against an invader, but the people of the state worked not only in the city, but also in the surrounding countryside. In a time of military crisis, a watchman was appointed. He would take a high vantage point on the city wall and keep a perpetual watch for the advance of the enemy. If the enemy were spotted, the watchman would sound a loud warning on his trumpet, alerting his people to the approaching danger. The parable then elaborates upon the different areas of responsibility in such a time of military crisis. The watchman's responsibility is to watch and to warn; if those duties are fulfilled, his work is done. The citizen's responsibility is to listen and to react; when the warning trumpet blast is heard, the citizen must seek the safety of the city's walls.

THE PARABLE OF THE WATCHMAN II

Ezekiel 33:1–20 (*cont'd*)

The interpretation of the parable is presented in two parts. The first part (verses 7–9) explicitly identifies Ezekiel as Israel's watchman. The enemy is identified as the "army of evil" that seeks to destroy the people of Israel. The prophet must watch for evil's arrival and warn his people of the disaster it brings. The people's responsibility is to heed the watchman's warning and flee from evil to the stronghold of good. Both watchman and people have clearly defined duties and responsibilities, yet both are mutually interdependent.

The second part of the interpretation (verses 10–20) is less directly related to the parable; it deals rather with objections raised against the fundamental teaching of the parable. The first objection is that the sinful past weighs so heavily upon the people that they cannot possibly escape from it, and hence cannot live. But such is not the case, the prophet declares. God does not act upon the past accumulation of evil, nor even upon the past accumulation of good; it is always the present attitude and action, and the commitment for the future, that are relevant. Thus the perpetual evil-doer is not beyond hope; turning from that evil to good, and attempting to right the wrongs that have been done, will lead to deliverance and life. Nor is the perpetual doer of good beyond danger; to turn from that good and do evil is to invite judgment and disaster. But this perspective invites a further objection: if this is the manner of God's dealing with mankind, is it not unjust? To paraphrase: if, after a lifetime of evil, a person repents and turns to good, is it not unfair that all the evil should be forgotten? And the reverse is equally unjust: after a lifetime of good, should a little lapse cancel out all the former benefits? Not so, implies the prophet.

The entire passage is rich in its theological implications; the teaching is not new, but is presented in different perspectives from the earlier passages of the book.

(i) *Individual and corporate responsibility:* the parable draws out both dimensions of responsibility. The watchman is responsible as an individual, both to God and to his fellow citizens, for faithfully fulfilling his duty. If he warns of danger, he has done his job; if he fails to warn, he is to be held responsible for all the terrible consequences. But he can only be held responsible for failing to warn; he cannot be responsible for the failure of people to respond to the warning. Thus the watchman stands alone in fulfilling his duty; he alone must answer for his faithfulness. But the responsibility as such extends beyond the individual; it embraces the community as a whole. Though he can only be held responsible for his own actions, those actions in turn affect multitudes of other people.

The principle of responsibility presented in the parable extends beyond the prophetic office to all forms of ministry, both lay and clerical. One is responsible to God only for one's own actions and the fulfilment of one's responsibilities. But because those responsibilities inevitably extend to influence the lives of others, individual responsibility always has a corporate dimension to it. And it is the corporate dimension that may make responsibility so terrifying; it is one thing to stand or fall by one's own actions, but another to know that others too stand or fall by those same actions. Yet ministry is always a form of service to others; if we were not responsible to others, we could do nothing for them. But in this parable we begin to perceive that ministry is not only a privilege, but also a risky business; it entails the risks of failure, of disappointment, of love spurned, and of warnings unheeded. There is no option, though: not to live with some responsibility for the lives of fellow human beings is not to live fully at all. Ezekiel's life, for all its grief and pain, was a fully human life.

(ii) *Justice and forgiveness*: in the opinion of many people, Ezekiel's view of God's actions in relation to human beings was not characterised by justice. In making such a claim, they failed to recognise both the nature of the relationship between a person and God, and the nature of forgiveness.

A superficial view of justice might indicate that we should be dealt with strictly in accordance with our actions. For a person normally good, the occasional bad lapse should not cancel out the credit balance of good—and vice versa! The trouble with such a notion of justice, as St Paul was to declare so forcibly in a later century, was that, at bottom, nobody was totally good (Rom. 3:9–20). If a totally holy God established the criterion of good, then in terms of justice alone, no human being would survive the test. The error was that of applying a rigid notion of justice to the fluid relationship with God. The prophet was concerned with how his people should live in relationship with God; the life of faith could not be reduced to a credit balance of good or bad deeds. Living with God was a vital process; from the divine perspective, it was only possible through the exercise of forgiveness, whereby the human partners in the relationship could continue to live in that relationship. From the human perspective, the continual turning to God in repentance permitted the receipt of forgiveness, so that life in the covenant relationship could continue.

The prophet does not affirm that God acts unjustly; he does declare that if justice alone were the criterion of relationship, there would be no hope. The solid principles of justice are tempered by mercy and the mystery of forgiveness, which alone make possible the continuity of life with God. And from the perspective of Christian theology, justice, mercy and forgiveness are all incorporated within the death of Christ, which in turn led to the resurrection and the possibility of continuing life with God.

THE FALL OF JERUSALEM

Ezekiel 33:21–33

[21]In the twelfth year of our exile, in the tenth month, on the fifth day of the month, a man who had escaped from Jerusalem came to me and said, "The city has fallen." [22]Now the hand of the Lord had been upon me the evening before the fugitive came; and he had opened my mouth by the time the man came to me in the morning; so my mouth was opened, and I was no longer dumb.

[23]The word of the Lord came to me: [24]"Son of man, the inhabitants of these waste places in the land of Israel keep saying, 'Abraham was only one man, yet he got possession of the land; but we are many; the land is surely given us to possess.' [25]Therefore say to them, Thus says the Lord God: You eat flesh with the blood, and lift up your eyes to your idols, and shed blood; shall you then possess the land? [26]You resort to the sword, you commit abominations and each of you defiles his neighbour's wife; shall you then possess the land? [27]Say this to them, Thus says the Lord God: As I live, surely those who are in the waste places shall fall by the sword; and him that is in the open field I will give to the beasts to be devoured; and those who are in strongholds and in caves shall die by pestilence. [28]And I will make the land a desolation and a waste; and her proud might shall come to an end; and the mountains of Israel shall be so desolate that none will pass through. [29]Then they will know that I am the Lord, when I have made the land a desolation and a waste because of all their abominations which they have committed.

[30]"As for you, son of man, your people who talk together about you by the walls and at the doors of the houses, say to one another, each to his brother, 'Come, and hear what the word is that comes forth from the Lord.' [31]And they come to you as people come, and they sit before you as my people, and they hear what you say but they will not do it; for with their lips they show much love, but their heart is set on their gain. [32]And, lo, you are to them like one who sings love songs with a

beautiful voice and plays well on an instrument, for they hear what you say, but they will not do it. [33]When this comes—and come it will!—then they will know that a prophet has been among them."

After a long period of dumbness, Ezekiel was at last given back the capacity of speech when the news was brought to those in exile of the fall of Jerusalem. The "twelfth year" of verse 21 should probably be emended to "eleventh year" (for which there is some evidence in ancient Hebrew manuscripts), thus dating the event in the winter months of 587/586 B.C., some six months after the fall of Jerusalem. As Ezekiel had declared at the time of his wife's death, his speech would be restored when a fugitive brought news of the city's fall (24:25–27).

It is easy to think that, in a time of great national crisis, people will finally come to their senses and grasp the reality of the situation. But, as the two parts of the prophecy which follows indicate, such is not the case. The prophet, employing powerfully his newly-restored capacity of speech, addresses first the people who still remained in the promised land (verses 23–29) and then those who continued to be his companions in exile.

The survivors in Israel, despite the collapse of Jerusalem and the defeat of the nation in war, were still totally blind to their perversion of the ancient faith that had culminated in national ruin. Rather than attempting to restore their faith in repentance, they were busily engaged in land-grabbing. Many of the former land-owners had been killed and others had been sent off into exile; the remaining citizens, too miserable to be taken seriously by the conquerors, were building a fortune for themselves in times of ruin. As we have seen several times in our own century, there are vast profits to be made from the chaos of a post-war period; the hyenas and hawks of the human race can build a fortune from the wreckage of human misery. But the survivors of Israel were not only grasping the land for themselves, but were brazenly and hypocritically justifying their actions in the language of religion. If one man, Abraham, deserved the land, surely the more numerous survivors of catastrophe had an even greater right to it (verse 24)?

The prophet declares the falsity of such presumption. Abraham was righteous, but the grasping survivors of catastrophe were the embodiment of unrighteousness, violent and bloodthirsty men, devoid of both morality and faith. And so we are presented with the extraordinary picture of the prophet *still* declaring judgment on the inhabitants of the promised land. They had totally failed to learn the lessons of the events taking place around them, and so still further divine judgment would come to pass for the small remnant remaining alive.

The second part of the prophet's address is directed to those still in exile with him. On the surface, the situation is positive. The prophet has gained some prestige, for his predictions have been fulfilled with horrifying accuracy, and so it became popular to listen to his words (verse 30). But while a prophet may hate to be perpetually ignored, he must be extremely careful if he becomes a popular figure. The people flock to hear the sermons of Ezekiel, as crowds might gather to hear the popular singer of love songs (verse 32). But just as those who listen to love songs do not practise love, so those who heard the prophet did not act on his words. The unpopular prophet had become popular, but his words no more penetrated the dull ears of his people in popularity then they had done in unpopularity.

The picture painted by the prophet's words at this crisis point in the history of the human race is a bleak one indeed. The city of Jerusalem and its temple lay in ruins; there was little hope that the faith of the Hebrews might survive. None of the calamities of history had been understood as divine judgment, despite the prophet's preaching. The survivors of the land continued as if nothing had happened, hoisting the old faith to justify their new circumstances. Those in exile took a new interest in the preaching of the prophet, but his words were as entertainment, not spurs to action. With the wisdom of hindsight, we can be amazed at the continuing obtuseness and blindness of the people, but our insight is marred by our inability to perceive our own blindness in a similar and contemporary crisis.

THE DELINQUENT SHEPHERDS

Ezekiel 34:1–16

¹The word of the Lord came to me: ²"Son of man, prophesy against the shepherds of Israel, prophesy, and say to them, even to the shepherds, Thus says the Lord God: Ho, shepherds of Israel who have been feeding yourselves! Should not shepherds feed the sheep? ³You eat the fat, you clothe yourselves with the wool, you slaughter the fatlings; but you do not feed the sheep. ⁴The weak you have not strengthened, the sick you have not healed, the crippled you have not bound up, the strayed you have not brought back, the lost you have not sought, and with force and harshness you have ruled them. ⁵So they were scattered, because there was no shepherd; and they became food for all the wild beasts. ⁶My sheep were scattered, they wandered over all the mountains and on every high hill; my sheep were scattered over all the face of the earth, with none to search or seek for them.

⁷"Therefore, you shepherds, hear the word of the Lord: ⁸As I live, says the Lord God, because my sheep have become a prey, and my sheep have become food for all the wild beasts, since there was no shepherd; and because my shepherds have not searched for my sheep, but the shepherds have fed themselves, and have not fed my sheep; ⁹therefore, you shepherds, hear the word of the Lord: ¹⁰Thus says the Lord God, Behold, I am against the shepherds; and I will require my sheep at their hand, and put a stop to their feeding the sheep; no longer shall the shepherds feed themselves. I will rescue my sheep from their mouths, that they may not be food for them.

¹¹"For thus says the Lord God: Behold, I, I myself will search for my sheep, and will seek them out. ¹²As a shepherd seeks out his flock when some of his sheep have been scattered abroad, so will I seek out my sheep; and I will rescue them from all places where they have been scattered on a day of clouds and thick darkness. ¹³And I will bring them out from the peoples, and gather them from the countries, and will bring them into their own land; and I will feed them on the mountains of Israel, by the fountains, and in all the inhabited places of the country. ¹⁴I will feed them with good pasture, and upon the mountain heights of Israel shall be their pasture; there they shall lie down in good grazing land, and on fat pasture they shall feed on the mountains of Israel. ¹⁵I myself will be the shepherd of my sheep, and I will make them lie down, says the Lord God. ¹⁶I will seek the lost, and

I will bring back the strayed, and I will bind up the crippled, and I will strengthen the weak, and the fat and the strong I will watch over; I will feed them in justice."

As the prophet continues the series of oracles associated with the fall of Jerusalem, his attention is now fixed on the leaders and kings of the chosen people. The "shepherds of Israel" were its rulers, those to whom the care of the flock (viz. the population as a whole) had been entrusted. The failure of the shepherds was already a chapter of history; the collapse of the holy city was merely the final instalment in a long record of incompetence and delinquency on the part of the shepherds. The oracle addressed to the shepherds is one of judgment for past failures. It is not a warning oracle, leaving open the possibility of repentance and change, for the damage had already been done. It declares the fate of the shepherds, but adds a note concerning the future care of the sheep. Taken as a whole, the prophet's words address: (i) the fate of the delinquent shepherds; (ii) the action of a new shepherd; (iii) the future of the sheep.

(i) *The fate of the delinquent shepherds* (verses 2–10). The condemnation of the shepherds for failure in their duty is comprehensive and devastating in its scope. They fed themselves well, but not their sheep. Indeed, though they did not lift a finger in fulfilling their pastoral duties, they knew how to profit from their position, dining on roast lamb and dressed in sheepskin jackets! And as they relaxed in the privileges of their position, the state of their flocks steadily declined. The sick and crippled sheep were not attended to, strays were left to wander, vulnerable to every beast of prey that sought a meal. Indeed, the shepherds had ceased to be shepherds; they had inherited flocks, they lived off the benefits of their inheritance, but they had never learned to act like shepherds and assume the burdens of responsibility. Transforming the pastoral metaphor, the rulers of Israel had profited from their positions of leadership, but had never assumed the responsibilities of leadership. They were like parasites in the fleeces of their flock, not leaders and guardians of their people.

This denunciation of the shepherds is sobering in that it evokes from all who have pastoral responsibilities an act of self-examination. To be a pastor, whether lay or clerical, is to have responsibility for other people; the responsibilities, in turn, bring with them certain rights and privileges. The pastoral role involves caring for others, not striving for oneself. But the prophetic denunciation reveals the capacity within each of us to fail as a pastor. It is a failure when one accepts the rights and privileges, but ignores the responsibilities. It is failure when one cares for one's self, but ignores the welfare of those entrusted to our care. And, as was true of the watchman's role (Chapter 33), failure as a shepherd leads not only to personal disaster, but results in terrible grief amongst the members of the flock. But perhaps worst of all is the divine declaration addressed to the delinquent pastors: "Behold, I am against the shepherds" (verse 10).

(ii) *The action of a new shepherd* (verses 11–16). When Ezekiel goes on to describe God as assuming the role of the Good Shepherd, he is not providing a new insight concerning God in the context of the Old Testament. One of the oldest titles of God in the Hebrew tradition was "Shepherd" (Gen. 49:24) and Psalm 23, amongst others, provides insight on Israel's understanding of God as a shepherd. Yet the prophet is saying something new, despite the familiarity of the notion of the Divine Shepherd in Hebrew theology. Throughout Israel's history, God had delegated the role of shepherd to kings and leaders amongst his people; they had been privileged to serve as under-shepherds, responsible to the Good Shepherd. In the failure of the under-shepherds, Ezekiel declares, God would act once again directly as Israel's shepherd.

When these verses are read in the light of the New Testament, one begins to perceive the way in which Jesus' conception of his ministry was shaped in part by the writings of Ezekiel. "I am the Good Shepherd," Jesus said (John 10:11); he was not merely describing a pastoral dimension to his ministry, but indicating, for those who could discern it, that his ministry was the unfolding of the divine shepherdship anticipated by Ezekiel. And the acts of Jesus were quite different from those of the delinquent shepherds. Whereas they had used the flock for the enrichment of their own lives, Jesus was the Good Shepherd who laid down his life for the sheep.

(iii) *The future of the sheep*. The verses describing the Good Shepherd also contain the promise of a new future for the sheep. They had been exploited, deserted, and exposed to terrible dangers under their former shepherds. In the new situation anticipated by the prophet, there would be a total change of circumstances: "I will feed them in justice," God declares (verse 16). This part of the prophet's declaration would have been a source of hope, not only to the survivors in Jerusalem, but also to Ezekiel's companions in exile.

Indeed, when all is said and done, it is the sheep that matter more than the shepherds. If there were no sheep, there would be no shepherds; if there were no people, there could be no rulers. And God's most fundamental concern, as expressed by the prophet, was for the people themselves. The words contain the terrors of judgment (verse 10), but the judgment of the shepherds is rooted in profound pastoral concern for the sheep. Thus the prophet's anticipation of a better future for his people is not simply a conviction that eventually justice would be done; it was also an insight into the love of God. The entire pastoral metaphor presupposes God's care and love. No shepherd can function without participating in that love; no sheep can live without experiencing that love. At long last the positive elements in Ezekiel's teaching are beginning to predominate.

THE FLOCK AND ITS FUTURE

Ezekiel 34:17–31

[17]"As for you, my flock, thus says the Lord God: Behold, I judge between sheep and sheep, rams and he-goats. [18]Is it not enough for you to feed on the good pasture, that you must tread down with your feet the rest of your pasture; and to drink of clear water, that you must foul the rest with your feet? [19]And must my sheep eat what you have trodden with your feet, and drink what you have fouled with your feet?

²⁰"Therefore, thus says the Lord God to them: Behold, I, I myself will judge between the fat sheep and the lean sheep. ²¹Because you push with side and shoulder, and thrust at all the weak with your horns, till you have scattered them abroad, ²²I will save my flock, they shall no longer be a prey; and I will judge between sheep and sheep. ²³And I will set up over them one shepherd, my servant David, and he shall feed them: he shall feed them and be their shepherd. ²⁴And I, the Lord, will be their God, and my servant David shall be prince among them; I, the Lord, have spoken.

²⁵"I will make with them a covenant of peace and banish wild beasts from the land, so that they may dwell securely in the wilderness and sleep in the woods. ²⁶And I will make them and the places round about my hill a blessing; and I will send down the showers in their season; they shall be showers of blessing. ²⁷And the trees of the field shall yield their fruit, and the earth shall yield its increase, and they shall be secure in their land; and they shall know that I am the Lord, when I break the bars of their yoke, and deliver them from the hand of those who enslaved them. ²⁸They shall no more be a prey to the nations, nor shall the beasts of the land devour them; they shall dwell securely, and none shall make them afraid. ²⁹And I will provide for them prosperous plantations so that they shall no more be consumed with hunger in the land, and no longer suffer the reproach of the nations. ³⁰And they shall know that I, the Lord their God, am with them, and that they, the house of Israel, are my people, says the Lord God. ³¹And you are my sheep, the sheep of my pasture, and I am your God, says the Lord God."

Although Chapter 34 is dominated in its entirety by the pastoral metaphor of the shepherd, the prophet's focus swings back and forth like a pendulum between the immediate crisis through which he lived, and the more distant future for which he hoped. Ezekiel began with a declaration of judgment against the shepherds, or rulers (verses 1–10), but then turned to a time when God would act as the Good Shepherd directly (verses 11–16). Now he turns back to the present, and describes the judgment of the sheep (verses 17–22), but that in turn moves his attention forward to the future and the full restoration of God's people (verses 23–31).

The swinging pendulum of the prophet's theme is an illustration in part of the immense struggle of faith being engaged within him. The proclamation of judgment at the time of Jerusalem's collapse is a pointer to what would be the future: there would be no bright future for the chosen people, who had failed so miserably in their calling. On the other hand, Ezekiel was one who knew God with extraordinary intimacy, having sensed his glory in the great vision with which his ministry began. And knowing God so deeply, he knows there yet remains a future for God's people. It is distant and elusive, not easily described in human speech, as this and other passages demonstrate. But it is a real and positive future, nevertheless; as Ezekiel declares these words to his companions, he is providing a gleam of hope to those who have come to the end of their road.

(i) *The judging of the flock* (verses 17–22). The shepherds or rulers have already been judged for their failure in pastoral responsibility, but the sheep themselves were not entirely free from blame. There were strong and weak beasts, and the stronger ones had exploited the weak for personal advantage. (*Note:* the judgment was between strong and weak animals, between good and evil, not between sheep and goats; flocks in the ancient world contained both sheep and goats, which is the point of the description in verse 17.)

The metaphorical development of the exploitation is striking in the manner in which it brings out the perversity in the human exercise of strength. The strong animals not only pushed forward to graze on the best grass but, when they had eaten their fill, they trampled on the rest to render it inedible for the weaker sheep. They pushed forward to drink the fresh water, but then stirred up the mud to make it undrinkable for their companions. It was not enough for them to partake first of the good things in life; they also destroyed those good things, so that their companions could not participate in them. In the metaphor the prophet is describing the rich and powerful segment of Hebrew society that was always grasping for itself, and never concerned for the welfare of its weaker neighbours.

The prophet's picturesque metaphor brings out starkly the latent perversity of human nature. First, there is greed. We push and shove, using all our strength to thrust aside our fellow human beings in order to achieve our goal. And having achieved the first goal, the discovery of power leads to a peculiar twist. We got what we wanted because we were strong, but the same strength could stop the weak from getting what they want; so, having partaken to the full, we destroy what remains to deny it to others. Such behaviour can be seen sometimes amongst children in their less likeable moods. It is equally prevalent amongst adults; but as with most adult evils, it is commonly cloaked with sophisticated rationalisations. But however well cloaked, our greed and perversity cannot remain hidden forever: "I myself will judge," says the Lord (verse 20).

(ii) *The future of the flock* (verses 23–31). The prophet declares that God would establish a new shepherd to take care of the flock, "my servant David" (verse 23). For a number of reasons, the statement is difficult to interpret. (a) Earlier in the chapter, the prophet had declared that God himself would assume the role of shepherd; now, he seems to indicate that the role would be passed to another. (b) The expression "my servant David" is not entirely clear. It should probably not be interpreted literally; the prophet does not anticipate a resurrection of the long-dead former king of Israel.

For all the difficulties, the prophet's statement clearly refers to the future, and presumably the distant future. A new covenant is anticipated (verse 25), which gives a clue to the significance of *David*; as, in David's time, an eternal covenant had been established, so too in the future that eternal covenant would be both renewed and established. It would be renewed in the sense that the former covenant with David was eternal; it would be established in the sense that the current covenant, in its temporal aspects at least, had clearly been terminated in the collapse of Jerusalem.

Ezekiel's prophecy of the future is difficult to interpret in detail, in part because its language is a continuation of the pastoral metaphor of the chapter as a whole. As in old Israel, David was a shepherd before he had become king, so in the future kingdom, David's successor would be a shepherd-king. The kingdom itself is described in terms of pastoral security; its citizens would be protected and have every provision made for their needs. And the shepherd called David is clearly closely related to God himself in this coming peaceful kingdom, for the prophecy ends: "You are my sheep, the sheep of my pasture, and I am your God, says the Lord God" (verse 31).

It is possible to read this chapter from a Christian perspective, as has already been indicated; Jesus, the Davidic Messiah, was the Good Shepherd, through whom a new covenant and new kingdom would be established. For Ezekiel's companions in exile the message would have been full of hope, but lacking nevertheless in clarity and sharpness of detail. The hope, though, was fundamental to their survival. As exiles, they were as sheep without a shepherd. Following the defeat of Jerusalem, they were partners to a covenant that had come to an end. They were the servants of a king who no longer ruled. They were vulnerable in an evil world, with no protector. And to these hapless folk the prophet's words brought an element of good cheer. They could not fully understand it but, though they themselves might not live long enough to see it, there remained nevertheless a future, one in which the love and care of God would be revealed once again to mankind.

THE DESOLATION OF MOUNT SEIR

Ezekiel 35:1–15

[1]The word of the Lord came to me: [2]"Son of man, set your face against Mount Seir, and prophesy against it, [3]and say to it, Thus says the Lord God: Behold, I am against you, Mount Seir, and I will stretch out my hand against you, and I will make you a desolation and a waste. [4]I will lay your cities waste, and you shall become a desolation; and you shall know that I am the Lord. [5]Because you cherished perpetual enmity, and gave over the people of Israel to the power of the sword at the time of their calamity, at the time of their final punishment; [6]therefore, as I

live, says the Lord God, I will prepare you for blood, and blood shall pursue you; because you are guilty of blood, therefore blood shall pursue you. ⁷I will make Mount Seir a waste and a desolation; and I will cut off from it all who come and go. ⁸And I will fill your mountains with the slain; on your hills and in your valleys and in all your ravines those slain with the sword shall fall. ⁹I will make you a perpetual desolation, and your cities shall not be inhabited. Then you will know that I am the Lord.

¹⁰"Because you said, 'These two nations and these two countries shall be mine, and we will take possession of them,'—although the Lord was there—¹¹therefore, as I live, says the Lord God, I will deal with you according to the anger and envy which you showed because of your hatred against them; and I will make myself known among you, when I judge you. ¹²And you shall know that I, the Lord, have heard all the revilings which you uttered against the mountains of Israel, saying, 'They are laid desolate, they are given us to devour.' ¹³And you magnified yourselves against me with your mouth, and multiplied your words against me; I heard it. ¹⁴Thus says the Lord God: For the rejoicing of the whole earth I will make you desolate. ¹⁵As you rejoiced over the inheritance of the house of Israel, because it was desolate, so I will deal with you; you shall be desolate, Mount Seir, and all Edom, all of it. Then they will know that I am the Lord."

This prophecy of doom, addressed to Mount Seir, seems at first strange in its context. An earlier portion of Ezekiel's book had been devoted exclusively to prophecies against foreign nations (Chapters 25–32); Chapter 35, though, belongs to that part of Ezekiel's ministry following the news of the defeat of Jerusalem, when the prophet's attention turned toward the future of the chosen people. But the oracle of doom to Mount Seir must be read in conjunction with the following passage (36:1–15), addressed to the mountains of Israel. The two passages together, both addressed poetically to "mountains", indicate God's future activities on behalf of his people and the land.

Mount Seir is another name for the nation called Edom, which has already been the subject of one of the prophet's short oracles (25:12–14). Edom was located to the south-east of the Dead Sea, on the eastern flanks of the Arabah; nowadays it is a part of the territory of the kingdom of Jordan. According to Hebrew tradition, the land was populated by the descendants of Esau, Jacob's brother, but despite this element of common ancestry there had been a long history of enmity between the citizens of Israel (Judah) and Edom.

Although the reason for Ezekiel's prophecy against Mount Seir/Edom at this point in his ministry remains uncertain, one may speculate that it was prompted by news that reached the prophet in exile. Indeed, the news may have been brought by the same refugee who told of Jerusalem's defeat. The substance of that news would have concerned Edom's complicity in Judah's collapse. They conspired with the Babylonian invaders in bringing about the defeat. And afterwards, when Judah lay in ruins, they saw an opportunity for themselves. The territory that formerly belonged to Judah now seemed to be free for the taking; the Edomites began to seize the land for themselves.

The substance of the prophecy against Mount Seir falls into three basic parts. (a) It begins with a declaration of God's enmity against Edom and the coming judgment of the nation (verses 1–4). The cities of the land, apparently secure in the mountainous territory of Seir from all external attack, would be made desolate, a wasteland on the border of the great desert that extended to the east. (b) There follows the first reason for Edom's coming judgment: they had "cherished perpetual enmity" against the chosen people, even at the time of their greatest calamity (verses 5–9). For generations, the two neighbouring states had squabbled over petty matters, but now in Judah's crisis, Edom had seized the opportunity to dispose of its neighbour once and for all. And in so doing, they were guilty of murder ("blood", verse 6). As Edom had been responsible in part for the slaughter of so many people, it would experience divine judgment in the slaughter of its own citizens. (c) A second reason is stated for Edom's coming judgment: they wanted Judah's collapse, so that they could take possession of a vacant land and make it their own (verses 10–15). Their hatred was mixed with envy, and they saw in Judah's demise an opportunity to add the rich lands of Israel and Judah to their own inventory of rather barren land to the east of the Arabah.

As is so often the case in the Old Testament, the description of evil in the ancient world seems to mirror accurately the modern world. Mount Seir was a land that had cultivated hatred from one generation to the next; no doubt it was in part justified, based on the memories of acts of injustice done against it in former centuries by its neighbour, Judah. But whatever the reasons, a nation that stores its hatred for another, cultivating it from one generation to another, is harbouring a rot within its soul. And Edom has its modern counterparts; there are still nations whose history is one of hatred for a neighbour. There are always reasons for the hatred, well-grounded in past injustices done to it by the neighbour. But a history of hatred, taught to children so that it might flourish in a coming generation, is ultimately a curse on any nation; like a cancer, it spreads through the body of the nation as a whole, bringing closer the day of its own demise. Nations, no less than individuals, need to learn the art of forgiveness, which alone can cut out the cancer in the body of the nation.

Pure hatred is a rare emotion; Edom's hatred was mixed with envy, in effect greed to grasp the possessions that belonged once to its neighbour. And hatred and greed mixed together are a dangerous recipe, creating within a nation or individual a terribly destructive force. There can be no full human life when these forces of evil remain rampant. At the heart of human living must be the recognition that we are loved by God and are required to love; we cannot love if hate abounds. And as we learn of the love of God, we discover above all that it is a self-giving love; love and greed cannot flourish together. Thus, whether as individuals or as the members of a nation, we must learn that hatred and greed can only be destroyed from our midst if love abounds. If they are not destroyed then, like Mount Seir, we shall hear the terrible divine words: "I am against you" (verse 3).

HOPE FOR THE MOUNTAINS OF ISRAEL

Ezekiel 36:1–15

[1]"And you, son of man, prophesy to the mountains of Israel, and say,

O mountains of Israel, hear the word of the Lord. [2]Thus says the Lord God: Because the enemy said of you, 'Aha!' and, 'The ancient heights have become our possession,' [3]therefore prophesy, and say, Thus says the Lord God: Because, yea, because they made you desolate, and crushed you from all sides, so that you became the possession of the rest of the nations, and you became the talk and evil gossip of the people; [4]therefore, O mountains of Israel, hear the word of the Lord God: Thus says the Lord God to the mountains and the hills, the ravines and the valleys, the desolate wastes and the deserted cities, which have become a prey and derision to the rest of the nations round about; [5]therefore thus says the Lord God: I speak in my hot jealousy against the rest of the nations, and against all Edom, who gave my land to themselves as a possession with wholehearted joy and utter contempt, that they might possess it and plunder it. [6]Therefore prophesy concerning the land of Israel, and say to the mountains and hills, to the ravines and valleys, Thus says the Lord God: Behold, I speak in my jealous wrath, because you have suffered the reproach of the nations; [7]therefore thus says the Lord God: I swear that the nations that are round about you shall themselves suffer reproach.

[8]"But you, O mountains of Israel, shall shoot forth your branches, and yield your fruit to my people Israel; for they will soon come home. [9]For, behold, I am for you, and I will turn to you, and you shall be tilled and sown; [10]and I will multiply men upon you, the whole house of Israel, all of it; the cities shall be inhabited and the waste places rebuilt; [11]and I will multiply upon you man and beast; and they shall increase and be fruitful; and I will cause you to be inhabited as in your former times, and will do more good to you than ever before. Then you will know that I am the Lord. [12]Yea, I will let men walk upon you, even my people Israel; and they shall possess you, and you shall be their inheritance, and you shall no longer bereave them of children. [13]Thus say the Lord God: Because men say to you, 'You devour men, and you bereave your nation of children,' [14]therefore you shall no longer devour men and no longer bereave your nation of children, says the Lord God; [15]and I will not let you hear any more the reproach of the nations, and you shall no longer bear the disgrace of the peoples and no longer cause your nation to stumble, says the Lord God."

The prophecy of doom addressed to Mount Seir (Chapter 35) is now balanced by this prophecy of hope addressed to Israel's mountains. The two prophecies together vividly contrast God's coming actions with the existing state of world affairs. Edom had survived the recent military disasters, but its future would be one of desolation; Israel's mountains now lay desolate, but for them there remained a bright future. But the prophecy of this passage must also be read in contrast to another of Ezekiel's prophecies. At an earlier point in his ministry the prophet had declared the coming desolation of Israel's mountains (6:1–7); now that the earlier prophecy had been fulfilled, the prophet sees beyond that desolation a new hope for the land of Israel.

The prophecy as such falls into two parts. (a) In a poetic address to the mountains, Ezekiel declares the coming judgment against Edom and all other foreign nations, who had gleefully participated in the first desolation of Israel's land (verses 1–7). The style of this section is somewhat stilted, suggesting to some scholars that an original short prophecy has been edited and expanded, and to others that the passion of the prophet's declaration has contributed to the unevenness of style. (b) The second part describes the new life that would return to the mountains of Israel. The land would once again be cultivated, its cities rebuilt, and its population restored. The post-war chaos of the promised land would eventually disappear, as it was restored to its former prosperity and beauty. This part of the prophecy may refer in part to the anticipated restoration of the land when the exiles returned eventually to their homes. But from the perspective of Ezekiel and his companions, the anticipation of a new future for the land could not be pinned down chronologically; in the larger context, the restoration of Israel's mountains would be just one part of a new work of salvation undertaken by God on behalf of his people.

This prophecy addressed to the mountains has its messages for human beings.

(i) *Beyond judgment, there lies hope.* The prophecy to the mountains in Chapter 6 was one of destruction and ruin; that in Chapter 36 is one of reconstruction and prosperity. The prophecies are separated by time and circumstance. Earlier in time, doom was foretold to a people busily engaged in the construction of their own future, devising evil schemes contrary to the will of

God. Now, later in time, all that has changed; when the people have finally recognised the futility of their ways, a new and God-given future can be revealed to them.

The experience of judgment is always painful, not least because we may perceive in the midst of it the way in which we have been instrumental in precipitating our own ruin. But God's word of judgment is not his last word. Beyond the desolation of the mountains (Chapter 6), there was a time of restoration (Chapter 36). And beyond the disasters of our lives, which we bring about as a consequence of our own folly, there lies also the possibility of restoration. As the wasteland may be replanted and newly populated, so too may human lives be re-established and lived with new zest. This truth was perceived by the prophet in a time of extreme darkness, when all the evidence militated against any declaration of hope. It was only possible because of Ezekiel's profound perception that, in the end, it was God's mercy and love that would triumph.

(ii) *Every person needs a home.* It is difficult for us sometimes to perceive the centrality of the land, with its mountains, in the minds of the Hebrews. Centuries before the life of the prophet, refugees in the wilderness had anticipated a land of their own. Their posterity had possessed the land and flourished in it for a while. Now, in Ezekiel's century, the people had lost their land; they could remember it as it used to be, but they knew it lay in desolation. And yet, the prophet declared, for all the disasters of their day, the land was still in a peculiar way the possession of God. Despite the encroachments of the Edomites, it would remain God's possession until one day it was restored to beauty and prosperity. And that secure knowledge that the land had a future would have been a source of strength to exiled Israelites; they might live far from its precious soil, but they would know the land was there. And over countless generations, down to the present century, the land has retained its significance to the Jewish people. It is a moving sight to see a Jew, escaped perhaps from a far nation in which he has lived in exile, arrive in Israel and kneel down and kiss the soil. The land is still there. And the same phenomenon may be seen among various peoples and nations. I know of Canadians in Nova Scotia who speak Gaelic and play the pipes; they know Scotland intimately, though they have never set foot on its soil. Yet they know the land is there, and they follow its fortunes with fascination, waiting patiently for the day when they can go and walk on the land from which their forefathers came.

Within most human beings there is a powerful identification with a particular land or place. And yet, from the Christian perspective, we must balance this recognition of the importance of land with the recognition that in this world we have no continuing city. God has prepared a city for those persons of faith, who recognise that life in this world is in so many ways a pilgrimage (Heb. 11:13–16). Our task is not to ignore this world, and dream only of the city that lies beyond; but there *is* another city beyond, and we can take strength from the knowledge of its existence to live life now to the full in the land in which God has placed us.

A NEW HEART AND A NEW SPIRIT

Ezekiel 36:16–38

[16]The word of the Lord came to me: [17]"Son of man, when the house of Israel dwelt in their own land, they defiled it by their ways and their doings; their conduct before me was like the uncleanness of a woman in her impurity. [18]So I poured out my wrath upon them for the blood which they had shed in the land, for the idols with which they had defiled it. [19]I scattered them among the nations, and they were dispersed through the countries; in accordance with their conduct and their deeds I judged them. [20]But when they came to the nations, wherever they came, they profaned my holy name, in that men said of them, 'These are the people of the Lord, and yet they had to go out of his land.' [21]But I had concern for my holy name, which the house of Israel caused to be profaned among the nations to which they came.

[22]"Therefore say to the house of Israel, Thus says the Lord God: It is not for your sake, O house of Israel, that I am about to act, but for the sake of my holy name, which you have profaned among the nations to which you came. [23]And I will vindicate the holiness of my great name, which has been profaned among the nations, and which you have

profaned among them; and the nations will know that I am the Lord, says the Lord God, when through you I vindicate my holiness before their eyes. ²⁴For I will take you from the nations, and gather you from all the countries, and bring you into your own land. ²⁵I will sprinkle clean water upon you, and you shall be clean from all your uncleannesses, and from all your idols I will cleanse you. ²⁶A new heart I will give you, and a new spirit I will put within you; and I will take out of your flesh the heart of stone and give you a heart of flesh. ²⁷And I will put my spirit within you, and cause you to walk in my statutes and be careful to observe my ordinances. ²⁸You shall dwell in the land which I gave to your fathers; and you shall be my people, and I will be your God. ²⁹And I will deliver you from all your uncleannesses; and I will summon the grain and make it abundant and lay no famine upon you. ³⁰I will make the fruit of the tree and the increase of the field abundant, that you may never again suffer the disgrace of famine among the nations. ³¹Then you will remember your evil ways, and your deeds that were not good; and you will loathe yourselves for your iniquities and your abominable deeds. ³²It is not for your sake that I will act, says the Lord God; let that be known to you. Be ashamed and confounded for your ways, O house of Israel.

³³Thus says the Lord God: On the day that I cleanse you from all your iniquities, I will cause the cities to be inhabited, and the waste places shall be rebuilt. ³⁴And the land that was desolate shall be tilled, instead of being the desolation that it was in the sight of all who passed by. ³⁵And they will say, 'This land that was desolate has become like the garden of Eden; and the waste and desolate and ruined cities are now inhabited and fortified.' ³⁶Then the nations that are left round about you shall know that I, the Lord, have rebuilt the ruined places, and replanted that which was desolate; I, the Lord, have spoken, and I will do it.

³⁷"Thus says the Lord God: This also I will let the house of Israel ask me to do for them: to increase their men like a flock. ³⁸Like the flock for sacrifices, like the flock at Jerusalem during her appointed feasts, so shall the waste cities be filled with flocks of men. Then they will know that I am the Lord."

As Ezekiel in this chapter continues to address his companions in exile, his attention is still directed to the future, and the new work that God would undertake amongst his chosen people. In many ways these verses contain the very essence of Ezekiel's theology, indicating not only what God would do, but also the reasons for his future actions.

The passage begins with a recollection of the past. Despite all their privileges, the people had abused the land that God had given them and acted sinfully in it; and so they had experienced divine judgment. The judgment of God, though fully deserved, had resulted in a negative consequence: the citizens of other nations had observed only that the Israelites had been given a land, but had failed to keep it. Thus, the whole point of election had failed; the people, who had been called to form a special nation in the world of human nations, had failed. Israel, which should have demonstrated to all mankind the holiness of the one true God, had revealed rather to the blurred sight of other nations only the picture of an inadequate national deity.

Thus God determined to act further, in order that his original purpose in the election of Israel might be fulfilled. He would act again, not for Israel's sake, for they had demonstrated their unworthiness, but for the "sake of his holy name" (verse 22); that is, his further actions would demonstrate the holiness of God to all mankind. God's new action would involve the radical transformation of his people. Whereas in the past they had been unclean, he would sprinkle fresh water on them and make them clean (verse 25). Whereas in the past they had been hard-hearted, unable to discern the truth and maintain the faith, he would give them a new living heart. The old spirit of evil and disobedience would be replaced by a new spirit, pliable to the will of God (verses 26–27).

What is particularly striking about this portion of Ezekiel's prophecy is the manner in which its focus is primarily upon the initiative of God, rather than the human response of the people. As the people had failed so miserably to respond to God and fulfil their purpose in the world, there would have to be radical surgery: the old stony hearts would be replaced with new living hearts and the old stubborn spirits replaced with God's life-giving spirit. Only then would the land be restored and become like the garden of Eden (verse 35). And only then would the chosen people form such a kingdom that all the nations of the world would perceive the holy hand of God at work in their midst.

Ezekiel, in his theology, has undertaken a radical reappraisal of the entire nature of Israel's covenant with God, and the way in which that covenant would achieve God's purposes in the world as a whole. When the covenant had first been formed at Mount Sinai, it had been for the purpose of establishing Israel as a nation; the covenant was in effect Israel's constitution, its Magna Carta. The nation was to have been a "kingdom of priests and a holy nation" (Exod. 19:6), demonstrating to all the world's peoples the holiness of the one true God. But Israel had failed in its calling, and even in judgment it had given to the world a false notion of the nature of God. And so Ezekiel perceives a new kind of covenant. The kingdom of God would no longer be in the form of a nation state, for the state of the chosen people had been singularly unsuccessful in its task of revealing God's righteousness to the world. Rather, God's new covenant would involve the radical, inner transformation of human beings. Those who received a new heart and a new spirit from God would reveal to the world God's true nature.

While Ezekiel's prophecy is directed to Israel, it has implications nevertheless for the gentile world. To be a Christian is to have received from God a new heart and a new spirit; it is to have received that radical spiritual surgery which will enable us to live our lives fully to the glory of God. And for the new covenant, which is the Christian faith, this transformation of heart and spirit is the prerequisite of membership. As, in Ezekiel's prophecy, the transformation of heart and spirit was preceded by the symbolic sprinkling of fresh water, so in Christianity the water of baptism symbolises the transformation of heart and spirit.

But for us, as for Israel, one of the hardest lessons to learn is that all this work of God is not for our sake alone, but for "the sake of his name". Through Israel and through the Church, God works to reveal his nature and character to all mankind. And if the heart and spirit have been truly transformed, it is impossible to live for oneself alone. It is hard to grasp in its fulness, but somehow our lives are to be the avenues through which God's holiness and will are made known to all the world.

THE VALLEY OF THE DRY BONES

Ezekiel 37:1–14

¹The hand of the Lord was upon me, and he brought me out by the Spirit of the Lord, and set me down in the midst of the valley; it was full of bones. ²And he led me round among them; and behold, there were very many upon the valley; and lo, they were very dry. ³And he said to me, "Son of man, can these bones live?" And I answered, "O Lord God, thou knowest." ⁴Again he said to me, "Prophesy to these bones, and say to them, O dry bones, hear the word of the Lord. ⁵Thus says the Lord God to these bones: Behold, I will cause breath to enter you, and you shall live. ⁶And I will lay sinews upon you, and will cause flesh to come upon you, and cover you with skin, and put breath in you, and you shall live; and you shall know that I am the Lord."

⁷So I prophesied as I was commanded; and as I prophesied, there was a noise, and behold, a rattling; and the bones came together, bone to its bone. ⁸And as I looked, there were sinews on them, and flesh had come upon them, and skin had covered them; but there was no breath in them. ⁹Then he said to me, "Prophesy to the breath, prophesy, son of man, and say to the breath, Thus says the Lord God: Come from the four winds, O breath, and breathe upon these slain, that they may live." ¹⁰So I prophesied as he commanded me, and the breath came into them, and they lived, and stood upon their feet, an exceedingly great host.

¹¹Then he said to me, "Son of man, these bones are the whole house of Israel. Behold, they say, 'Our bones are dried up, and our hope is lost; we are clean cut off.' ¹²Therefore prophesy, and say to them, Thus says the Lord God: Behold, I will open your graves, and raise you from your graves, O my people; and I will bring you home into the land of Israel. ¹³And you shall know that I am the Lord, when I open your graves, and raise you from your graves, O my people. ¹⁴And I will put my Spirit within you, and you shall live, and I will place you in your own land; then you shall know that I, the Lord, have spoken, and I have done it, says the Lord."

Ezekiel once again describes the substance of a dramatic vision in order to convey to his companions the prophetic word of God. We are not informed of the date of this vision, though the despair experienced by his fellow exiles (verse 11) indicates that it must have taken place shortly after the fall of Jerusalem, when his companions felt that they were as dead men with no future. As with his previous experience of vision, Ezekiel felt as if he were bodily transported away from his home in exile and set down in another place, a valley.

The vision itself is striking with respect both to its setting and the action undertaken. The valley was full of human bones, scattered haphazardly over its desert floor; the bones were extremely dry, as if they had baked in the sun for many months. The scene was one of death, as if a great regiment of human beings had been lost in a desert and died from lack of food and water. As Ezekiel surveyed this terrible scene, a question was put to him by God: "Can these bones live?" The prophet's reply should probably be paraphrased: "You know the answer to that. Of course they can't live!" And then God addressed Ezekiel again and told him, in effect, to preach to the bones. As an experienced prophet, Ezekiel must have felt many times in the past that he was preaching to the dead, but never so dramatically as on this occasion; and when he began to declare God's word, the results were equally startling. He preached to the bones, declaring that God would restore them to life, and even as he spoke, his sermon was accompanied by a cacophany of clanking as the dead bones began to come together. Then, before the prophet's eyes, the reconstructed skeletons were fitted with sinew and muscles and clothed with skin. They now looked marvellous, their skeletal appearance removed, but still they were dead. Again, the prophet was commanded to speak; addressing the four winds, he invited the spirit (RSV "breath") of God to enter the reconstituted bodies and give them life. As he spoke, life was imparted: a great host of living persons stood up in the valley where formerly only corpses had been.

After the description of the vision, an interpretation is provided (verses 11–14). It is important to read the interpretation carefully, for the nature of the vision is such that, if we are not careful, we will impose upon it a meaning not intended by the author. The people in exile had complained, "Our bones are dried up, and our hope is lost" (verse 11). The collapse of

Jerusalem had seemed to drive the nails into the coffin that was their exile; there was no more hope of a return and new life in their homeland. But again the prophet was commanded to speak: the graves of exile would be opened (verse 13) and the people would return to their homeland with the gift of new life. The prophecy, in other words, is not concerned with any theology of resurrection from the dead, an insight which is never clearly attained in the Old Testament period; rather, its focus is on the restoration of moribund exiles to new life in their original homeland.

The prophecy provides, nevertheless, an extraordinary insight into the life-giving capacity of God. To a people whose life seemed to be over, a declaration of new life was made. To those whose existence had become a form of living death, new horizons of hope were revealed.

We must perceive the contemporary significance of the passage in a broader context than that of the theology of individual resurrection. The valley of dry bones typifies the human race as a whole, exiled from God their Creator, and therefore missing that fulness of life which God planned for every creature. And the proclamation of the prophet becomes the proclamation of the gospel, that there may be a fulness of life for all mankind in a new land. For the valley is like the world as a whole, populated by those who live (as did the exiles), but in truth have no life. And the message of hope to those in exile may become a message of hope to all: it is that the Spirit of God imparts fulness of life to all creatures.

A STORY OF TWO STICKS

Ezekiel 37:15–28

¹⁵The word of the Lord came to me: ¹⁶"Son of man, take a stick and write on it, 'For Judah, and the children of Israel associated with him'; then take another stick and write upon it, 'For Joseph (the stick of Ephraim) and all the house of Israel associated with him'; ¹⁷and join them together into one stick, that they may become one in your hand. ¹⁸And when your people say to you, 'Will you not show us what you

mean by these?' [19]say to them, Thus says the Lord God: Behold, I am about to take the stick of Joseph (which is in the hand of Ephraim) and the tribes of Israel associated with him; and I will join with it the stick of Judah, and make them one stick, that they may be one in my hand. [20]When the sticks on which you write are in your hand before their eyes, [21]then say to them, Thus says the Lord God: Behold, I will take the people of Israel from the nations among which they have gone, and will gather them from all sides, and bring them to their own land: [22]and I will make them one nation in the land, upon the mountains of Israel; and one king shall be king over them all; and they shall be no longer two nations, and no longer divided into two kingdoms. [23]They shall not defile themselves any more with their idols and their detestable things, or with any of their transgressions; but I will save them from all the backslidings in which they have sinned, and will cleanse them; and they shall be my people, and I will be their God.

[24]"My servant David shall be king over them; and they shall all have one shepherd. They shall follow my ordinances and be careful to observe my statutes. [25]They shall dwell in the land where your fathers dwelt that I gave to my servant Jacob; they and their children and their children's children shall dwell there for ever; and David my servant shall be their prince for ever. [26]I will make a covenant of peace with them; it shall be an everlasting covenant with them; and I will bless them and multiply them, and will set my sanctuary in the midst of them for evermore. [27]My dwelling place shall be with them; and I will be their God, and they shall be my people. [28]Then the nations will know that I the Lord sanctify Israel, when my sanctuary is in the midst of them for evermore."

Yet again, the prophet is instructed to enact a parable in the presence of his people; the story, and its visible enactment, would communicate forcefully to the audience the substance of God's message to those in exile.

Ezekiel was to take two sticks and write on each of them. The inscription on one stick would indicate that it represented the southern kingdom of Judah; that on the other stick ("For Joseph") would associate it with the northern kingdom of Israel, which had ceased to exist as an independent state more than a hundred years before Ezekiel's time. Then, placing the two sticks end to end, the prophet was to grasp them with one hand; as he held up the sticks for his audience to see, they would appear to be a single stick, the join between them covered by the grasping hand. The enacted part of the story was designed to elicit from the audience a question concerning the meaning of the actions (verse 18), and an answer was to be given.

God would take the two kingdoms of his chosen people, both of which had ceased to exist as free kingdoms; grasped by the divine hand, the two kingdoms would become one again, as they had been in the far-off time of King David. In order to achieve this reunification, God would bring together his people from the various lands of exile to which they had been scattered and resettle them in the promised land. The joining of the two nations would be marked by the appointment of a single king, as had been the case in the past. And all the idols and evils that had culminated in the split of the former united kingdom would be removed; the unity of the new kingdom would survive on the basis of a cleansing of the people undertaken by God (verse 23). The king of this united people would be a new David; their covenant would be a covenant of peace. And in the midst of the people would be God's sanctuary, representing the divine presence and purifying power.

This oracle embodies many of the difficulties in interpreting the concluding chapters of Ezekiel's book, but also illuminates still further the nature of God in his dealings with his people.

(i) It is difficult to know how to apply or interpret the oracle. The northern kingdom no longer existed, and many of its peoples had been scattered and long absorbed by other cultures. How could it be restored to the land? Recognising the mystery, several cults and sects in recent centuries have sought to identify themselves with the lost tribes of Israel, and thus find a place in prophecy. But it is safer to recognise the necessary element of mystery involved in any language addressing the future. The main thrust of the prophecy is that *all* of God's people would somehow participate in the future restoration; how this could be is not known, yet it is the essence of the prophet's affirmation.

(ii) It is clear, with the benefit of hindsight, that the prophecy concerns a distant future. The preceding passage, concerning the dry bones, could be interpreted simply in terms of exiles returning to their homeland. But this oracle moves out of the realm of history, as we commonly understand it, and anticipates a future time in which God would bring a new kind of reality into being. While the precise significance of each part of the prophecy may elude us, the broad thrust is clear: God had not forgotten his people and had determined their restoration.

(iii) One of the capacities of God is vividly illustrated in this story; it is the ability to create oneness where formerly that unity had been fractured. The human tendency of evil always precipitates brokenness and segregation amongst human beings; it is only the firm hand of God that can create unity out of the fragments of human society.

(iv) The oracle had a twist in it for those who heard it first. Those in exile, who had recently learned of the defeat of their homeland, were immensely concerned about themselves and their own future. Long since, they had ceased to wonder whether or not there was a future for their relatives in the northern kingdom, which had been defeated in war in 722 B.C. But where human memory ceases, often through selfish lack of concern for others, the divine memory is still at work. All God's people were important to him, whether from Joseph or Judah; all would eventually share in this salvation.

It is good to be reminded, from the later perspective of Christian theology, that the divine will for salvation extends to all mankind. For there is within us a deeply selfish tendency, commonly cloaked in various kinds of piety, that would limit the grace of God to a few. Ezekiel's companions, concerned only about their own plight and future, were reminded that God's goodness extended beyond themselves to include others. So should we, and as God's new people, we should particularly here think of his old people, Israel.

PROPHECIES CONCERNING GOG

Ezekiel 38:1-9

[1]The word of the Lord came to me: [2]"Son of man, set your face toward

Gog, of the land of Magog, the chief prince of Meshech and Tubal, and prophesy against him ³and say, Thus says the Lord God: Behold, I am against you, O Gog, chief prince of Meshech and Tubal; ⁴and I will turn you about, and put hooks into your jaws, and I will bring you forth, and all your army, horses and horsemen, all of them clothed in full armour, a great company, all of them with buckler and shield, wielding swords; ⁵Persia, Cush, and Put are with them, all of them with shield and helmet; ⁶Gomer and all his hordes; Beth-togarmah from the uttermost parts of the north with all his hordes—many peoples are with you.

⁷"Be ready and keep ready, you and all the hosts that are assembled about you, and be a guard for them. ⁸After many days you will be mustered; in the latter years you will go against the land that is restored from war, the land where people were gathered from many nations upon the mountains of Israel, which had been a continual waste; its people were brought out from the nations and now dwell securely, all of them. ⁹You will advance, coming on like a storm, you will be like a cloud covering the land, you and all your hordes, and many peoples with you."

The series of prophecies concerning Gog, contained in Chapters 38–39, are among the most difficult parts of the entire book of Ezekiel to interpret. For some sober commentators the difficulties have seemed insuperable, and though the individual words and verses have been interpreted, little sense has emerged from the chapters as a whole. Others have freely interpreted the chapters in terms of the events of their own time, little troubled apparently by the extreme improbabilities of their interpretations. But whatever position one takes on these chapters, it is wise at the beginning to recognise the difficulties of interpretation.

(i) The first difficulty is the literary difficulty; it concerns the significance of the present location of these chapters in the Book of Ezekiel.

The forty-eight chapters of the Book of Ezekiel as a whole contain, as we have already seen, a variety of materials from different points in the prophet's life and ministry. From one perspective, Chapters 1–37 contain the principal substance of the book; Chapters 40–48 contain an appendix, in which the chief focus is on God's temple in the restoration of the promised land. The appendix is an elaboration of the reference, which we have just looked at, to God's sanctuary in the closing portion of the book's main part (37:27–28). Between the main portion of the book and its appendix are these two chapters concerning Gog. Is the location significant, or could the chapters equally well have been placed after Chapters 40–48? There is no sure resolution of this difficulty.

(ii) A related difficulty concerns the authorship of these chapters. Are they from Ezekiel, or from one of the prophet's later disciples, or an editor who compiled the prophet's work and saw fit to add these prophecies to them? Again there can be little certainty; my feeling is that they are from Ezekiel, but their subject matter has made it difficult for those responsible for the book's transmission to fit them into the larger mosaic of Ezekiel's thought.

(iii) Are the chapters to be interpreted along the lines employed with respect to the foreign nation oracles (Chapters 25–32), or should they be viewed as a kind of apocalypse, describing the end of the times? From one perspective, they appear similar to foreign nation oracles, and thus rooted in ancient historical realities. Gog may well be Gyges, a 7th century prince of Lydia (which is located in western Asia Minor), but the "land of Magog" (verse 2) is unknown. Meshech and Tubal (verse 2) were territories in Asia Minor, and other places referred to have known geographical locations. Yet, for all the geographical and historical realism of these chapters, they are also characterised by an atmosphere that might be called "apocalyptic geography". Certainly, in New Testament times, the chapters were interpreted in an apocalyptic fashion (see, e.g. Rev. 20:8), indicating that it was then believed that their substance referred to a still distant future.

(iv) The difficulty of knowing whether the chapters should be interpreted historically or apocalyptically is compounded by a further difficulty. Ezekiel's book is striking for the absence of reference to a judgment on Babylon. As has been observed over many centuries, persecution has a striking influence on the art of writing. And if Ezekiel, a captive in Babylon, wanted to write about Babylon, he would certainly not have named it openly. So it is possible that these two chapters contain what might be called subversive writing, necessarily opaque in substance, and probably kept hidden during its early existence. Later, when the captivity lay in the past, the writings could be made public and added to the Book of Ezekiel, but by then the deliberate obscurity of the original manuscript became a veil obscuring the sense from future readers. The key to unlock them, available to Ezekiel's contemporaries, had been lost.

Though there is no simple resolution to the kinds of difficulty summarised above, they do establish certain horizons within which the interpreter may proceed cautiously. Summarised in negative and positive terms, they may be expressed as follows. (a) From a negative perspective, one must be careful not to interpret these prophecies confidently on the assumption that they are simply predictions of the twentieth (or any other) century. It has been popular with some recent interpreters to take Magog to be Russia, Meshech to be Moscow, and Tubal to be Tobolsk. To put it mildly, such a procedure is hazardous; it illuminates more the mysteries and biases of the modern mind than it does the mind of the prophet. (b) From a positive perspective, a recognition of the uncertainties must press the interpreter to seek to identify the prophet's principal message in these chapters. That message, stated broadly, is that God is the master of human history. More precisely, God's purpose in his mastery of history is to make his holiness known to all human nations (38:16, 23 and 39:7, 13). If we grasp that the evil machinations of men and nations fall under the judgment of God, and that God's judgment demonstrates his holiness to all mankind, then we are close to grasping the main thrust of these two curious chapters in the Book of Ezekiel, whether they concern in their details a nation or nations of Ezekiel's own time or are an allegory of the last days.

THE ATTACK OF GOG

Ezekiel 38:10–23

[10]"Thus says the Lord God: On that day thoughts will come into your mind, and you will devise an evil scheme [11]and say, 'I will go up against the land of unwalled villages; I will fall upon the quiet people who dwell securely, all of them dwelling without walls, and having no bars or gates'; [12]to seize spoil and carry off plunder; to assail the waste places which are now inhabited, and the people who were gathered from the nations, who have gotten cattle and goods, who dwell at the centre of the earth. [13]Sheba and Dedan and the merchants of Tarshish and all its villages will say to you, 'Have you come to seize spoil? Have you assembled your hosts to carry off plunder, to carry away silver and gold, to take away cattle and goods, to seize great spoil?'

[14]"Therefore, son of man, prophesy, and say to Gog, Thus says the Lord God: On that day when my people Israel are dwelling securely, you will bestir yourself [15]and come from your place out of the uttermost parts of the north, you and many peoples with you, all of them riding on horses, a great host, a mighty army; [16]you will come up against my people Israel, like a cloud covering the land. In the latter days I will bring you against my land, that the nations may know me, when through you, O Gog, I vindicate my holiness before their eyes.

[17]"Thus says the Lord God: Are you he of whom I spoke in former days by my servants the prophets of Israel, who in those days prophesied for years that I would bring you against them? [18]But on that day, when Gog shall come against the land of Israel, says the Lord God, my wrath will be roused. [19]For in my jealousy and in my blazing wrath I declare, On that day there shall be a great shaking in the land of Israel; [20]the fish of the sea, and the birds of the air, and the beasts of the field, and all creeping things that creep on the ground, and all the men that are upon the face of the earth, shall quake at my presence, and the mountains shall be thrown down, and the cliffs shall fall, and every wall shall tumble to the ground. [21]I will summon every kind of terror against Gog, says the Lord God; every man's sword will be against his brother. [22]With pestilence and bloodshed I will enter into judgment with him; and I will rain upon him and his hordes and the many peoples that are with him, torrential rains and hailstones, fire and brimstone. [23]So I will show my greatness and my holiness and make myself known in the eyes of many nations. Then they will know that I am the Lord."

Gog assembled an enormous army, an alliance drawn from nations at the remotest parts of the known world (verses 2–6). This army, confident in its own strength, conceived a plot (verse 10). The promised land and its restored people offered an immensely tempting military target: the land was unfortified, its cities and villages having no walls and its people living peacefully and quietly going about their business. It would be the easiest thing in the world for Gog and his allies to invade this defenceless land and seize its spoils for themselves. And so the plan was prepared and then put into operation in a military attack.

But when the military campaign is launched, it is foiled by a factor not taken into account by Gog and his armies of evil. Though Israel is defenceless, God is its defender; summoning a great earthquake, he creates havoc in the midst of the invading army (verses 19–22). The earthquake creates such panic that the invaders turn upon themselves and fight each other in the terrible confusion of the day. The military campaign that was to have been so easy turns to an immense defeat. God's people have not raised a hand to defend themselves, but God brings about victory through his mastery of the powers of nature.

As the prophecy unfolds, gradually its theological significance in the context of Ezekiel's thought becomes clearer.

(i) The prophecy addresses a theological dilemma. Already Ezekiel has anticipated and declared a time in which the chosen people would return from their exile and live again in their promised land in peace. But when that time came, the nations of the world would still exist; the power and evil that many of them represented would still be a threat to Israel. It is not impossible that the seeming permanence of the Babylonian Empire started him on this train of thought. Be that as it may, he nevertheless has a vision of a distant world in which in spite of evil God's good would be established. The battle which he describes is thus in essence a final "cosmic" battle in which evil would eventually be eliminated and righteousness be victorious.

Any theological resolution of the persistence of evil is bound to be expressed in terms of conflict, for both literally and metaphorically evil continues to struggle against the survival of goodness in the world. Thus Ezekiel's portrayal of a final and great battle is a projection onto an apocalyptic screen of the battle that has always existed in our world between good and evil. His picture is extracted, as it were, from the framework of all human history and painted now on this single apocalyptic canvas. And the prophet's portrayal of events in these gloomy chapters is, at bottom, an extraordinary statement of faith; ultimately, the world's evil will be conquered by the direct intervention of God in the world's affairs.

(ii) Throughout the scene, the initiative in action lies with God. Gog and his allies thought it was they who schemed the great military plot, but in reality it was the action of God (verse 16). The forces of evil thought they would win a victory over a defenceless nation, but it was God who would conquer them. It is the prophet's conviction, not only that God is the only one who ultimately can conquer evil in the world, but also that such conquest is part of the divine will for the world.

Given the violent character of Ezekiel's world, and indeed the continuing violence of our own century, it is not easy to share the prophet's hope. Yet he declared his hope of the ultimate conquest of evil and establishment of peace in a world at least as bleak as our own. Reaching above the empirical evidence of the perpetuity of evil, he saw a better world beyond, and he invites all to share in that vision.

THE CONQUEST OF GOG AND BEYOND

Ezekiel 39:1–29

[1]"And you, son of man, prophesy against Gog, and say, Thus says the Lord God: Behold, I am against you, O Gog, chief prince of Meshech and Tubal; [2]and I will turn you about and drive you forward, and bring you up from the uttermost parts of the north, and lead you against the mountains of Israel; [3]then I will strike your bow from your left hand, and will make your arrows drop out of your right hand. [4]You shall fall upon the mountains of Israel, you and all your hordes and the peoples

that are with you; I will give you to birds of prey of every sort and to the wild beasts to be devoured. ⁵You shall fall in the open field; for I have spoken, says the Lord God. ⁶I will send fire on Magog and on those who dwell securely in the coastlands; and they shall know that I am the Lord.

⁷"And my holy name I will make known in the midst of my people Israel; and I will not let my holy name be profaned any more; and the nations shall know that I am the Lord, the Holy One in Israel. ⁸Behold, it is coming and it will be brought about, says the Lord God. That is the day of which I have spoken.

⁹"Then those who dwell in the cities of Israel will go forth and make fires of the weapons and burn them, shields and bucklers, bows and arrows, handpikes and spears, and they will make fires of them for seven years; ¹⁰so that they will not need to take wood out of the field or cut down any out of the forests, for they will make their fires of the weapons; they will despoil those who despoiled them, and plunder those who plundered them, says the Lord God.

¹¹"On that day I will give to Gog a place for burial in Israel, the Valley of the Travellers east of the sea; it will block the travellers, for there Gog and all his multitude will be buried; it will be called the Valley of Hamon-gog. ¹²For seven months the house of Israel will be burying them, in order to cleanse the land. ¹³All the people of the land will bury them; and it will redound to their honour on the day that I show my glory, says the Lord God. ¹⁴They will set apart men to pass through the land continually and bury those remaining upon the face of the land, so as to cleanse it; at the end of seven months they will make their search. ¹⁵And when these pass through the land and any one sees a man's bone, then he shall set up a sign by it, till the buriers have buried it in the Valley of Hamon-gog. ¹⁶(A city Hamonah is there also.) Thus shall they cleanse the land.

¹⁷"As for you, son of man, thus says the Lord God: Speak to the birds of every sort and to all beasts of the field, 'Assemble and come, gather from all sides to the sacrificial feast which I am preparing for you, a great sacrificial feast upon the mountains of Israel, and you shall eat flesh and drink blood. ¹⁸You shall eat the flesh of the mighty, and drink the blood of the princes of the earth—of rams, of lambs, and of goats, of bulls, all of them fatlings of Bashan. ¹⁹And you shall eat fat till you are filled, and drink blood till you are drunk, at the sacrificial feast which I am preparing for you. ²⁰And you shall be filled at my table with horses and riders, with mighty men and all kinds of warriors,' says the Lord God.

²¹"And I will set my glory among the nations; and all the nations shall see my judgment which I have executed, and my hand which I have laid on them. ²²The house of Israel shall know that I am the Lord their God, from that day forward. ²³And the nations shall know that the house of Israel went into captivity for their iniquity, because they dealt so treacherously with me that I hid my face from them and gave them into the hand of their adversaries, and they all fell by the sword. ²⁴I dealt with them according to their uncleanness and their transgressions, and hid my face from them.

²⁵"Therefore thus says the Lord God: Now I will restore the fortunes of Jacob, and have mercy upon the whole house of Israel; and I will be jealous for my holy name. ²⁶They shall forget their shame, and all the treachery they have practised against me, when they dwell securely in their land with none to make them afraid, ²⁷when I have brought them back from the peoples and gathered them from their enemies' lands, and through them have vindicated my holiness in the sight of many nations. ²⁸Then they shall know that I am the Lord their God because I sent them into exile among the nations, and then gathered them into their own land. I will leave none of them remaining among the nations any more; ²⁹and I will not hide my face any more from them, when I pour out my Spirit upon the house of Israel, says the Lord God."

In the continuing description of the battle, there are elements of repetition from the previous chapter and some further amplifications are provided. The defeat of the invading forces of evil would be complete and their elimination total. And, as a consequence of the defeat, God's name would be known in Israel and no longer profaned amongst the other nations of the world (verse 7). Then, in a series of rather morbid scenes, there are described the mopping-up operations that would follow the battle. The weapons left strewn about the field of battle would be so numerous that they would provide the local population with a seven-year supply of firewood. So vast would be the pile of corpses in the cemetery valley, that travellers would be unable to pass through the valley and the burial details would take seven months to complete their tasks. Eventually all the dead would be buried and the land would be cleansed.

The prophecy thus continues to elaborate upon the total defeat and destruction of the forces of evil in the final cataclysmic battle. As with all apocalyptic language, the description is vivid and symbolic, though not to be interpreted literally. The emphasis in this portion of the prophecy is on the totality of the destruction of the forces of evil that would eventually be achieved by the divine intervention. And some of the minor points of the description highlight the victory in a striking way. After most forms of human conflict, the weapons that remain are salvaged for future wars. But the prophet is describing essentially a war to end all wars, and so the weapons of war can finally be put to a useful purpose; they can be burned in the fire and add a little warmth to a cold world.

In the last portion of the prophecy concerning Gog, the prophet emphasises again the totality of the defeat and slaughter of the forces of evil. The birds of prey and wild beasts are invited to assemble and feast upon the carcases of the slain (verses 17–20). The scene supplements the preceding passage (describing the burial of the dead), rather than follows it chronologically. The participation of beasts in the demise of the defeated stresses the finality of the event; human beings were to have been the masters and stewards of the world of nature, according to the pattern of creation, but in their pursuit of evil they have become at last the victims of the natural order.

When the battle was finished, God's glory would at last be established (verses 21–29). All the world's remaining nations would know beyond any doubt that God was the master of human history, and that his mastery was exercised in righteousness. And both Israel and the nations would know that Israel's former defeat and captivity were not a sign of the weakness of Israel's God, but rather a demonstration of his judgment of sin. His ultimate power and concern for his people would be demonstrated in his restoration of them to the promised land, there to live in peace.

At the end of the prophecy concerning Gog it is, above all, the prophet's faith which stands out in stark relief. He spoke of the eventual triumph of good in an evil world, but at the time of speaking his experience was only of evil, of Babylon and her like and what they had done and were doing. He foresaw the eventual re-establishment of his people in the promised land, though at the time of speaking more refugees were joining him from the debris of a broken Jerusalem. He spoke of the ultimate defeat of evil nations, though his experience was that of exile and captivity in Babylon. From an objective and empirical perspective, there was a kind of insanity to all his words; none of them was supported by the least evidence of world events of that time. But Ezekiel had seen a vision of God and his sight was no longer the same as that of other mortals; knowing the greatness and goodness of God, he was able to perceive a world arising in the future in which war and evil would be no more. He would not himself see it, and he did not know when its day would dawn, but dawn it would.

A NEW VISION

Ezekiel 40:1–4

[1]In the twenty-fifth year of our exile, at the beginning of the year, on the tenth day of the month, in the fourteenth year after the city was conquered, on that very day, the hand of the Lord was upon me, [2]and brought me in the visions of God into the land of Israel, and set me down upon a very high mountain, on which was a structure like a city opposite me. [3]When he brought me there, behold, there was a man, whose appearance was like bronze, with a line of flax and a measuring reed in his hand; and he was standing in the gateway. [4]And the man said to me, "Son of man, look with your eyes, and hear with your ears, and set your mind upon all that I shall show you, for you were brought here in order that I might show it to you; declare all that you see to the house of Israel."

The last nine chapters of the book (40–48) provide a kind of self-contained appendix; the content of these chapters is described as the substance of a vision which the prophet experienced in the year 573 B.C. (verses 1–2). Thus, this portion of the book comes from the later period of the prophet's life and is among the last of the dated prophecies in the Book of Ezekiel. The chapters are concerned with the temple, the land, and the people in the restored Israel that has already been anticipated in earlier prophecies. They are not easy chapters to read and interpret, in part because of the great attention to detail on matters that may seem to us of little moment. And the style of writing is somewhat erratic, suggesting to many commentators that these chapters contain several additions from persons other than Ezekiel. But although editorial additions are clearly present, the majority of the contents of these chapters is typical of Ezekiel, whose background in a priestly family gave him a natural interest in matters related to the temple.

The writing is apocalyptic in style (as were Chapters 38–39), expressing in a profoundly symbolic manner the nature of the restored Israel that God would establish in the future. From a human perspective, they may be viewed as the result of more than a decade of reflection on the prophet's part; as he continued to live in exile, conscious of the evils that brought to an end the old Israel, he began to perceive what an ideal Israel would be like. The years of reflection culminate in the extraordinary vision, introduced in these verses, in which the prophet's various hopes for the future are given firm but symbolic shape.

To describe the chapters as an appendix may be a little misleading. They are an appendix in the sense that they form a self-contained literary unit, but in other ways they form an integral part of the prophet's book. Just as the prophet's ministry opened with a great vision (Chapters 1–3), so too it ends with one. And just as, in an early vision of Jerusalem, the prophet had declared God's departure from Jerusalem and the temple (Chapters 8–11), so now he anticipates God's return. The collapse and fall of Jerusalem and Judah, which have been the historical substance of so much of the Book of Ezekiel, are here balanced by the rebuilding and restoration of the promised land.

While the details of the vision (e.g. the precise measurements of the reconstructed temple) may seem to offer little by way of spiritual edification to the modern reader of these chapters, nevertheless the great principles of Ezekiel's vision of a renewed Israel become clear in the chapters as a whole. God would be present among his people, and they would find the fulfilment of their lives in the worship of God. Although expressed in language that seems sometimes alien to a twentieth-century gentile world, the chapters communicate the fundamental truth that the meaning and end of human existence are to be found in the knowledge and the worship of God.

In the context of the vision, the prophet was set down on a mountain, overlooking a city. Standing at the gate of the city was a being who addressed the prophet and declared that he was to be Ezekiel's guide. What the prophet saw, with that mysterious figure by his side, is described in the following verses and chapters.

THE OUTER COURT

Ezekiel 40:5–27

5And behold, there was a wall all around the outside of the temple area, and the length of the measuring reed in the man's hand was six long cubits, each being a cubit and a handbreadth in length; so he measured the thickness of the wall, one reed; and the height, one reed. 6Then he went into the gateway facing east, going up its steps, and measured the threshold of the gate, one reed deep; 7and the side rooms, one reed long, and one reed broad; and the space between the side rooms, five cubits; and the threshold of the gate by the vestibule of the gate at the inner end, one reed. 8Then he measured the vestibule of the gateway, eight cubits; 9and its jambs, two cubits; and the vestibule of the gate was at the inner end. 10And there were three side rooms on either side of the east gate; the three were of the same size; and the jambs on either side were of the same size. 11Then he measured the breadth of the opening of the gateway, ten cubits; and the breadth of the gateway, thirteen cubits. 12There was a barrier before the side rooms, one cubit on either side; and the side rooms were six cubits on either side. 13Then he measured the gate from the back of the one side room to the back of the other, a breadth of five and twenty cubits, from door to door. 14He measured also the vestibule, twenty cubits; and round about the vestibule of the gateway was the court. 15From the front of the gate at the entrance to the end of the inner vestibule of the gate was fifty cubits. 16And the gateway had windows round about, narrowing inwards into their jambs in the side rooms, and likewise the vestibule had windows round about inside, and on the jambs were palm trees.

¹⁷Then he brought me into the outer court; and behold, there were chambers and a pavement, round about the court; thirty chambers fronted on the pavement. ¹⁸And the pavement ran along the side of the gates, corresponding to the length of the gates; this was the lower pavement. ¹⁹Then he measured the distance from the inner front of the lower gate to the outer front of the inner court, a hundred cubits.

Then he went before me to the north, ²⁰and behold, there was a gate which faced toward the north, belonging to the outer court. He measured its length and its breadth. ²¹Its side rooms, three on either side, and its jambs and its vestibule were of the same size as those of the first gate; its length was fifty cubits, and its breadth twenty-five cubits. ²²And its windows, its vestibule, and its palm trees were of the same size as those of the gate which faced toward the east; and seven steps led up to it; and its vestibule was on the inside. ²³And opposite the gate on the north, as on the east, was a gate to the inner court; and he measured from gate to gate a hundred cubits.

²⁴And he led me toward the south, and behold, there was a gate on the south; and he measured its jambs and its vestibule; they had the same size as the others. ²⁵And there were windows round about in it and in its vestibule, like the windows of the others; its length was fifty cubits, and its breadth twenty-five cubits. ²⁶And there were seven steps leading up to it, and its vestibule was on the inside; and it had palm trees on its jambs, one on either side. ²⁷And there was a gate on the south of the inner court; and he measured from gate to gate toward the south, a hundred cubits.

Ezekiel's visonary tour of the city begins outside the eastern gate of the outside wall of the outer court of the temple area. He is led by his angelic guide and seems to function like an archaeologist's assistant; as the guide measures and calls out the proportions of different parts of the structures, Ezekiel duly notes them.

To visualise Ezekiel's temple tour as a whole, one must visualise what an ancient temple was like. Surrounding the temple building was an inner courtyard, the outer boundaries of which were marked by a wall. Beyond that wall lay an outer courtyard, and its outer limit was also marked by a wall. The orientation of the entire structure was east-west. The wall of the outer courtyard had gates in its eastern, northern, and southern sides, as did the wall of the inner courtyard; the western wall was bounded by the temple proper. Ezekiel's tour began at the eastern gate, through which he passed into the outer courtyard. After examining the various rooms in the outer courtyard, he was conducted first to the north gate and then to the south gate for an examination of each. What emerged most clearly from an examination of each part of the outer court, its walls, gates and rooms, was the extraordinary care and symmetry with which the whole was constructed. The building and its various parts were finely proportioned and had been constructed with precision and care.

It is not easy for the average modern reader to become enthralled by the number of cubits in the measurement of a courtyard gate, in a building without real existence! Yet it is wise to recognise the problem as lying within ourselves, rather than in the ancient text. For one who has never held a rod or felt the urge to fish, a fly-fisher's compendium offers little fascination. For one who has never ridden a motorcycle, the motorcycle magazines offer no interest at all. But a fisherman can spend hours enjoying a book on fishing. A motorcycling enthusiast can read with fascination the technical specifications of a new machine. And Ezekiel, whose initial upbringing had been for service in the temple, must have been enthralled with the vision of God's restored temple, and he recorded the details of the vision with an architect's care and thoroughness. We can sense the enthusiasm, even if we find it hard to share it. But we can also perceive how the fascination was with a subject loftier than fly-fishing or motorcycles! The temple was the place that symbolised God's presence amongst his people. As such, it deserved the closest attention; it was only a building, but it represented nevertheless the presence of God in the world.

THE INNER COURT

Ezekiel 40:28–49

²⁸Then he brought me to the inner court by the south gate, and he

measured the south gate; it was of the same size as the others. [29]Its side rooms, its jambs, and its vestibule were of the same size as the others; and there were windows round about in it and in its vestibule; its length was fifty cubits, and its breadth twenty-five cubits. [30]And there were vestibules round about, twenty-five cubits long and five cubits broad. [31]Its vestibule faced the outer court, and palm trees were on its jambs, and its stairway had eight steps.

[32]Then he brought me to the inner court on the east side, and he measured the gate; it was of the same size as the others. [33]Its side rooms, its jambs, and its vestibule were of the same size as the others; and there were windows round about in it and in its vestibule; its length was fifty cubits, and its breadth twenty-five cubits. [34]Its vestibule faced the outer court, and it had palm trees on its jambs, one on either side; and its stairway had eight steps.

[35]Then he brought me to the north gate, and he measured it; it had the same size as the others. [36]Its side rooms, its jambs, and its vestibule were of the same size as the others; and it had windows round about; its length was fifty cubits, and its breadth twenty-five cubits. [37]Its vestibule faced the outer court, and it had palm trees on its jambs, one on either side; and its stairway had eight steps.

[38]There was a chamber with its door in the vestibule of the gate, where the burnt offering was to be washed. [39]And in the vestibule of the gate were two tables on either side, on which the burnt offering and the sin offering and the guilt offering were to be slaughtered. [40]And on the outside of the vestibule at the entrance of the north gate were two tables; and on the other side of the vestibule of the gate were two tables. [41]Four tables were on the inside, and four tables on the outside of the side of the gate, eight tables, on which the sacrifices were to be slaughtered. [42]And there were also four tables of hewn stone for the burnt offering, a cubit and a half long, and a cubit and a half broad, and one cubit high, on which the instruments were to be laid with which the burnt offerings and the sacrifices were slaughtered. [43]And hooks, a handbreadth long, were fastened round about within. And on the tables the flesh of the offering was to be laid.

[44]Then he brought me from without into the inner court, and behold, there were two chambers in the inner court, one at the side of the north gate facing south, the other at the side of the south gate facing north. [45]And he said to me, This chamber which faces south is for the priests who have charge of the temple, [46]and the chamber which faces north is for the priests who have charge of the altar; these are the sons

of Zadok, who alone among the sons of Levi may come near to the Lord to minister to him. ⁴⁷And he measured the court, a hundred cubits long, and a hundred cubits broad, foursquare; and the altar was in front of the temple.

⁴⁸Then he brought me to the vestibule of the temple and measured the jambs of the vestibule, five cubits on either side; and the breadth of the gate was fourteen cubits; and the sidewalls of the gate were three cubits on either side. ⁴⁹The length of the vestibule was twenty cubits, and the breadth twelve cubits; and ten steps led up to it; and there were pillars beside the jambs on either side.

The prophet's conducted tour of the visionary temple now progresses from the outer court to the inner court; he gains access to the inner court via the southern gate, which was virtually identical with the three gates in the wall of the outer court. It was not a simple "garden gate", but an elaborate structure, having small rooms with doors opening on to the passage way, and a porch or vestibule on the outside, looking towards the outer court. As with many ancient castles, the gate was a massive and powerful structure. Ezekiel continued to an examination of the gates in the east and north walls of the inner court; they had the same dimensions as those of the south gate. By the vestibule of the gate in the north wall, a number of tables were located; they were used for the sacrificial activity of the temple, the slaughter of animals to be used in sacrifice and the storage of the butcher's tools that were used by the priests.

Inside the inner court were two dormitories, located on the north and south sides of the court, for the use of the priests. The priests in the northern room were responsible for the service of the temple building; those in the southern room were responsible for the altar, which was located just outside the temple proper, on its east side. After examining the rooms, the prophet was led across the square inner courtyard and brought to the vestibule of the temple itself, the sacred building that was so carefully protected by the inner and outer walls and courts.

It is difficult for a modern reader to grasp the impressiveness and symbolism of the structure through which Ezekiel was conducted. It was more than just a splendid church, though some of our older churches and cathedrals contain the same symbolism. Each part of the structure had a religious function. As the prophet passed from the outside world to the outer court, from the outer court to the inner court, and then in the inner court to the vestibule of the temple itself, there was a mounting sense of climax. From the secular world, access was gained, gradually, to an inner sacred sanctuary. And the very architecture of the temple contributed to a process of introspection that was required of the worshipper in liturgical practice. "Who shall ascend the hill of the Lord and who shall stand in his holy place?" the priests used to ask of people coming to worship (Ps. 24:3). The answer was clear: "He who has clean hands and a pure heart," and the very structure of the temple, with its progression from outer world to inner sanctuary, reminded those who entered of the privilege and sanctity of the act of worship.

For Ezekiel, though, that possibility of worship in the real temple had ceased to exist. In reality, he was an exile; far away in Jerusalem, the once splendid temple lay in ruins. Only in the vision did this marvellous temple exist; it was a sign to him that God would not always be absent from his people, but that a time would come again in which the chosen people could not only worship God, but know his presence in their midst.

THE NEW TEMPLE

Ezekiel 41:1–26

> ¹Then he brought me to the nave, and measured the jambs; on each side six cubits was the breadth of the jambs. ²And the breadth of the entrance was ten cubits; and the sidewalls of the entrance were five cubits on either side; and he measured the length of the nave forty cubits, and its breadth, twenty cubits. ³Then he went into the inner room and measured the jambs of the entrance, two cubits; and the breadth of the entrance, six cubits; and the sidewalls of the entrance, seven cubits. ⁴And he measured the length of the room, twenty cubits, and its breadth, twenty cubits, beyond the nave. And he said to me, This is the most holy place.

⁵Then he measured the wall of the temple, six cubits thick; and the breadth of the side chambers, four cubits, round about the temple. ⁶And the side chambers were in three stories, one over another, thirty in each story. There were offsets all around the wall of the temple to serve as supports for the side chambers, so that they should not be supported by the wall of the temple. ⁷And the side chambers became broader as they rose from story to story, corresponding to the enlargement of the offset from story to story round about the temple; on the side of the temple a stairway led upward, and thus one went up from the lowest story to the top story through the middle story. ⁸I saw also that the temple had a raised platform round about; the foundations of the side chambers measured a full reed of six long cubits. ⁹The thickness of the outer wall of the side chambers was five cubits; and the part of the platform which was left free was five cubits. Between the platform of the temple and the ¹⁰chambers of the court was a breadth of twenty cubits round about the temple on every side. ¹¹And the doors of the side chambers opened on the part of the platform that was left free, one door toward the north, and another door toward the south; and the breadth of the part that was left free was five cubits round about.

¹²The building that was facing the temple yard on the west side was seventy cubits broad; and the wall of the building was five cubits thick round about, and its length ninety cubits.

¹³Then he measured the temple, a hundred cubits long; and the yard and the building with its walls, a hundred cubits long; ¹⁴also the breadth of the east front of the temple and the yard, a hundred cubits.

¹⁵Then he measured the length of the building facing the yard which was at the west and its walls on either side, a hundred cubits.

The nave of the temple and the inner room and the outer vestibule ¹⁶were panelled and round about all three had windows with recessed frames. Over against the threshold the temple was panelled with wood round about, from the floor up to the windows (now the windows were covered), ¹⁷to the space above the door, even to the inner room, and on the outside. And on all the walls round about in the inner room and the nave were carved likenesses ¹⁸of cherubim and palm trees, a palm tree between cherub and cherub. Every cherub had two faces; ¹⁹the face of a man toward the palm tree on the one side, and the face of a young lion toward the palm tree on the other side. They were carved on the whole temple round about; ²⁰from the floor to above the door cherubim and palm trees were carved on the wall.

²¹The doorposts of the nave were squared; and in front of the holy place was something resembling ²²an altar of wood, three cubits high, two cubits long, and two cubits broad; its corners, its base, and its walls were of wood. He said to me, "This is the table which is before the Lord." ²³The nave and the holy place had each a double door. ²⁴The doors had two leaves apiece, two swinging leaves for each door. ²⁵And on the doors of the nave were carved cherubim and palm trees, such as were carved on the walls; and there was a canopy of wood in front of the vestibule outside. ²⁶And there were recessed windows and palm trees on either side, on the sidewalls of the vestibule.

Having passed through the outer and inner courts, the prophet is conducted at last to the temple itself. One must envisage a large building, rectangular in shape, with a single door in the east wall. The interior of the building had three rooms, access to each being gained by doors that became successively narrower. First there was a vestibule, beyond that a nave (the "holy place"), and finally a small inner room, the "holy of holies". Although access to the inner part of the temple was possible only through its vestibule, there were further structures attached to the outside wall of the temple building. On the north and south sides of the temple building stairways provided access to the three stories, each having thirty storage rooms, built outwards from the inner, solid walls of the temple.

First, the prophet passed through the vestibule into the nave, or holy place, to which (in real life, as distinct from vision) he would have been permitted access by virtue of his priestly background (the laity worshipped in the court). His guide passed on alone into the innermost sanctuary and then came out again to report the measurements. Then they moved outside again to examine the platform on which the whole temple was set and the stairways leading upwards to the three levels of storage rooms. Behind the temple, on its west side, was a further large building, probably also designed for storage purposes.

Inside the temple building the prophet examined in detail the furnishing and decorations. The three doors, providing access to the vestibule, nave and inner sanctuary, were each double doors, meeting in the middle; each side of the door in turn was hinged, so that the doors could be folded back and would fit flush to the wall. In the nave there was the table that symbolised God's presence with, and provision for, his people. The walls were panelled and decorated with designs of palm trees and cherubim.

The focal point of this entire structure was the innermost room of the temple, the "holy of holies", to which ordinary mortals did not have access (not even Ezekiel in his vision). In the history of the real (as distinct from visionary) temple, only the High Priest could enter the innermost sanctuary, and that happened only once a year on the Day of Atonement. The entire structure, the outer and inner courts and the temple building itself, were all in a sense a part of the protection of this inner room, which symbolised the divine presence in the very heart of Israel.

In a literal sense, God's presence cannot be focused and limited to a single spot in the world; there can be no geographical or architectural constraints on a deity who is transcendent. But a too casual view of a God who is both transcendent and immanent, both beyond the world and yet permeating every part of it, has certain dangers. On the one hand, God may seem to be so distant as to be not really present; on the other hand, the belief in his presence everywhere may lead us to take it for granted. The nature of the temple and its innermost sanctuary in Ezekiel's vision strikes a balance. God is indeed present in the world, but that presence should not be recognised casually; it is a holy presence, an extraordinary privilege, and to be treated with appropriate awe.

ROOMS FOR THE PRIESTS

Ezekiel 42:1–20

¹Then he led me out into the inner court, toward the north, and he brought me to the chambers which were opposite the temple yard and opposite the building on the north. ²The length of the building which was on the north side was a hundred cubits, and the breadth fifty cubits. ³Adjoining the twenty cubits which belonged to the inner court, and facing the pavement which belonged to the outer court, was

gallery against gallery in three stories. ⁴And before the chambers was a passage inward, ten cubits wide and a hundred cubits long, and their doors were on the north. ⁵Now the upper chambers were narrower, for the galleries took more away from them than from the lower and middle chambers in the building. ⁶For they were in three stories, and they had no pillars like the pillars of the outer court; hence the upper chambers were set back from the ground more than the lower and the middle ones. ⁷And there was a wall outside parallel to the chambers, toward the outer court, opposite the chambers, fifty cubits long. ⁸For the chambers on the outer court were fifty cubits long, while those opposite the temple were a hundred cubits long. ⁹Below these chambers was an entrance on the east side, as one enters them from the outer court, ¹⁰where the outside wall begins.

On the south also, opposite the yard and opposite the building, there were chambers ¹¹with a passage in front of them; they were similar to the chambers on the north, of the same length and breadth, with the same exits and arrangements and doors. ¹²And below the south chambers was an entrance on the east side, where one enters the passage, and opposite them was a dividing wall.

¹³Then he said to me, "The north chambers and the south chambers opposite the yard are the holy chambers, where the priests who approach the Lord shall eat the most holy offerings; there they shall put the most holy offerings—the cereal offering, the sin offering, and the guilt offering, for the place is holy. ¹⁴When the priests enter the holy place, they shall not go out of it into the outer court without laying there the garments in which they minister, for these are holy; they shall put on other garments before they go near to that which is for the people."

¹⁵Now when he had finished measuring the interior of the temple area, he led me out by the gate which faced east, and measured the temple area round about. ¹⁶He measured the east side with the measuring reed, five hundred cubits by the measuring reed. ¹⁷Then he turned and measured the north side, five hundred cubits by the measuring reed. ¹⁸Then he turned and measured the south side, five hundred cubits by the measuring reed. ¹⁹Then he turned to the west side and measured, five hundred cubits by the measuring reed. ²⁰He measured it on the four sides. It had a wall around it, five hundred cubits long and five hundred cubits broad, to make a separation between the holy and the common.

The final part of the account of the visionary temple focuses on two buildings designed for the use of the priests. The description is not easy to interpret with any precision. There were two buildings, similar in structure, located respectively on the north and south sides of the main temple. They appear to have been located somewhat towards the west of the temple proper, adjacent perhaps to the large storage building due west of the temple. These two buildings served a threefold purpose: (a) they were refectories in which the priests ate the portions of offerings allotted to them; (b) they were for the storage of offerings; (c) they were changing rooms, for the priestly attire used in the inner court had to be exchanged for different clothes before the priests passed back to the outer court of the temple.

Finally, the prophet was led back through the courtyards to the exterior of the temple, where his angelic guide took the external measurements of the building complex as a whole. It was five hundred cubits square, or approximately eight hundred feet long by eight hundred feet wide; there is no indication as to the height of the various parts. The wall that was around the temple separated the holy world that lay within and the common world outside.

In this part of the vision the description has been of the temple buildings, but there has been one thing notable for its absence: for all the symbolism of the temple, no reference has been made to the actual living presence of God within the temple. Indeed, without the divine presence the building was merely a structure, not a temple, and years earlier the prophet had predicted the Lord's departure from his temple and holy city (Chapters 10–11). Now the scene has been set for the return of God's glory to the temple, which is described in the next episode of the vision.

GOD'S RETURN TO THE TEMPLE

Ezekiel 43:1–12

[1]Afterward he brought me to the gate, the gate facing east. [2]And behold, the glory of the God of Israel came from the east; and the

sound of his coming was like the sound of many waters; and the earth shone with his glory. ³And the vision I saw was like the vision which I had seen when he came to destroy the city, and like the vision which I had seen by the river Chebar; and I fell upon my face. ⁴As the glory of the Lord entered the temple by the gate facing east, ⁵the Spirit lifted me up, and brought me into the inner court; and behold, the glory of the Lord filled the temple.

⁶While the man was standing beside me, I heard one speaking to me out of the temple; ⁷and he said to me, "Son of man, this is the place of my throne and the place of the soles of my feet, where I will dwell in the midst of the people of Israel for ever. And the house of Israel shall no more defile my holy name, neither they, nor their kings, by their harlotry, and by the dead bodies of their kings, ⁸by setting their threshold by my threshold and their doorposts beside my doorposts, with only a wall between me and them. They have defiled my holy name by their abominations which they have committed, so I have consumed them in my anger. ⁹Now let them put away their idolatry and the dead bodies of their kings far from me, and I will dwell in their midst for ever.

¹⁰"And you, son of man, describe to the house of Israel the temple and its appearance and plan, that they may be ashamed of their iniquities. ¹¹And if they are ashamed of all that they have done, portray the temple, its arrangement, its exits and its entrances, and its whole form; and make known to them all its ordinances and all its laws; and write it down in their sight, so that they may observe and perform all its laws and all its ordinances. ¹²This is the law of the temple: the whole territory round about upon the top of the mountain shall be most holy. Behold, this is the law of the temple."

Prior to this point, Ezekiel's vision has been in the form of a tour of the restored temple; an angelic guide had led him from one part of the temple to another, to examine and measure its structure. Now the vision reaches its climax; God returns to the temple and then addresses Ezekiel from its innermost holy place. The remainder of the vision (and the book) is concerned with the substance of the final message that Ezekiel is to convey to his people. This climactic portion of the prophet's vision falls into three parts.

(i) *God's return to the temple* (verses 1–5). Having completed his guided tour, the prophet returned to the gate in the temple's east wall; this was the main gate, for the whole temple was constructed in such a fashion that it faced toward the east. Standing at the eastern gate, the prophet saw a vision within his vision; the new vision was that of the return of God's glory to its earthly dwelling. For the prophet, the new vision was reminiscent both of his initial vision of God's glory near the River Chebar, with which his ministry began (Chapter 1), and of the more horrifying vision of God's departure from the temple (Chapters 10–11), which had preceded the collapse of Jerusalem and the destruction of its temple. As the sun rose in the east and cast its first morning rays on the temple's eastern gate, so too did God's glory shine on the eastern gate, before passing through and coming to rest in the innermost sanctuary of the temple itself. The prophet, still in a visionary state, felt himself conveyed from the eastern gate to the temple's inner court, just outside the building within which God's glory now rested.

The importance of this part of the prophet's vision cannot be overestimated. The very essence of Israel's religion focused upon the privilege they had been granted of fellowship with the living God in the world. Yet Israel's past evil had created a world in which God could no longer be present. The people had created their own kind of hell, a world in which God's presence could not be known. But now, in his vision, the prophet sees God's glory and presence return to the world of human existence. The return is in vision, not yet in reality, but it augurs well for the future, for there can be no future hope unless God is present in the human world. And so the prophet's vision so many centuries ago carries a perpetual message. We have created a world of such evil proportions that the presence of God within it might seem impossible; without that presence, and without the possibility of fellowship with God, human life loses its potential for meaning. But God is always returning to his world, always coming back to his people; before that renewed presence can be known, however, the reason for the departure of God's glory is stressed once again.

(ii) *The voice from the temple* (verses 6–9). Standing in the inner court, but outside the temple building, the prophet now hears a voice addressing him from within the temple; the voice is that of God, whose glory is located in the innermost sanctuary. First, the Lord declares that the place of his presence is indeed his home, his symbolic dwelling in the midst of his chosen people. Then there is a statement addressed to Israel: the people must no longer defile the place of God's residence by their acts of idolatry and associated practices. If they would put aside their evil practices, God's presence would remain with them for ever.

The message from within the temple is simple and yet profound. It comes from the universal God, the creator of the world who cannot be contained within the universe itself; yet it concerns the presence of that God amongst mortal human beings. God wills to dwell in the presence of men and women, yet can only do so as they turn from evil to good and seek to restore the sanctity of their world. And whether it is the temple of old Israel, the world itself, or even the temple which is the human body, we are reminded by the prophet not only that God seeks to dwell there, but also that his presence can only be known among those who consciously turn aside from evil. The vision thus probes to the heart of human life: we do not discover the meaning of living unless we discover also the presence and fellowship of God, but we cannot know that presence if our evil eliminates its residence in our midst.

(iv) *The commission to the prophet* (verses 10–12). The prophet is given instructions to address his people and describe to them the restored temple and all its laws, the substance of his vision. His description is to be both oral and written; the inscribed account would serve as a permanent record for future generations. For Ezekiel, with his priestly background, the whole substance of the vision was glorious; indeed, for his people, whose existence was given meaning by the symbolism of the temple in their midst, the visionary scene would have been equally glorious and full of hope. And though we may not easily grasp the excitement of the account of the temple and its laws that follows, we can at least sense the thrill that it would have imparted to prophet and people alike.

"Where there is no vision, the people perish" (Prov. 29:18, AV). To a people almost devoid of hope, the late Martin Luther

King described a vision from the mountain top and restored the flickering flame of hope. And to a people in exile in the throes of despair, Ezekiel was to describe a vision and restore to them a vestige of hope. To only a few persons is granted the privilege of seeing the extraordinary vision of God and perceiving the change that his presence could make to an evil and sad world. But all may participate in the vision and work towards its fulfilment. And the vision with which the Church is entrusted is similar to that of the prophet: it is of a world in which the presence of God may be made known through the proclamation of the gospel of God's presence in the world in the person of Jesus Christ.

THE ALTAR AND ITS CONSECRATION

Ezekiel 43:13–27

¹³"These are the dimensions of the altar by cubits (the cubit being a cubit and a handbreadth): its base shall be one cubit high, and one cubit broad, with a rim of one span around its edge. And this shall be the height of the altar: ¹⁴from the base on the ground to the lower ledge, two cubits, with a breadth of one cubit; and from the smaller ledge to the larger ledge, four cubits, with a breadth of one cubit; ¹⁵and the altar hearth, four cubits; and from the altar hearth projecting upward, four horns, one cubit high. ¹⁶The altar hearth shall be square, twelve cubits long by twelve broad. ¹⁷The ledge also shall be square, fourteen cubits long by fourteen broad, with a rim around it half a cubit broad, and its base one cubit round about. The steps of the altar shall face east."

¹⁸And he said to me, "Son of man, thus says the Lord God: These are the ordinances for the altar: On the day when it is erected for offering burnt offerings upon it and for throwing blood against it, ¹⁹you shall give to the Levitical priests of the family of Zadok, who draw near to me to minister to me, says the Lord God, a bull for a sin offering. ²⁰And you shall take some of its blood, and put it on the four horns of the altar, and on the four corners of the ledge, and upon the rim round about; thus you shall cleanse the altar and make atonement for it. ²¹You shall also take the bull of the sin offering, and it shall be burnt in the appointed place belonging to the temple, outside the sacred area. ²²And on the second day you shall offer a he-goat without

blemish for a sin offering; and the altar shall be cleansed, as it was cleansed with the bull. 23When you have finished cleansing it, you shall offer a bull without blemish and a ram from the flock without blemish. 24You shall present them before the Lord, and the priests shall sprinkle salt upon them and offer them up as a burnt offering to the Lord. 25For seven days you shall provide daily a goat for a sin offering; also a bull and a ram from the flock, without blemish, shall be provided. 26Seven days shall they make atonement for the altar and purify it, and so consecrate it. 27And when they have completed these days, then from the eighth day onward the priests shall offer upon the altar your burnt offerings and your peace offerings; and I will accept you, says the Lord God."

The substance of the prophet's vision now returns to a description of parts of the temple area and regulations concerning the temple's future use. At first sight these verses seem to be something of an anti-climax, after the account of the return of God's glory to the temple. But there is an important transition to be observed: in the initial description of the visionary temple, the prophet perceived a splendid building which was not being used. Now, as the description of the vision continues, the scene as such is supplemented by instructions concerning the inauguration and use of this splendid building. At the very heart of the temple was its altar; the prophet first describes the altar, and then indicates the procedures by which it would be put to use once again. In these concluding portions of the prophet's vision particularly, some parts of the original account may have been supplemented by the additions of the prophet's editors and disciples.

(i) *The description of the altar* (verses 13–17). The altar was a large, stone structure located in the inner court of the temple compound. The construction, as described here, is reminiscent of a much larger structure familiar in ancient Babylon, the *ziggurat*, of which some remains may still be seen by the modern traveller in southern Iraq. (See also Dr Gibson's commentary on *Genesis*, volume 1, pp. 204ff.) The altar stood on a stone base which was a little less than two feet high. The altar as such comprised three large stone blocks, namely two pedestal blocks, and on top the altar hearth. Each block was slightly smaller, giving a stepped appearance to the structure as a whole. Rising from the top block, the altar hearth, were four "horns", or protrusions, at each corner. The whole structure was more than twelve feet high, and access to the top was gained by means of the steps on the eastern side of the altar. It was on the temple's altar that the sacrifices were offered which would restore, and make possible the continuation of, the relationship between Israel and God.

The altar was a reminder not only of the gap that separates human beings from God, but also of the possibility of that gap being bridged. Human life finds its meaning in the relationship with God, but evil humans may not commune with the holy God. Only when human evil has been dealt with is communion with God possible. And thus the altar of Ezekiel's visionary temple reminds us of another altar, in the form of a cross, on which a perfect sacrifice at last achieved the bridging of that gap that separates human beings from their God.

(ii) *The laws for the use of the altar* (verses 18–27). Nothing was to be casual in the use of the restored temple; the new altar could not be put to use immediately, as if there had been no break in the functioning of the temple. For one week the priests of the family of Zadok were to offer special sacrifices upon the altar, the purpose of which was specifically to cleanse it and sanctify it for its proper and perpetual usage, namely the offering of sacrifices on behalf of human beings.

In our modern age, it is not easy at first to grasp the significance of a week of special religious activity designed only to "purify" a structure made of stone! We can see, in ceremonial terms, that the process served to separate the sacred from the profane, but still the significance of the procedure is hard to grasp. Stone is stone, whether sanctified or not. Yet, as is so often the case, though the activity was directed to the altar, the impact of that activity was impressed upon the minds and hearts of the worshippers. And by the end of the week it would have dawned on them fully the extent to which the altar both was, and symbolised, a special place. It could not be a casual matter to approach God at the altar, seeking forgiveness for human evil and the restoration of relationship with God. And yet that was what the altar represented: the place where the relationship with God was restored and maintained. And the process of sanctifying the altar as such would impress upon the minds of all what an extraordinary privilege it was for human beings to approach God and be granted the gift of relationship.

ADMISSION TO THE SANCTUARY

Ezekiel 44:1–14

¹Then he brought me back to the outer gate of the sanctuary, which faces east; and it was shut. ²And he said to me, "This gate shall remain shut; it shall not be opened, and no one shall enter by it; for the Lord, the God of Israel, has entered by it; therefore it shall remain shut. ³Only the prince may sit in it to eat bread before the Lord; he shall enter by way of the vestibule of the gate, and shall go out by the same way."

⁴Then he brought me by way of the north gate to the front of the temple; and I looked, and behold, the glory of the Lord filled the temple of the Lord; and I fell upon my face. ⁵And the Lord said to me, "Son of man, mark well, see with your eyes, and hear with your ears all that I shall tell you concerning all the ordinances of the temple of the Lord and all its laws; and mark well those who may be admitted to the temple and all those who are to be excluded from the sanctuary. ⁶And say to the rebellious house, to the house of Israel, Thus says the Lord God: O house of Israel, let there be an end to all your abominations, ⁷in admitting foreigners, uncircumcised in heart and flesh, to be in my sanctuary, profaning it, when you offer to me my food, the fat and the blood. You have broken my covenant, in addition to all your abominations. ⁸And you have not kept charge of my holy things; but you have set foreigners to keep my charge in my sanctuary.

⁹"Therefore thus says the Lord God: No foreigner, uncircumcised in heart and flesh, of all the foreigners who are among the people of Israel, shall enter my sanctuary. ¹⁰But the Levites who went far from me, going astray from me after their idols when Israel went astray, shall bear their punishment. ¹¹They shall be ministers in my sanctuary, having oversight at the gates of the temple, and serving in the temple; they shall slay the burnt offering and the sacrifice for the people, and they shall attend on the people, to serve them. ¹²Because they minis-

tered to them before their idols and became a stumbling block of iniquity to the house of Israel, therefore I have sworn concerning them, says the Lord God, that they shall bear their punishment. ¹³They shall not come near to me, to serve me as priest, nor come near any of my sacred things and the things that are most sacred; but they shall bear their shame, because of the abominations which they have committed. ¹⁴Yet I will appoint them to keep charge of the temple, to do all its service and all that is to be done in it."

Ezekiel's vision of the restored temple continues but, in the following chapters, the visionary element is reduced, and much of the text has the form of regulations pertaining to the sanctuary's use. Many scholars consider that a secondary element has been added to the prophet's original narrative in these chapters. While Ezekiel's vision concerned a future and ideal temple, many of the verses that follow, legislative in form, appear to mirror the very real functional concerns that pertained to the actual usage of the temple, once its service was started again after the return from exile. This passage begins with a continuation of the vision (verses 1–3), and then provides regulations with respect to foreigners (verses 4–9) and Levitical ministers (verses 10–14).

(i) *The closure of the east gate* (verses 1–3). The prophet, still in his visionary state, is conducted by his guide back to the eastern gate in the outer wall of the outer court: through this gate, he had seen the Lord enter on his return to the temple. The prophet is told that this gate would remain closed; the closure would be a reminder to all of God's passage through it in his return to his holy temple. Only the king would be allowed to sit in the gate, there to eat in the presence of God; he would enter it through the vestibule from the temple's outer court.

The closure of the gate is significant in many ways. When those who entered the temple via the north and south gates for the first time asked why the east gate was closed, they would be told that the Lord, who had once left his temple, had returned again by means of the east gate. But, perhaps more significantly, the closure of the gate may be indicative of the Lord's intention never again to leave his sanctuary. He had left once before, a consequence of the evil of his people; in the restored temple, for use in the worship of a renewed people, his presence would be permanent. So the closed gate is not an ominous symbol, but a hopeful one; a people, who by their actions had caused the divine departure, would again know the permanent presence of their God.

(ii) *Regulations concerning foreigners* (verses 4–9). It had become the custom in former years to employ foreigners (especially foreign slaves) in the variety of menial tasks which were essential to the proper functioning of the temple. The foreigners, while not necessarily evil persons as such, were alien to the faith and worship of Israel; they were "uncircumcised in heart and flesh" (verse 7) meaning that, both literally and emotionally, they were not a part of the covenant community.

This legislative portion of the vision, expressed as the words of God to the prophet, is critical of Israel, not the foreigners. To the foreign servants of the temple had been delegated a variety of tasks: they were janitors, doormen, cleaners, assistants in various sacrificial activities, and the like. Their tasks as such held no particular appeal, and those responsible for the temple in the past had no doubt been glad of the regiment of foreign servants placed at their disposal. But using the foreigners had betrayed a fundamental misunderstanding of the temple's place at the heart of the covenant community. It may be that few people like to wield a broom or function as doormen, yet they were honest and worthy tasks, a vital part of the functioning of the temple as a whole. And, whether in ancient Israel or the modern Church, the privilege of divine service is misunderstood if the "dirty" jobs are delegated without thought and the "honourable" ones retained. Every role in the service of the sanctuary is important, that of the cleaner no less than that of the priest; it may not always appear to be so in human estimation, but these verses represent the divine estimation.

(iii) *The Levitical ministers* (verses 10–14). The tasks unassigned by the exclusion of foreigners from the temple would have to be assumed by some other group of persons. They were to be assumed by Levites, specifically those groups of Levites who, in former days, had left the true faith to serve in the idolatrous country shrines that had dotted the landscape and hillsides of ancient Judah. Their past activities were such that these Levites could not stand directly before God, functioning as priests. They could, nevertheless, participate fully in the worship of the temple, assisting the assembled congregation in their tasks. Though there is a judgmental theme running through these verses, there is also a theme of grace and mercy. Those whose past activities might seem for all time to have excluded them from participation in the divine worship, would yet be able to partake in the worship of Israel in its new temple.

THE RESPONSIBILITIES OF THE ZADOKITE PRIESTS

Ezekiel 44:15–31

15"But the Levitical priests, the sons of Zadok, who kept the charge of my sanctuary when the people of Israel went astray from me, shall come near to me to minister to me; and they shall attend on me to offer me the fat and the blood, says the Lord God; 16they shall enter my sanctuary, and they shall approach my table, to minister to me, and they shall keep my charge. 17When they enter the gates of the inner court, they shall wear linen garments; they shall have nothing of wool on them, while they minister at the gates of the inner court, and within. 18They shall have linen turbans upon their heads, and linen breeches upon their loins; they shall not gird themselves with anything that causes sweat. 19And when they go out into the outer court to the people, they shall put off the garments in which they have been ministering, and lay them in the holy chambers; and they shall put on other garments, lest they communicate holiness to the people with their garments. 20They shall not shave their heads or let their locks grow long; they shall only trim the hair of their heads. 21No priest shall drink wine, when he enters the inner court. 22They shall not marry a widow, or a divorced woman, but only a virgin of the stock of the house of Israel, or a widow who is the widow of a priest. 23They shall teach my people the difference between the holy and the common, and show them how to distinguish between the unclean and the clean. 24In a controversy they shall act as judges, and they shall judge it according to my judgments. They shall keep my laws and my statutes in all my appointed feasts, and they shall keep my sabbaths holy. 25They shall not defile themselves by going near to a dead person; however, for father or mother, for son or daughter, for brother or unmarried sister they may defile themselves. 26After he is defiled, he shall count for himself seven days, and then he shall be clean. 27And on the day that he goes into the holy place, into the inner court, to minister in the holy place, he shall offer his sin offering, says the Lord God.

28"They shall have no inheritance; I am their inheritance: and you shall give them no possession in Israel; I am their possession. 29They shall eat the cereal offering, the sin offering, and the guilt offering; and every devoted thing in Israel shall be theirs. 30And the first of all the first fruits of all kinds, and every offering of all kinds from all your offerings, shall belong to the priests; you shall also give to the priests the first of your coarse meal, that a blessing may rest on your house. 31The priests shall not eat of anything, whether bird or beast, that has died of itself or is torn."

The legislation concerning the service of the temple is now addressed to the worship at the altar as such, and the responsibilities of priests descended through Zadok for the conduct of that worship. The opening verses are curious; earlier in the book, the prophet had been fierce in his condemnation of these priests (e.g. 22:26), but now seems to indicate they had remained faithful (verse 15). Either the words are the addition of a later hand (no doubt a Zadokite one), or they reflect a selective sense: *some* of the Zadokite priests had remained faithful to God in the old days of apostasy.

The description of priestly regulations and duties that follows is similar in principle to the legislation contained in Exodus (e.g. 39:27–29) and Leviticus (e.g. 21:1–9). In their dress, appearance, and personal hygiene, the priests were to be clean, both literally and in terms of ritual purity. The same sense of cleanliness was to be maintained in such matters as marriage and encounters with the dead. They had responsibility for religious education, legal consulting and adjudication, and the conduct of worship at the temple's altar. Their whole life was to be the service of God, in itself all sufficient; they were not to supplement that sufficiency with the inheritance of possessions or the ownership of land (although the chapters that follow confuse this last point: see 45:3–4).

At first these verses appear to add little to the other extensive portions of the Old Testament, especially in Exodus and Leviticus, in which detailed legislation is provided concerning the behaviour and responsibility of the priesthood. And yet, for all their repetitive character, the verses do serve to emphasise an important point. The priests, who represented the people as a whole before God, were to be scrupulous in maintaining ritual purity which in turn was to be the outer clothing of an inner ethical purity. And the scrupulousness of their behaviour and activity in the temple's worship would serve constantly to remind the assembled worshippers of their own need of ethical purity in approaching God to worship. The failures of the past, among both priests and people alike, had been moral failures. Taking religion and God for granted, they had casually resorted to worship in the free moments between their acts of moral turpitude. There could be no ultimate distinction between life outside the temple and life within its precincts. Those who would worship a holy God must seek to live a holy life. Indeed, it was only in the pursuit of a holy life that the failure to attain it completely would become apparent, and hence the need for forgiveness, integral to all worship, would become the more evident.

THE ALLOCATION OF THE LAND

Ezekiel 45:1-8

[1]"When you allot the land as a possession, you shall set apart for the Lord a portion of the land as a holy district, twenty-five thousand cubits long and twenty thousand cubits broad; it shall be holy throughout its whole extent. [2]Of this a square plot of five hundred by five hundred cubits shall be for the sanctuary, with fifty cubits for an open space around it. [3]And in the holy district you shall measure off a section twenty-five thousand cubits long and ten thousand broad, in which shall be the sanctuary, the most holy place. [4]It shall be the holy portion of the land; it shall be for the priests, who minister in the sanctuary and approach the Lord to minister to him; and it shall be a place for their houses and a holy place for the sanctuary. [5]Another section, twenty-five thousand cubits long and ten thousand cubits

broad, shall be for the Levites who minister at the temple, as their possession for cities to live in.

⁶"Alongside the portion set apart as the holy district you shall assign for the possession of the city an area five thousand cubits broad, and twenty-five thousand cubits long; it shall belong to the whole house of Israel.

⁷"And to the prince shall belong the land on both sides of the holy district and the property of the city, alongside the holy district and the property of the city, on the west and on the east, corresponding in length to one of the tribal portions, and extending from the western to the eastern boundary of the land. ⁸It is to be his property in Israel. And my princes shall no more oppress my people; but they shall let the house of Israel have the land according to their tribes."

The substance of the prophet's vision moves from the sanctuary and its priests to the allocation of one portion of the restored holy land. The land as a whole, and its division amongst the various tribes, are examined in more detail in Chapters 47–48; here, only one portion of the land is considered, that in which the temple and the holy city were to be located. Specifically, Ezekiel is told that in the division and allocation of the restored land, one portion of it would be given directly to the Lord, in contrast to the remainder which would be divided amongst the people.

The piece of land described in this passage was an area of approximately sixty-four square miles (25,000 cubits being approximately eight miles); as with the layout of the temple, the squareness of the territory symbolised its perfection. The region was subdivided, by east-west boundaries, into three strips of land. To the north lay a strip of approximately twenty-five square miles, for the use of the Levites who ministered in the temple. To the south of that (the middle of the three strips) lay a section of land with the same area, both for the use of the priests, but also as the location of the sanctuary (located in a smaller, square plot of land within the strip). The most southerly strip of land was smaller, half the size of the two to its north (about twelve and a half square miles); it was granted to the city, and thus belonged to the nation as a whole. To the east and west of the sixty-four square mile region, the land was allocated to the prince; to the north and south lay the tribal lands. (The description of the prince's land is followed by a critical note: in the past, kings had expropriated the land belonging to others but, having their own land in the restored state, there would be no further expropriations.)

The entire description of this portion of the restored land and its subdivision continues to be characterised by the visionary quality of its context. Though clearly the prophet is thinking of his real homeland, he describes what might be called visionary geography. Taken literally, the temple would be outside (to the north of) the holy city, in a different strip of land. But it is the symbolism of the vision that is significant. Initially, it is the symbolism of perfection that is uppermost: the total territory is perfectly square, as is appropriate for the land given to God. But the more significant symbolism is perceived when this particular strip of land is recalled in its larger geographical context. From the days of Abraham and Moses, the chosen people had looked forward to having a land of their own. For a while they had possessed a land, though in Ezekiel's time the years of possession were already a thing of the past. But still, in exile, the people looked forward to returning to their land. The land that would belong to the people is described later in the vision (Chapters 47–48); first, the prophet reminds his people that at the heart of their land, God's land would be located. The land they would possess would be the gift of God; the presence in its midst of this sacred territory would be a reminder of the God who granted them the land in the first place, and made possible the life-giving commodities which were the fruit of that land.

As in the heart of Israel's land God's plot was to be located, so too in every human life the divine presence must be located at centre. For the significance of the whole land was to be found at the centre; in the centre strip, at its central point, was the sanctuary which symbolised God's presence. And our own lives, however diverse their territory and character, require a focal point: it is the recognition that God is central to human living.

THE DUTIES OF THE PRINCE

Ezekiel 45:9–17

9"Thus says the Lord God: Enough, O princes of Israel! Put away violence and oppression, and execute justice and righteousness; cease your evictions of my people, says the Lord God.

10"You shall have just balances, a just ephah, and a just bath. 11The ephah and the bath shall be of the same measure, the bath containing one tenth of a homer, and the ephah one tenth of a homer; the homer shall be the standard measure. 12The shekel shall be twenty gerahs; five shekels shall be five shekels, and ten shekels shall be ten shekels, and your mina shall be fifty shekels.

13"This is the offering which you shall make: one sixth of an ephah from each homer of wheat, and one sixth of an ephah from each homer of barley, 14and as the fixed portion of oil, one tenth of a bath from each cor (the cor, like the homer, contains ten baths); 15and one sheep from every flock of two hundred, from the families of Israel. This is the offering for cereal offerings, burnt offerings, and peace offerings, to make atonement for them, says the Lord God. 16All the people of the land shall give this offering to the prince in Israel. 17It shall be the prince's duty to furnish the burnt offerings, cereal offerings, and drink offerings, at the feasts, the new moons, and the sabbaths, all the appointed feasts of the house of Israel: he shall provide the sin offerings, cereal offerings, burnt offerings, and peace offerings, to make atonement for the house of Israel."

The concluding verses of the preceding section, referring to land allocated to princes, provide the bridge to this legislative passage concerning the duties of the prince in the restored land. The introductory verse (9) sets the context in which the whole passage is to be understood: Israel's rulers in the past had frequently exercised their power corruptly. They had employed violence and oppression to secure their goals, and had evicted people from their land. There would still be a royal house in the restored land of Ezekiel's vision, but it would be required to rule according to the principles of justice and righteousness.

(i) First, the prince was to be responsible for a national standards' system of weights and measures. The dry and liquid systems of measure described in verses 10–12 had in the past been subject to all kinds of abuse in the hands of unscrupulous merchants. When food, for example, was purchased, a light measure was used, so that the purchaser got less than that to which he was entitled. But when the same purchaser sold a commodity to the dealer, a heavy weight was employed, so that he was paid less for his commodity than its real value. Amos and other prophets had condemned the practice in ancient Israel. And even archaeology illustrates the issue: inscribed weights have been excavated in Israel, but those with the same inscriptions are not always the same weight. Since inevitably the future society would have a basis in the supply and provision of goods, it was essential that all business be conducted honestly; it would be the responsibility of the prince to ensure the establishment of just standards.

Thus, in these verses, the great vision of a restored land is suddenly narrowed in focus to the matter of measures and weights. Yet the prophet's concern is human and pertains to justice. It is in precisely such matters as measurement, in themselves apparently insignificant, that the foundations of injustice may be established. The rich and strong may exploit the poor and weak; a society is divided into "haves" and "have-nots". It is not the theoretical issues of wealth and property as such with which the prophet is concerned, but the even more fundamental issue of justice. No society can thrive where injustice prospers. The society which the prophet anticipated would be characterised by justice, especially in all the variety of transactions between human beings. And any nation that would have a just society must be as concerned with the details that comprise justice, such as weights and measures and fair dealings, as was the prophet in this account of his vision.

(ii) The princes were also to be responsible for making offerings on behalf of the people (verses 13–17). First the offerings that the people were to make, in kind and in particular (and modest) proportion, are specified. Then the procedure is established: first, the people would give their offerings to the prince, whose duty in turn would be to provide all the requirements necessary for the maintenance of the full system of worship at the sanctuary.

The perspective provided by these verses indicates the wholeness of life as the prophet perceived it. The sacrifices and offerings were to make atonement for Israel, to retain its relationship with God. Yet the capacity to make such offerings would be a direct consequence of God's gift to his people in crops and cattle. The capacity to give to God is always predicated upon the prior gift of God to human beings. Only from what he provides, may we return to the ultimate Giver. And in the act of returning, we are reminded of the constant need for the relationship with God to be restored and maintained. But it is not foolish to return to the Giver a portion of what he gave to us. He does not need it, but we need to give it, partly to learn that the essence of living is giving, and partly to destroy the illusion that what we have was acquired by our own strength.

As things turned out, a royal house did not survive in the restored community after the exile, and in that particular Ezekiel was wrong. But the central message of this portion of Ezekiel's great vision was relevant, whether Israel had a king or not; and it is still relevant today.

THE PURIFICATION AND WORSHIP OF THE TEMPLE

Ezekiel 45:18–25

[18]"Thus says the Lord God: In the first month, on the first day of the month, you shall take a young bull without blemish, and cleanse the sanctuary. [19]The priest shall take some of the blood of the sin offering and put it on the doorposts of the temple, the four corners of the ledge of the altar, and the posts of the gate of the inner court. [20]You shall do the same on the seventh day of the month for any one who has sinned through error or ignorance; so you shall make atonement for the temple.

[21]"In the first month, on the fourteenth day of the month, you shall celebrate the feast of the passover, and for seven days unleavened bread shall be eaten. [22]On that day the prince shall provide for himself and all the people of the land a young bull for a sin offering. [23]And on the seven days of the festival he shall provide as a burnt offering to the Lord seven young bulls and seven rams without blemish, on each of the

seven days; and a he-goat daily for a sin offering. ²⁴And he shall
provide as a cereal offering an ephah for each bull, an ephah for each
ram, and a hin of oil to each ephah. ²⁵In the seventh month, on the
fifteenth day of the month and for seven days of the feast, he shall
make the same provision for sin offerings, burnt offerings, and cereal
offerings, and for the oil."

The legislative instructions concerning the use of the sanctuary
continue in this portion of the account of the vision. It contains
three short sections pertaining to the initiation and continuing
usage of the restored sanctuary; each short section is concisely
written and presupposes a general knowledge of the religious
rituals and festivals which are referred to here.

(i) The purification of the temple (verses 18–20). The purification of the altar has already been described (43:18–27); now a
similar process is to be employed for the temple as a whole. But
whereas the former was a single event, the action described here
seems to have been anticipated as a regular, annual ceremony.
On New Year's Day special sacrifices were to be offered; blood
from the sacrificial animal was to be daubed at particular points of
the temple and its precinct, to symbolise the cleansing. A similar
procedure was to be repeated halfway through the year, at the
beginning of the seventh month.

(ii) The celebration of Passover (verses 21–24). This ancient
and significant festival of Israel's faith, recalling the redemption
of Israel from slavery in Egypt, was to continue to be celebrated
in the restored temple. The prince, whose responsibility as collec-
tor of tithes and offerings has already been described (45:9–17),
was to provide the various sacrificial animals and foodstuffs required for the celebration. Though the festival would take place
in a distant and restored future temple, the symbolism of the
Passover would remain significant to the worshippers. They
were, and would always be, a redeemed people; the commemora-
tion and thanksgiving for that redemption would always remain a
central feature of their lives.

(iii) The celebration of the Festival of Ingathering (verse 25).
This Festival, referred to here simply as "the feast", was the
agricultural festival celebrating God's provision of the harvest. It,

too, would continue to be observed, with the provisions being seen to by the prince. Not only was redemption to be recalled in Passover, but thanks were perpetually to be offered for the provision of the food that made the continuation of physical life possible.

Again, as it turned out, the legislations for the liturgies described here were not put into practice after the exile exactly as the prophet foresaw; but again, that is a minor matter compared with the deeper meaning which had always been attached to these great occasions and would continue to be attached to them in the future.

REGULATIONS CONCERNING WORSHIP

Ezekiel 46:1–15

1"Thus says the Lord God: The gate of the inner court that faces east shall be shut on the six working days; but on the sabbath day it shall be opened and on the day of the new moon it shall be opened. 2The prince shall enter by the vestibule of the gate from without, and shall take his stand by the post of the gate. The priests shall offer his burnt offering and his peace offerings, and he shall worship at the threshold of the gate. Then he shall go out, but the gate shall not be shut until evening. 3The people of the land shall worship at the entrance of that gate before the Lord on the sabbaths and on the new moons. 4The burnt offering that the prince offers to the Lord on the sabbath day shall be six lambs without blemish and a ram without blemish; 5and the cereal offering with the ram shall be an ephah, and the cereal offering with the lambs shall be as much as he is able, together with a hin of oil to each ephah. 6On the day of the new moon he shall offer a young bull without blemish, and six lambs and a ram, which shall be without blemish; 7as a cereal offering he shall provide an ephah with the bull and an ephah with the ram, and with the lambs as much as he is able, together with a hin of oil to each ephah. 8When the prince enters, he shall go in by the vestibule of the gate, and he shall go out by the same way.

9"When the people of the land come before the Lord at the appointed feasts, he who enters by the north gate to worship shall go out by the south gate; and he who enters by the south gate shall go out by the north gate: no one shall return by way of the gate by which he entered, but each shall go out straight ahead. ¹⁰When they go in, the prince shall go in with them; and when they go out, he shall go out.

¹¹"At the feasts and the appointed seasons the cereal offering with a young bull shall be an ephah, and with a ram an ephah, and with the lambs as much as one is able to give, together with a hin of oil to an ephah. ¹²When the prince provides a freewill offering, either a burnt offering or peace offerings as a freewill offering to the Lord, the gate facing east shall be opened for him; and he shall offer his burnt offering or his peace offerings as he does on the sabbath day. Then he shall go out, and after he has gone out the gate shall be shut.

¹³"He shall provide a lamb a year old without blemish for a burnt offering to the Lord daily; morning by morning he shall provide it. ¹⁴And he shall provide a cereal offering with it morning by morning, one sixth of an ephah, and one third of a hin of oil to moisten the flour, as a cereal offering to the Lord; this is the ordinance for the continual burnt offering. ¹⁵Thus the lamb and the meal offering and the oil shall be provided, morning by morning, for a continual burnt offering."

This continuation of the legislative material pertaining to the worship of the temple contains a variety of regulations concerning the conduct and requirements of worshippers.

(i) The Sabbath and the first of the month (verses 1–8). Although worship and sacrifices were offered on a daily basis in the temple, Sabbath days and the first day of each new month (viz. "the new moon", the calendar being a lunar system) were times of special worship. Throughout the week, the eastern gate of the temple's inner court was kept closed, but it was opened each Sabbath and on the first day of each month. The people as a whole would worship in the outer court; they could look through the eastern gate to the altar in the inner court where the sacrifices were offered, but they were not permitted to enter. Only the prince could pass through the vestibule of the eastern gate; he was not to go directly into the inner court, but was allowed to stand by the inner gatepost and observe the priests offer his offerings. There then follows a list of the various offerings specified for the Sabbath worship and for the first day of the month, which the prince provided on behalf of his people as a whole (verses 4–7).

(ii) The approach to worship at Festivals (verses 9–12). At the great Festivals that punctuated Israel's "church calendar", vast crowds of people came to the temple from all over the land to participate in the celebration. With the arrival of such great crowds, the actual worship undertaken in the temple precinct could quickly become a disorderly shambles, unless precautions were taken to ensure the orderly conduct of crowds. This regulation specifies how the crowds were to proceed through the temple area (specifically the outer court) during the Festival. A line would enter the court through the north gate, processing slowly through the court and exiting by means of the south gate. Concurrently, another line of pilgrims would enter via the south gate and pass out through the north gate. The two columns would pass each other in the courtyard. The prince would accompany the line of worshippers, perhaps leading one of the two columns. In this manner, order would be kept, but every pilgrim would enjoy the privilege of passing through the precincts of the great temple. There follow regulations concerning the nature of certain offerings on Festival days (verse 11), and the procedure by which the prince could make a free-will offering, over and above that stipulated by regulation.

(iii) The daily offerings (verses 13–15). The section concludes with specifications concerning the daily offerings to be provided by the prince. For although the great moments of worship were the Sabbath days and Festival days, no day was to go by without the proper conduct of the worship of God.

This collection of regulations concerning worship in the temple is a reminder of the diversity of Israel's worship, its daily continuity and its annual highlights. Every day there was to be worship in the temple. Every seventh day there was special worship, in remembrance of creation and redemption. And at special points throughout the year, there were great Festivals, highlighting God's redemptive acts on behalf of his people. And the maintenance of this rhythm of worship, integral to the prophet's vision of the restored temple, would contribute to the healthy rhythm of the spiritual life of God's people. And, no less than in the past, we continue to require the rhythms of worship, the simplicity of the daily act no less than the splendour of the great festival. Whether it be Christmas Day or a Tuesday in February, the life of worship must continue, if the health of the inner person is to prosper.

THE PRINCE'S PROPERTY

Ezekiel 46:16–18

> [16]"Thus says the Lord God: If the prince makes a gift to any of his sons out of his inheritance, it shall belong to his sons, it is their property by inheritance. [17]But if he makes a gift out of his inheritance to one of his servants, it shall be his to the year of liberty; then it shall revert to the prince; only his sons may keep a gift from his inheritance. [18]The prince shall not take any of the inheritance of the people, thrusting them out of their property; he shall give his sons their inheritance out of his own property, so that none of my people shall be dispossessed of his property."

This short piece of legislation concerning the disposition of the prince's property seems at first out of place, following the regulations about worship. But the larger context is clear; there has already been reference to the division of part of the restored land (45:1–8), and the theme returns in Chapter 48. These verses concern only the prince and the disposition of royal lands. From his holdings, the prince was entitled to distribute land to others. To his sons he could give land as an outright gift, without encumbrance; to his servants he could only give land on a leasehold basis. The servant who received land could keep and use it for a specified time, but then on the expiry of the lease it must return to the royal family. All leases terminated in the "year of liberty" (verse 17), presumably the fiftieth year or Jubilee Year (see Lev. 25:8–17). Thus, the gift of a lease could be a valuable commodity to a faithful servant, but ultimately the royal lands would all revert to the crown.

Verse 18 provides a clue about the deeper concerns that underlie this short piece of legislation. To a large extent Israel's social structure was based on land-holding. To each of the tribes, land was allotted; the land provided them not only with a livelihood, but also with the commodities from which they contributed to the worship and upkeep of the temple. The prince would also be a significant land-holder in this vision of the restored Israel. But past historical experience had taught the people to be wary of royal power in the matter of land holdings. The greedy kings of the past had exercised their formidable powers for the expropriation and acquisition of new territories; they strengthened thereby their own position, weakened those of the tribes, and contributed over time to the break-up of the social structure upon which the nation was based. The legislation in these verses both protects the long-term security of the royal land holdings, but also thereby undermines the need of a king who had a shortage of land to cast a covetous eye on the lands of others.

Implicit in the legislation is a recognition of the potential for corruption implicit in the possession and exercise of power. A prince would in Ezekiel's view be necessary in the new land, but a prince's power was always potentially dangerous. This law recognises the perquisites appropriate to the royal position, but seeks to control them in such a fashion as to reduce the temptation to abuse the exercise of authority.

TEMPLE KITCHENS

Ezekiel 46:19–24

[19]Then he brought me through the entrance, which was at the side of the gate, to the north row of the holy chambers for the priests; and there I saw a place at the extreme western end of them. [20]And he said to me, "This is the place where the priests shall boil the guilt offering and the sin offering, and where they shall bake the cereal offering, in order not to bring them out into the outer court and so communicate holiness to the people."

[21]Then he brought me forth to the outer court, and led me to the four corners of the court; and in each corner of the court there was a court—[22]in the four corners of the court were small courts, forty cubits long and thirty broad; the four were of the same size. [23]On the inside, around each of the four courts was a row of masonry, with hearths

made at the bottom of the rows round about. ²⁴Then he said to me, "These are the kitchens where those who minister at the temple shall boil the sacrifices of the people."

The visionary character of the narrative is now resumed: the prophet was conducted into the inner court of temple to the row of priestly chambers that flanked it. At the western end of these chambers he was invited to inspect the kitchens, in which certain meat offerings were boiled and cereal offerings baked. The kitchens were located in the inner court, because the culinary activity, albeit mundane, was a part of the central sacrificial process and therefore to be kept separate from the outer court in which the great mass of worshippers assembled from time to time. At the four corners of the outer courtyard there were located four further mini-courts, also serving as kitchens. In these four kitchen areas the Levitical servants of the temple would cook those portions of the sacrifices and offerings of which the worshippers as a whole would partake.

The legislation, for all its initially curious character, is a reminder that the temple worship included amongst its activities the simple fellowship of eating. That which was given to God in worship was also a provision, in part, for the consumption of the assembled priests and people. The participation symbolised not only fellowship with God and fellow human beings, but also the provision God made for the most simple, yet essential, of all human needs, namely food. And we are reminded too that worship was not limited to silent awe or spoken words, but included the activity of eating and the fellowship that comes from sharing food together.

THE GREAT RIVER FROM THE TEMPLE

Ezekiel 47:1–12

¹Then he brought me back to the door of the temple; and behold, water was issuing from below the threshold of the temple toward the east (for the temple faced east); and the water was flowing down from below the south end of the threshold of the temple, south of the altar.

²Then he brought me out by way of the north gate, and led me round on the outside to the outer gate, that faces toward the east; and the water was coming out on the south side.

³Going on eastward with a line in his hand, the man measured a thousand cubits, and then led me through the water; and it was ankle-deep. ⁴Again he measured a thousand, and led me through the water; and it was knee-deep. Again he measured a thousand, and led me through the water; and it was up to the loins. ⁵Again he measured a thousand, and it was a river that I could not pass through, for the water had risen; it was deep enough to swim in, a river that could not be passed through. ⁶And he said to me, "Son of man, have you seen this?"

Then he led me back along the bank of the river. ⁷As I went back, I saw upon the bank of the river very many trees on the one side and on the other. ⁸And he said to me, "This water flows toward the eastern region and goes down into the Arabah; and when it enters the stagnant waters of the sea, the water will become fresh. ⁹And wherever the river goes every living creature which swarms will live, and there will be very many fish; for this water goes there, that the waters of the sea may become fresh; so everything will live where the river goes. ¹⁰Fishermen will stand beside the sea; from En-gedi to En-eglaim it will be a place for the spreading of nets; its fish will be of very many kinds, like the fish of the Great Sea. ¹¹But its swamps and marshes will not become fresh; they are to be left for salt. ¹²And on the banks, on both sides of the river, there will grow all kinds of trees for food. Their leaves will not wither nor their fruit fail, but they will bear fresh fruit every month, because the water for them flows from the sanctuary. Their fruit will be for food, and their leaves for healing."

As the vision continues, the prophet is conducted from the kitchen area of the inner court back to the entrance of the temple building on its east side. Standing there, he sees a stream of water which flows from beneath the south side of the threshold or platform on which the temple is built; emerging from the south side of the temple, the stream of water flows in an easterly direction, south of the altar, and passes under the outside wall of the inner court. Then the prophet is conducted to the outside of the temple precinct, via the north gate; standing to the east of the temple, he sees the flow of water emerging from beneath the wall, just south of the eastern gate of the outer court.

The prophet and his guide now take a walk along the river bank for a little more than a mile. After each one third of a mile (a thousand cubits), they check the water of the river. At the first stop, the waters are only ankle-deep, but by the second stop they are knee-deep. By the third stop, the waters are waist-deep, and a third of a mile further down, the waters can only be forded by swimming. "Have you seen this?" his guide asks, meaning, "Do you understand the significance of this?" As the water flows away from the temple spring, it gets deeper, but without the aid of joining tributaries; the river is a miraculous stream of water. Retracing his steps along the river bank towards the temple, Ezekiel notices for the first time the luxuriant trees that flourish beside the river.

The prophet's guide describes to him the course of the river beyond the limit of their short excursion. Leaving the temple's east side, the waters drop through the rough country east of Jerusalem into the Arabah, the great rift valley through which the Jordan flows. This new river flows into the Dead Sea, the large salt lake more than a thousand feet below sea level, whose briny waters can support no life. But as the fresh waters of the river flow into it, the Dead Sea becomes the Sea of Life: the salt is transformed to freshness. Fish and aquatic creatures begin to flourish, and the formerly deserted shores of the sea become populated by the fishermen who move there to seek a living from its waters. The swamps and marshes along the coast retain their character so that, despite the transformation, the sea continues to provide its former single blessing—salt. But elsewhere, by river bank and beach, the trees flourish, providing fruit for food and leaves of medicinal value.

In this part of the narrative, the visionary character of the account is heightened and the picture the prophet sees is like that of a new paradise established in the world. As in the garden of Eden the four great rivers from God's mountain provided for the sustenance of life, so here the river from God's temple transforms the wilderness and the salt sea into a fruitful and life-giving area. The realms of the earth, which had seemed to former writers to be under a dreadful curse, are to be transformed into a luscious garden. But the prophet is not prophesying a physical and geographical transformation; rather, in the symbolism of his vision, he is anticipating the extraordinary transformation that would overcome the people of Israel, when once again the temple in their midst was the residence of God.

We begin to see the transformation that may be effected when God's presence is at centre. Ezekiel's vision was of a temple, in its tiniest detail, but his concern was for an entire nation and all its people. When God was present in the midst of his people and land, the driest and saltiest areas of wilderness would be restored to life. And so we perceive from the prophet's vision how important it is, in any restoration, to get to the heart of the matter. Only with God's presence firmly re-established in the centre, the temple, could there be new life and restoration. And what was true for Israel is true for the Church. When God's presence is firmly established at the centre, the blessing of that presence flows out to transform the wilderness with life-giving waters.

THE BOUNDARIES OF THE RESTORED LAND

Ezekiel 47:13–23

[13]Thus says the Lord God: "These are the boundaries by which you shall divide the land for inheritance among the twelve tribes of Israel. Joseph shall have two portions. [14]And you shall divide it equally; I swore to give it to your fathers, and this land shall fall to you as your inheritance.

[15]"This shall be the boundary of the land: On the north side, from the Great Sea by way of Hethlon to the entrance of Hamath, and on to Zedad, [16]Berothah, Sibraim (which lies on the border between Damascus and Hamath), as far as Hazerhatticon, which is on the border of Hauran. [17]So the boundary shall run from the sea to Hazarenon, which is on the northern border of Damascus, with the border of Hamath to the north. This shall be the north side.

[18]"On the east side, the boundary shall run from Hazar-enon between Hauran and Damascus; along the Jordan between Gilead and the land of Israel; to the eastern sea and as far as Tamar. This shall be the east side.

¹⁹"On the south side, it shall run from Tamar as far as the waters of Meribath-kadesh, thence along the Brook of Egypt to the Great Sea. This shall be the south side.

²⁰"On the west side, the Great Sea shall be the boundary to a point opposite the entrance of Hamath. This shall be the west side.

²¹"So you shall divide this land among you according to the tribes of Israel. ²²You shall allot it as an inheritance for yourselves and for the aliens who reside among you and have begotten children among you. They shall be to you as native-born sons of Israel; with you they shall be allotted an inheritance among the tribes of Israel. ²³In whatever tribe the alien resides, there you shall assign him his inheritance, says the Lord God."

The legislative character of the account returns in these verses, which are introduced as God's word to the prophet concerning the boundaries and internal division of Israel's restored land. The land had originally been divided amongst the people following their initial settlement in the promised land. Now, the prophet envisages a new return from exile and a new division of territory amongst the chosen people. Although the boundaries are similar to those of other geographical accounts (e.g. Num. 34:1–12), the allocation of land to the tribes is quite different.

The eastern and western boundaries of the restored land are easy to grasp; those to the south and especially the north are more difficult to determine, given the relative obscurity of some of the geographical terms employed. The western boundary was the coast of the Mediterranean Sea (the "Great Sea"). The eastern boundary began in the region of the headwaters of the Jordan, followed the river Jordan south, and continued along the western shore of the Dead Sea. The northern boundary began on the coast of the Mediterranean, somewhere in the vicinity of Tyre, and extended in an easterly direction to a point north of the Sea of Galilee. In the south, the line extended from just south of the Dead Sea, through the Negeb to the Mediterranean coast. While the extent of the envisaged land is similar to that of Solomon's kingdom (e.g. 1 Kings 8:65), it should be noted that it does not include any of the territory to the east of the Jordan Valley, which was possessed by some of the tribes in the original settlement of the land. The entire land of Ezekiel's vision lies to the west of the Jordan Valley and the Arabah.

In the summary comments concerning the allocation of the land (verses 21–23), a further new note is added. Formerly land had only been allocated to the tribes, and then subdivided amongst their full Hebrew members. But in the restored land, even aliens (immigrants) would be entitled to hold land and participate fully in life with their fellow countrymen.

In reading this part of the narrative it is important to remember the context. The vision of a restored land is seen by one in exile; the prophet has no land and is cut off from the land to which he once belonged. Without permanent residence, he envisages a time when all his people will live permanently once again in a God-given land. But Ezekiel is not only an exile, but also an alien. And as an alien in captivity, he has no special privileges and no right to hold land. But in the restored land of Israel, even aliens would have rights and privileges, provided at the injunction of God. It was this vision of a restored and better land that was to sustain the prophet and his companions in exile. But the deeper source of sustenance was not the land itself, of which the boundaries are described here in such detail, but rather it was the presence of God in the land. Ezekiel gives expression to the hunger latent in all persons, not simply to be a land-owner, but rather to reside in a place in which God's presence may be known intimately.

THE DIVISION OF THE LAND

Ezekiel 48:1–29

[1]"These are the names of the tribes: Beginning at the northern border, from the sea by way of Hethlon to the entrance of Hamath, as far as Hazar-enon (which is on the northern border of Damascus over against Hamath), and extending from the east side to the west, Dan, one portion. [2]Adjoining the territory of Dan, from the east side to the west, Asher, one portion. [3]Adjoining the territory of Asher, from the east side to the west, Naphtali, one portion. [4]Adjoining the territory of

Naphtali, from the east side to the west, Manasseh, one portion. [5]Adjoining the territory of Manasseh, from the east side to the west, Ephraim, one portion. [6]Adjoining the territory of Ephraim, from the east side to the west, Reuben, one portion. [7]Adjoining the territory of Reuben, from the east side to the west, Judah, one portion.

[8]"Adjoining the territory of Judah, from the east side to the west, shall be the portion which you shall set apart, twenty-five thousand cubits in breadth, and in length equal to one of the tribal portions, from the east side to the west, with the sanctuary in the midst of it. [9]The portion which you shall set apart for the Lord shall be twenty-five thousand cubits in length, and twenty thousand in breadth. [10]These shall be the allotments of the holy portion: the priests shall have an allotment measuring twenty-five thousand cubits on the northern side, ten thousand cubits in breadth on the western side, ten thousand in breadth on the eastern side, and twenty-five thousand in length on the southern side, with the sanctuary of the Lord in the midst of it. [11]This shall be for the consecrated priests, the sons of Zadok, who kept my charge, who did not go astray when the people of Israel went astray, as the Levites did. [12]And it shall belong to them as a special portion from the holy portion of the land, a most holy place, adjoining the territory of the Levites. [13]And alongside the territory of the priests, the Levites shall have an allotment twenty-five thousand cubits in length and ten thousand in breadth. The whole length shall be twenty-five thousand cubits and the breadth twenty thousand. [14]They shall not sell or exchange any of it; they shall not alienate this choice portion of the land, for it is holy to the Lord.

[15]"The remainder, five thousand cubits in breadth and twenty-five thousand in length, shall be for ordinary use for the city, for dwellings and for open country. In the midst of it shall be the city; [16]and these shall be its dimensions: the north side four thousand five hundred cubits, the south side four thousand five hundred, the east side four thousand five hundred, and the west side four thousand and five hundred. [17]And the city shall have open land: on the north two hundred and fifty cubits, on the south two hundred and fifty, on the east two hundred and fifty, and on the west two hundred and fifty. [18]The remainder of the length alongside the holy portion shall be ten thousand cubits to the east, and ten thousand to the west, and it shall be alongside the holy portion. Its produce shall be food for the workers of the city. [19]And the workers of the city, from all the tribes of Israel, shall till it. [20]The whole portion which you shall set apart shall be

twenty-five thousand cubits square, that is, the holy portion together with the property of the city.

21"What remains on both sides of the holy portion and of the property of the city shall belong to the prince. Extending from the twenty-five thousand cubits of the holy portion to the east border, and westward from the twenty-five thousand cubits to the west border, parallel to the tribal portions, it shall belong to the prince. The holy portion with the sanctuary of the temple in its midst, 22and the property of the Levites and the property of the city, shall be in the midst of that which belongs to the prince. The portion of the prince shall lie between the territory of Judah and the territory of Benjamin.

23"As for the rest of the tribes: from the east side to the west, Benjamin, one portion. 24Adjoining the territory of Benjamin, from the east side to the west, Simeon, one portion. 25Adjoining the territory of Simeon, from the east side to the west, Issachar, one portion. 26Adjoining the territory of Issachar, from the east side to the west, Zebulun, one portion. 27Adjoining the territory of Zebulun, from the east side to the west, Gad, one portion. 28And adjoining the territory of Gad to the south, the boundary shall run from Tamar to the waters of Meribath-kadesh, thence along the Brook of Egypt to the Great Sea. 29This is the land which you shall allot as an inheritance among the tribes of Israel, and these are their several portions, says the Lord God."

The land to be allocated to the tribes was divided in the middle by a strip of land, extending from the eastern boundary to the west, which has already been apportioned between the prince, the temple, the city, and the Levites (see 45:1–9). The description of the allocation of land which now follows begins with an account of the division of the land that lay to the north of this central territory. Being somewhat larger than its southern counterpart, the northern territory was to be divided among seven tribes, while the southern territory was to be divided among five tribes.

The division of the northern territory (verses 1–7) was into a series of horizontal strips of land, extending east-west. All were bounded by the borders of the land as such on the east and west, but adjoined their neighbours' territories on the south and north sides. The strips of land, beginning in the north, were to be allocated as follows: Dan, Asher, Naphtali, Manasseh, Ephraim,

Reuben, and Judah. Dan's northern boundary was that of the
nation as a whole: Judah's southern boundary was that of the
central strip of special land running through its midst. The division of the land, as envisaged by Ezekiel, has little or no relationship with the territories originally held by the tribes in bygone
centuries. The point of the narrative is not that the tribes would
get their old land back, but rather that in the new land, each tribe
would have its assigned and rightful place. And again it should be
stressed that each tribe would have land, even those of the northern kingdom that had ceased to exist more than a century before
Ezekiel's birth. None of God's people would be forgotten in the
great restoration; all would have a place in the divine scheme of
things.

The description of the central strip of land and its internal division
(verses 8–22) is essentially an elaboration of the earlier account of
the same territory provided in 45:1–9. The central strip had a
square block in the middle, subdivided between the city, the
temple and the Levites. The land on either side of the block,
extending to the Mediterranean in the west and the Arabah in the
east, belonged to the prince. None of this land could be sold or
"alienated", for though in a certain sense it was allocated to
particular persons, ultimately it was all considered to be land
belonging especially to God, flanked on its northern and southern
borders by the land allocated to the tribes.

The land assigned to the city is described in greater detail here
than in Chapter 45; the smallest of the three strips of land that
together comprised the central block of land, it was to be used for
the benefit of the citizens, who would not be landowners in the
same sense as their relatives in the tribal territories. In the midst
of this territory would be the city itself, surrounded by a thin strip
of open land. Surrounding the open land would be agricultural
land. The citizens of the city would be assigned the care and tilling
of this land, so that its produce could support the needs of the
inhabitants, thus making the city independent and not subject to
the "charity" of the tribal territories. For all its visionary character, the narrative is also permeated by a remarkable degree of

practicality and realism. The entire central strip of land running through the restored nation would be self-sustaining and independent.

The description of the southern portion of the restored land (verses 23–29) balances that of the northern portion given earlier in the chapter (verses 1–7). Again, the territory was divided into east-west strips; the northern boundary began at the southern edge of the central strip of land (verses 8–22) and the territory extended south to the Negeb and the southern boundary of the land as a whole (47:13–23). The strips of land, beginning in the north, were assigned as follows: Benjamin, Simeon, Issachar, Zebulon, and Gad. There were five tribes in the southern region, as distinct from seven in the north, presumably because the southern territory was smaller and somewhat less rich than that in the north. As before, the land was divided amongst tribes that had formerly belonged to two separate states, Israel and Judah, though all the land in this narrative had originally belonged to Judah.

THE CITY OF GOD

Ezekiel 48:30–35

> 30"These shall be the exits of the city: On the north side, which is to be four thousand five hundred cubits by measure, 31three gates, the gate of Reuben, the gate of Judah, and the gate of Levi, the gates of the city being named after the tribes of Israel. 32On the east side, which is to be four thousand five hundred cubits, three gates, the gate of Joseph, the gate of Benjamin, and the gate of Dan. 33On the south side, which is to be four thousand five hundred cubits by measure, three gates, the gate of Simeon, the gate of Issachar, and the gate of Zebulun. 34On the west side, which is to be four thousand five hundred cubits, three gates, the gate of Gad, the gate of Asher, and the gate of Naphtali. 35The circumference of the city shall be eighteen thousand cubits. And the name of the city henceforth shall be, The Lord is there."

Ezekiel's book concludes with an account of the City of God. It is described as a city of perfect proportions. Each of the walls on the four sides of the city was of the same length (4,500 cubits); in each wall, three gates were placed, each one representing one of the tribes of Israel, and all symbolising the free access by which all the members of the tribes would be admitted to the city. The conception of the tribes in this account differs somewhat from that underlying the preceding narrative concerning the division of the land. In the latter passage, Levi (the priestly tribe) was not considered to be a tribe holding territory, and the two half-tribes, Ephraim and Manasseh, were listed separately, thereby keeping the number of land-holding tribes at twelve. But in this passage, which is concerned to stress the accessibility to the city for every one of the chosen people, the original and complete list of tribes is used, with Joseph in place of Ephraim and Manasseh. No person would be denied access to the City of God.

The most striking feature of these closing verses is to be found in the new name given to the city: it is to be called *Yahweh-shammah*, or "the Lord is there". It was to be known, not for its architecture or symmetrical design, but for the presence in its midst of Israel's God. And more than the measurements of its walls or the location of its gates, it was the divine presence that would make the city holy.

The concluding verses of the book indicate the wholeness and completeness of the prophet's vision and ministry as a whole. From one perspective, it is a sad book; it begins with Ezekiel in exile, cut off from the land he loved so dearly, and it ends nearly a quarter of a century later with the same prophet still in exile. For all his vision, the prophet's lot has remained the same: his place in life has not moved from the alien soil of Babylon. Yet we perceive how the prophet's vision has outstripped the physical experience of his life. Whereas his ministry began and ended in exile, he has moved from desolation to hope. The miserable huts of captivity in which he and his companions lived have faded behind the vision of the perfect, four-square city. Faith has outstripped experience, but the longing for an actual return to his homeland has been replaced by a vision of the restored land, in which, above all else, "the Lord is there" (verse 35).

As we leave Ezekiel's book, it may not be with any sense of having mastered every mystery and solved every problem. Yet the last verses of the prophet's book provide a clue to the meaning of the whole. We leave the book with the memory of a man who lived in a world from which God seemed to be absent. Yet such was his vision that he perceived a new world, with God at its centre; world events had not changed in such a way as to encourage this vision, but he had transcended the negative and empirical evidence of his time to grasp the better world beyond. He was not a visionary, in the sense of being cut off from any awareness of reality; indeed, more than most people, he grasped the terrors and torments of his time. But knowing God, he could see beyond, and his longing for a future was for a world in which all men and women might know the reality of God's presence more intimately. And if, albeit only partially, we have shared in this vision of an extraordinary prophet, then we leave his book with a permanent gain.

FURTHER READING

The following is a brief selection of books that may be of assistance in the further study of the Book of Ezekiel. Those marked with an *asterisk* are introductory, while those without are more detailed and advanced studies.

*K. W. Carley, *The Book of the Prophet Ezekiel* (The Cambridge Bible Commentary on the New English Bible) (Cambridge University Press, 1974)

G. A. Cooke, *A Critical and Exegetical Commentary on the Book of Ezekiel* (The International Critical Commentary) (T. and T. Clark, 1936)

W. Eichrodt, *Ezekiel: A Commentary* (The Old Testament Library) (SCM Press, 1970)

*C. G. Howie, *The Book of Ezekiel: The Book of Daniel* (The Layman's Bible Commentary, Volume 13) (John Knox Press, 1961)

*J. B. Taylor, *Ezekiel: An Introduction and Commentary* (The Tyndale Old Testament Commentaries) (Tyndale Press, 1969)

J. W. Wevers, *Ezekiel* (New Century Bible) (Oliphants, 1969)